More Praise for *In Due Season*

"Paul Wilkes's *In Due Season* takes the reader on a moving journey through an extraordinary era's thickets of American Catholic life and belief—opening at last into wisdom, affirmation, and hope."

> —James Carroll, author, *Practicing Catholic* and
> *An American Requiem,* winner of the National Book Award.

"Paul Wilkes is a rare creature: someone who writes about religion in a way that's both insightful and riveting. He combines personal experience with reportage and canny analysis like few others."

> —Steven Waldman, editor-in-chief, Beliefnet.com

"*In Due Season* is Paul Wilkes's *The Seven Storey Mountain*. Profoundly influenced by Thomas Merton, Wilkes is uniquely himself in these pages, honest and brave in his search for God."

> —Brother Patrick Hart, O.C.S.O., was Thomas Merton's last
> secretary and continues to edit Merton's writings and
> serve as General Editor of the Monastic Wisdom Series
> of Cistercian Publications

"*In Due Season* is ripe and ready for picking. St. Augustine is all smiles with this confessional autobiography of decadence and redemption set in the parched haunts of East Coast literati."

> —Donald Cozzens, author, *Faith That Dares to Speak*

Books by Paul Wilkes

Nonfiction

Beyond the Walls: Monastic Wisdom for Everyday Life

The Seven Secrets of Successful Catholics

The Good Enough Catholic: A Guide for the Perplexed

And They Shall Be My People: An American Rabbi and His Congregation

The Education of an Archbishop

In Mysterious Ways: The Death and Life of a Parish Priest

Merton: By Those Who Knew Him Best

Companions Along the Way

Six American Families

These Priests Stay

Trying Out the Dream: A Year in the Life of an American Family

∞

Fiction

Temptations

∞

For Children

Fitzgo, the Wild Dog of Central Park

My Book of Bedtime Prayers

∞

Lilly Endowment Grant

Best Practices from America's Best Churches

Excellent Catholic Parishes: The Guide to Best Places and Practices

Excellent Protestant Congregations: The Guide to Best Places and Practices

IN DUE
SEASON

A Catholic Life

Paul Wilkes

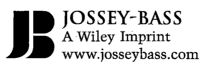

JOSSEY-BASS
A Wiley Imprint
www.josseybass.com

Published by Jossey-Bass
A Wiley Imprint
989 Market Street, San Francisco, CA 94103-1741—www.josseybass.com

Jossey-Bass books and products are available through most bookstores. To contact Jossey-Bass directly call our Customer Care Department within the U.S. at 800-956-7739, outside the U.S. at 317-572-3986, or fax 317-572-4002.

Jossey-Bass also publishes its books in a variety of electronic formats. Some content that appears in print may not be available in electronic books.

Library of Congress Cataloging-in-Publication Data:
Wilkes, Paul, date.
  In due season : a Catholic life / Paul Wilkes.
     p.   cm.
  ISBN 978-0-470-42333-2 (cloth)
   1. Wilkes, Paul, date   2. Catholics—United States—Biography.   I. Title.
  BX4705.W55748A3   2009
  282.092—dc22
  [B]
                                                        2008050162

Printed in the United States of America
FIRST EDITION
HB Printing   10 9 8 7 6 5 4 3 2 1

CONTENTS

AS GOOD AS IT GETS?

GETTING BEARINGS

LIFE, LIVED

RETURNING

. . . so that people might seek God,
even perhaps grope for him and find him,
though indeed he is not far from any one of us.

—Acts 17:27

OO

And he shall be like a tree
which is planted near the running waters,
which shall bring forth its fruit,
in due season.

— Psalm 1

AUTHOR'S NOTE

This is one man's story, of a life that has seen its share of dark days and those filled with light. It is a life shared with many people, through the good times and the not so good, and as I write about those people, these are but snapshots, taken from my angle, at that time, in that place. To retell the story of my life, I used letters, photos, journal entries, interviews, and other research, in addition to calling on my own memory. I have attempted to reconstruct events and conversations as accurately as possible and to the best of my memory. If I have made any mistakes, in fact, tone, or context, they are unintentional. In a very few cases, where it was appropriate, names and identities have been changed. All else in the book is fact—at least as best I could recall and relate it.

INTRODUCTION

I have spent much of my adult life watching people, asking them questions, and eventually writing about what I observed and heard. Some were famous people, others unknown. Each had a story to tell, as everyone does, given the opportunity.

In my writing life, it was not long before I came to the conclusion that there are but few truly extraordinary people. Most of us are ordinary. Yet we, the ordinary, are placed in the extraordinary circumstances of our lives; how we respond is unpredictable, and what we eventually become, endlessly fascinating. Our story is certainly our own, but universal in so many ways. "The human condition" is what this is often called, for lack of a neater category.

I am one of those ordinary people.

As I look back over the first part of my life, I realize that this ordinary man has lived in extraordinary times and has been shaped by extraordinary events and people. Recollecting and reassembling the various shards, scraps, and fragments of my life, I find that some of the most horrific moments were gateways to grace. Some of the potentially holiest were mere tin idols. I have changed dramatically, and I have remained the same person I was from childhood. It is so for all of us.

Woven through the events and years that I write about is a search for God. I hope that doesn't sound presumptuous, but trying to understand who God is and what he might want has occupied me from a very young age. I had a rich religious upbringing, but beyond that, it just seemed to make sense. After all, why was I alive, but to aspire to come close to him, please him, understand him? If I am made in his image, I must be destined to be something like him—impossible as that might sound.

But, as most of us have found, God does not speak to us directly, giving us specific instructions on what to do with our lives. Rather he speaks to us through people we meet, places we are in, the decisions with which we are confronted. At least that has been my experience.

I think that most of you will nod and see a part of yourself at some point on the bumpy, twisting path that is my life. Not that my life is at all exemplary; it is not. But what I have tried to do here is to be as honest as I could in its telling. When people asked me what I was working on, I said, "the story of my days on this planet," not wanting to call it an autobiography—that sounded much too grand for such an ordinary life— or a memoir, which sounded far too self-conscious. So let it be what it is: a story, a true story, about an ordinary man's search for God and for life's meaning.

IN DUE SEASON

PART ONE

FORMATION

THE SEVENTH CHILD

ON SEPTEMBER 12, 1938, WHILE ADOLPH HITLER, with a fiery speech to the Party Congress in a vast hall in Nuremberg, was giving birth to his dream of National Socialism, Margaret Wilkes, already the mother of six, was stoically gritting her teeth in a cramped hospital delivery room at St. Luke's Hospital in Cleveland, Ohio. She was laboring to bear her seventh child, hardly, for her, a dream. Of course, the two events had no linkage, nor were they in any sense of equal importance.

Only that I was the child born on that fateful day.

Margaret had passed between the tall, elegant pillars of St. Luke's entrance and presented herself to the admissions desk at about 10:30 PM the night before. This in itself was extraordinary; she had never been in a hospital before. All her other children had been delivered at home by good Dr. Brown, by the light of a kerosene lamp, in a humble house in the anthracite coalfields of Pennsylvania, where the family had lived until recently. When Margaret learned that she would be required to pay the customary daily rate of $1.29 for the remains of that day—such were the inflexible rules for mothers on welfare, which, embarrassingly enough, she was at the time—she took her small canvas bag and returned to the waiting room. Every penny counted, especially with this new baby coming. She sat quietly and alone, watching the clock, trying not to call attention to herself as the contractions increased in rapidity and strength. At midnight, she once again presented herself at the admissions desk and was immediately whisked into the brightly lit delivery room.

She had awoken with a start shortly after going to bed that night. The pains low in her belly were both familiar and rhythmic. She whispered to her husband, Paul, "It's time." He rose sleepily from the bed, but she told him that no, he did not have to go with her. Although Paul was still among the some 3.3 million men then formally unemployed, his work at forty cents an hour with the Works Progress Administration (WPA) provided at least some semblance of dignity and served as the gateway for collecting free food and clothing for his family at the local center up on Buckeye Road. His work as a WPA carpenter required him to be on the job promptly at seven the next morning. Margaret took her small bag, packed with clean underwear, her best flannel nightgown, toothbrush, and a small jar of salt and baking soda—her dentifrice of choice and necessity—and walked the two miles to the hospital.

My mother, Margaret, then thirty-eight years old, was a stocky, compact woman of about five foot two. She had the square, solid shoulders of the Slovak peasant stock from which she was descended, reddish, rough hands from washing the family's clothes on a scrubbing board with homemade soap. She wore no makeup, not even lipstick. She was not a woman prone to smiling; her milky blue eyes seemed to hold only the assurance of the inevitable as the birth drew near.

This pregnancy, somehow negotiated in the windowless attic of her mother-in-law's tiny house on East 111th Street in the company of the other six children, was hardly looked upon as a fortunate occurrence. Having to live in an attic, treated no better than dusty trunks and out-of-season clothes, crowded together with her children, who slept crossways, three to a sagging bed, was bad enough. But it was better than being homeless, which had been a distinct possibility when the family, penniless and in a borrowed Model T Ford, were forced to leave a house in Pennsylvania that had been built by her husband but reclaimed by the state for taxes owed.

In fact, this pregnancy could not have come at a worse time. Her husband had almost saved the $100 required to join Local 11 of the United Brotherhood of Carpenters and Joiners of America. Soon, Margaret had already carefully planned, they would be off "the dole" and would no longer have to borrow the neighbor's rusty wagon to bring home the bug-infested bags of wheat and the uniformly green dresses and brown shoes that placed the Wilkes girls, then 14, 12, 10, and 4, on the truly needy side of the thin line dividing simple Depression-era want from poverty.

Paul and Margaret's relatives were scandalized by Paul's seemingly gluttonous sexual insistence and her impractical fecundity. When Margaret told her sister Rose—who was then living in her own shame back in Pennsylvania with a young son born out of wedlock—Rose's eyes widened. "Take something strong," she advised, as if the child should be flushed away with some strong chemical, like those used to clear clogged drains. But Margaret would have none of the abortifacients then available from the hollow-eyed gypsy women who lived in shacks bordering the trolley car barns down on Woodhill Road. "God will provide," she bravely said, even as she wondered how she and her husband could feed still another mouth.

The birth, some eight hours later, was uneventful. And when her husband arrived after work that day, he found a seven-pound boy sleeping peacefully in his wife's arms.

Unlike his wife, Paul had no trouble smiling. His wool cap cocked at a jaunty angle, the faint whiff of bottom-shelf whiskey and draft beer on his breath, a faint brown dribble of Havana Blossom chewing tobacco at the corner of his mouth, Paul Wilkes Sr. seemed to view the world at once bemusedly and benignly. Everything would work out. It was this attitude that drove his wife mad. No, everything would not necessarily work out. Right now, nothing was right. And besides, if she couldn't afford lipstick, he shouldn't afford a double shot of Corby's and a bottle of Erin Brew. For Margaret, disaster awaited the unwary. For Paul, life unfolded as it would, so what was there to worry about?

Deep in the Great Depression, Paul and Margaret Wilkes could hardly have known that even more catastrophic world events were afoot. The armies of the furious man in Nuremberg were poised to swallow up their first bites of Europe, eventually including the Slovak land from which their own parents had escaped over forty years before. It was then part of the Austro-Hungarian empire, which would have been news to them. They did not even know the village their parents had come from, only that wherever it was, there was not enough of its poor soil to be divided once again among family members. Rather than starve, they had come to the place they called *Amerike*.

Survival had been the focus for the Vlk, as they were called before the name was Americanized, and the Salanskys, Margaret's people. For that was all that they knew, serfs that they were, trying as best they could to live under feudal kings and princes, greedy landowners in their native land, and then under capricious mine owners in their new homeland. Now they owed allegiance to a more benevolent leader, far distant from their daily lives—Franklin Delano Roosevelt. At least he had kept them from starving.

But it would be wrong to sum up their lives—and their humble heritage up to this point—only in terms of possessions or status. For there was a side to their lives that transcended the vagaries of this earth. There may have been no widely known Slovak kings or books or inventors or artists—such as the French or British or German or Italian or Irish immigrants could claim. But Paul and Margaret Wilkes were members of the most important royal family the world had ever known, something that no depth of poverty could erase. They were Catholic—and their new son would be soon baptized into this one true faith. Others might succeed in *this* world, but they were sure they would prevail in the next. Their Catholic Church in America was itself a magnificent, sprawling, and unified empire. While non-Catholic America still regarded their growth warily, working-class Catholics built schools and churches in great number. Devotions to the Blessed Mother were sung and uttered by churches full of the faithful, nuns wore distinctive garb, priests were never seen in public without a Roman collar. On the altar, the Mass was intoned in an unchanging Latin. Little had changed since the Council of Trent, the sixteenth-century response to Luther's heresies.

When asked what name should be written on the birth certificate of this, the latest member, Paul and Margaret looked at one another. They already had a Thomas and an Edward. The girls were Pauline, Marian, Francis, and Margaret. Without much further discussion, they simply named the child Paul, with no middle name, after his father.

And so my life began.

OO

Before bedtime, my six sisters and brothers and I would kneel, in order, oldest to youngest, before my mother at the edge of our breakfast nook table to say our nightly prayers. It was here that my early relationship— as narrow and perhaps misguided as it then was—with God began. My father had covered the table's worn, wooden, cracked surface with yellow Formica, the newest modern rage, and we secretly imagined that its use surely marked us as true Americans. But of course, in almost every way, our outward lives were, like that Formica, very much a veneer on a much thicker piece of American life, of which we knew very little.

There were benches on either side of the table, and my mother, droopy-eyed from her work as a housekeeper up in Shaker Heights for the Chadwick family—they, the wealthy makers of the Chadwick automobile that had faded into history, but whose money remained quite plentiful and readily accessible—as well as from all the washing, cooking, baking, sewing, and mending that a large family required, would sit there to hear our various cries to heaven. My brothers and sisters knelt on the glistening linoleum floor, scrubbed bare and polished each Saturday afternoon. This was an accepted portion of self-inflicted pain, penance for sins; after all, prayer was magnified in direct proportion to the time spent and pain endured. God surely listened better if you were at least uncomfortable, preferably in agony. I, however, knelt on a grate that brought heat from our coal furnace into the kitchen. Such a penitential act in one so young might be misunderstood by those who were not members of an immigrant Catholic family in the 1940s. But ours was a Church that believed in the purifying effects of suffering. Our pope, Pius XII, already looked like a cadaver. Our churches were populated with statues that did not shy away from depicting glistening blood, gaping wounds, and pain-filled, mournful, heaven-cast eyes.

The grate's checkered pattern of forged steel offered me the opportunity to come close to God in the surest way I then knew—through suffering. For this was a distant God, large and all-enveloping, whose Son I saw hanging from the cross at the front of our church. His followers readily suffered. "Hail Mary, full of grace, the Lord is with thee. . . . Our Father who art in heaven, hallowed . . ." As the prayers I had been learning from the Notre Dame sisters at St. Benedict's grade school passed my lips, my mind was often elsewhere, with the martyrs of my faith. In a courtyard next to St. Sebastian, my hands behind my back, just like his; arrows piercing my chest, just like his. By a river's edge with Jesuit missionaries, a wild-eyed Iroquois ripping out my fingernails with his teeth. In a Roman amphitheatre among my young, brave friends, with lions tearing at our flesh as we calmly said our Hail Marys together. In an Italian village like eleven-year-old Maria Goretti, protecting my virginity—whatever that was—from some brutish thug.

Catholicism of this time is so easy to parody, but to a child like me it made perfect mythic sense. Especially when so much of the world was out of reach. Here was a sure path to greatness, open to the modest of birth and sinew, open to those brave enough to trudge step-by-step in the footprints of the ages. This temporal world was passing; what else was there to do but pile up treasure in heaven? Each painful moment on that grate mattered and counted. It was a simple world, with ironclad, nonnegotiable rules and guarantees. What else to aspire to, except sainthood?

On the Formica-like surface of my life, I was an overly talkative, distracted, and often disobedient child. Actually, there was nothing more I wanted than to be a saint. As I knelt on that grate, the numbing sensations radiating up my legs and into my hips were at once excruciating painful and wonderfully comforting. I was on the path to becoming that saint. No one knew that, but I was. What were a few piddling years of difficulty when compared to an eternity of divine pleasure? As I look back on those days, there is no anger, only affection. There was a simplicity and honesty about such an approach to God.

In parishes like mine, St. Benedict's, priests provided one of the few comforts of this alien land by speaking the native Slovak tongue for the half million who had immigrated around the turn of the century. In crowded parish school classrooms we were kept apart from non-Catholic influences so that we might preserve our faith, under assault by a Protestant-dominated American culture. For we were a perfect society, the Church complete in itself, neither having nor needing nor seeking much of a relationship to the world. The Baltimore Catechism answered any question we might have, let us know exactly where we stood with God, when we were going astray, and how far. We were taught to "mortify" our senses, avoid temptation or even the "near occasion" of sin. It was incomprehensible that if we would marry—a state decidedly inferior to becoming a nun or priest, which only the holiest among us aspired to— we would not marry anyone other than another Catholic, preferably a Slovak one.

∞

Although I was a member of this huge family, I always had the sense of being alone in the world. Perhaps I felt this way because my older siblings and parents seemed "the family" and then there was me, separated by four years and a chasm that only widened with time. It was not that I was unloved or uncared for. The one picture of me from my early years—taken by a professional at Woolworth's Five and Dime up on Buckeye Road—shows luxuriant, chin-length curls, held neatly back by a barrette, framing a chubby, smiling face. An obviously indulged, slightly petulant . . . little girl. Was it that my mother knew that girls were more malleable and hoped to reprogram my maleness as much or for as long as she could? Or had she already sensed in me—as mothers can do just by the tone of a child's cry or the way a breast is taken or the position while sleeping—that I would not be a cooperative crew member on this fragile family bark sailing stormy and uncharted American waters?

Because my siblings were older and my parents were working, I was something of a feral creature, raising myself, cautiously ranging out into the neighborhood that surrounded our one-and-a-half-story shingled house at 11412 Forest Avenue. I would follow the horse-drawn wagon with a man calling out "Paperricks, paperricks" (which only much later I would decode as a Yiddish plea for scrap "paper" and "rags") as it rattled over Forest Avenue's red bricks. I peered at women in babushkas as they hurried back from the crossroads of 116th and Buckeye Road, having stopped at fruit and vegetable markets, the butcher shop, the bakery, each its own province. Ours was more a medieval village than the result of modern city planning. The men were plumbers and lathe operators, electricians, tin smiths, masons; each of their homes could have just as easily had a guild crest out in front. They were hard-working men, blessed with the dignity of a job after the scourge of the Depression. Cleveland's mills and factories were happy to have them, an intact, stable workforce, willing to toil in whatever conditions they found so that they could provide for their large families.

Any house that I went into had clean floors, an icebox with drip pan beneath, a garden in the rear, an older-model car in the driveway, and usually the familiar smell of cabbage, onion, or bread. Jews, blacks? At the time, I didn't even know the Hungarians, who lived in St. Margaret's, a neighboring parish and autonomous fiefdom not much further away than our own St. Benedict's, but in the opposite direction, across 116th Street.

Our house, with its two downstairs bedrooms, a dining room used only on holidays, and a living room not used at all, had a largely unfinished attic into which my father crafted two more bedrooms to provide more room for the seven of us and my mother's mother, Anna Salansky, who had come to live with us after her husband died. A full basement contained the furnace; a huge coal bin; and a small, two-burner stove on which my mother heated washing water, boiled the white clothes in huge copper tubs, and rendered homemade soap. There was a loom, where clothing and sheets past patching or mending commingled, to be reincarnated as colorful rag rugs. Clotheslines ran the length of the basement, for drying clothes throughout the long Cleveland winter. A cool fruit cellar held jars of tomatoes, plums, peppers, and pickles my mother had preserved. There was a single bathroom with the luxury of store-bought Ivory soap for our weekly bath. The payments were $41 a month, and with my father and mother working and my older brothers and sisters selling newspapers, clerking, or working at the parish house, the idea was to "double up" on the payment so that the house would soon be ours. No one wanted to relive the horror of those years in the in-laws' dusty attic just a few blocks away. My father would have done anything never to have to repeat the humiliation of facing that perspiring, smooth-skinned man in the rumpled suit who, one hot day in 1936, told him that a bank and not Paul Wilkes now owned the house he and his children were illegally occupying. Each day as he mounted the steps to our tiny porch, my father hesitated before opening the back door. It was a sign of reverence. And thanksgiving.

My mother and father's mentality was a post-Depression ode to scarcity interwoven with the reality of a country at war. The tissue-thin foil wrapping from the occasional stick of Juicy Fruit chewing gum was carefully separated from its inner layer and annealed onto an ever-expanding ball in the pantry. No length of string was ever thrown away, no can not flattened, no glass jar ever discarded—for everything there was another season, another use. The war effort was really no effort at all for families like mine. Waste was unheard of, sinful in fact. Food was precious, a gift from the God who both provided and demanded careful accounting of its proper use. Even the cornmeal mush with browned butter that was our standard Friday night dinner was treasured down to the last congealed dollop. During the war, my mother always had extra ration stamps to give to other families. We would not consume more than our fair share. We would walk lightly on this earth, barely leaving a footprint. There was an ominous, unspoken sense that our life hung by a thread and that any false move could be disastrous.

And yet to walk as a visitor through the back door on Forest Avenue, onto the scrubbed, waxed linoleum, was to be treated royally. Whatever food that was already prepared was yours, and if a serving bowl was emptied, it was an embarrassment, for you may have wanted a bit more. Our humble icebox became a cornucopia of delights, our stove forever burning bright. Stuffed cabbage, chicken soup with my mother's homemade noodles, perogi, garlic sausage, huge loaves of Martinovic's Bakery rye bread with caraway seeds. If family members knew not to ask for another slice of bread or not to tarry during mealtime lest that errant piece of meatloaf or pork chop be snapped up by someone else, ours was a house in which the visitor never felt any want.

Strangely enough, I never felt poor—there always was enough to go around, enough for anyone who would walk through our doors. Even a pathetic pots-and-pans salesman would get a sale if he looked as though he needed it.

Those who came to our house were neighbors and relatives mostly. Sit, have a "biffer," as my father called it—the boilermaker, the Slovak's cocktail, aphrodisiac, anesthetic. Corby's was the whiskey, preferably a double shot. P.O.C. (Pride of Cleveland) or Erin Brew was the beer, and that was the order in which you drank, the whiskey warm and the beer at the temperature of our fruit cellar in the basement, the icebox considered far too aggressively chilly for something as savory as this.

The men's talk—which I listened to as I took their empty glasses away with the drop or two remaining as my reward—was of hard work, unfair bosses, and low pay. The shots and beers made the men stronger and wiser on those Sundays, which began with Mass and ended, by early afternoon, in an alcoholic haze. But instead of planning the revolution that would free them from these bonds, taking on roles in their unions or otherwise plotting a way out of the indentured servitude their own grandfathers knew firsthand, they inevitably turned on themselves. After all, what were they but "dumb hunkies." Somehow, they deserved it.

They were living in a land of supposed unbounded possibility, and although being an American was a point of enormous pride, it was far too large a concept to have much of an impact on their lives. Voting was an almost arrogant act. Accomplishment was a cursed word; to be a fore-man or supervisor was to take a lesser—not greater—place in the world, one of privilege and not dignified by labor. It was unholy, a form of pros-titution of a man's most sacred parts—his back, his hands. To think of higher education as a road out was not even considered. Keep your head down; don't ask for or, worse yet, expect too much.

My father never talked about religion or politics or world events, or made grand pronouncements, even deep into a Sunday's drinking with family or friends. But every so often, sometimes spurred by my lazi-ness—the windows I was supposed to paint, porch glider assemble, grass cut—he would say, obliquely, yet with great seriousness, as if he were imparting the very essence of his being, "When a man pays you for eight hours' work, you give him nine." For him it was a sacred oath. Only later in life would I realize it was little different from the scrip-tural admonishment to walk an extra mile if asked for only one. Work, even unrequited and unrewarded hard work, not only had dignity; it was the source of holiness. This way of facing the world was always within one's control, even when little else was. And so it was that Catholicism, combined with the suffering of a long-oppressed people, contained the perfect construct for us. Suffering was true nobility, and certainly within our grasp.

Whereas my mother and father may have agonized over their country's survival and their own, for a young boy like me, the war effort was more of a great adventure. I could pray fervently for the safety of our troops, and wish the agonizing death of Zero pilots and Panzer tank crews. As I memorized the Our Father and Hail Mary, I memorized the names and numbers of our airplanes and can recite them to this day: P-51 Mustang, P-48 Flying Tiger, B-24 Liberator. Jackie Kerner and I took turns with the one plastic .45 pistol and single helmet we had between us, climbing trees and jumping off low garages, killing and being killed, alternately Tojo and GI Joe. In our front window, next to the sign that told Johnny, the ice deliveryman, to leave 25, 50, 75, or 100 pounds of ice (depending on the season), was a single blue star representing my brother Tom, who was in the Navy. Other houses had two and three blue stars. A few had a gold star. When we passed, we knew to make the sign of the cross.

∞

Although America was involved in this war, and such places as Europe and Japan actually must have existed, it was the squarish red brick building of St. Benedict's four blocks away on the corner of Lamontier and East Boulevard that was truly the focal point of our lives. From an early age, I understood that God was the proper center of our lives, all life, in good times and bad. If you asked Cleveland ethnics where they lived, it was always their parish, not their street address, they gave. St. Benedict's was administered by Benedictine monks, every one of them a Slovak and—so it was hoped—role models for us, this cowlicked horde of boys at the parish grade school. There, class by class, we lined up for daily Mass, with a Notre Dame sister in her distinctive horseshoe-shaped headpiece to synchronize our choreographed genuflections with a clicker folded into her smooth hand.

Some of those nuns were no more than children themselves, having ardently joined directly from grade school and, because of the burgeoning numbers of children in Catholic schools, quickly returned to the classroom after but a year or two of college. Nonetheless, they were superb teachers in their fifty-student classrooms, explaining how letters were formed; sentences diagrammed; numbers added, subtracted, multiplied, and divided. How little I knew of their secret, quiet life, shoehorned as they were, fifteen of them, into a tiny convent adjoining the school. They were so restrained, so regimented. They never perspired, even on the hottest day. Their skin was a uniform pale color. They would wipe a table, tuck their handkerchief into their billowing sleeve, enter a room, or sit down in precisely the same way. Their novitiate was a holy uniformity, instilling in them a mentality of seeking perfection, being part of something far bigger than themselves. The best girls from each eighth-grade class would be honored when they were asked to follow in these soft footsteps.

Our four priests presided as lords of the Slovak manor, still at the time when the parish priest was educated far better than anyone in the flock and his authority was unquestioned. Empty liquor cases (not cheap Corby's, to be sure) on their back porch (built by my father, who was rewarded with two holy pictures for his work) told of a far different life than that of the sisters. On those rare occasions when I went to the priests' spacious house with my mother to obtain *oplatki,* the Christmas wafer, and give our offering, it smelled of cigar smoke. Our pastor, Father Leo, was not a man to smile, and his priests took the cue that a stern face and stern penances in the confessional booth were needed to keep these uneducated masses in check.

The best boys from each eighth-grade class were encouraged to be priests, the highest calling. Not me. My report cards read a steady stream of A's and B's in academic subjects and consistent D's in "cooperation," "dependability," "industriousness," and that seminal virtue of virtues, "guidance of action by reason." "I am very disappointed in Paul's work and in his attitude. He makes no effort to improve" were the damning words on the bottom of one report card.

Each morning in our parish church, a place suffused with an otherworldly ochre light, the holy smell of incense and burning beeswax candles enveloping us, I peered up to a priest (certainly not the likes of us!) reverently facing the altar, his stiff fiddleback chasuble properly keeping us from the mysteries that he alone could negotiate. He whispered in Latin to a God that surely was not the same God to whom I directed my prayers each night. I wanted to know this other God, this bigger, grander God, but for now I had to settle for my own. My God was a smaller God, gimlet-eyed, scrutinizing my every move.

"Please help me to sit still."

"Please don't let Jeanette Smolko write my name on the board when sister leaves."

"Please forgive me for kissing my cousin Nancy when we hid in that pile of coats on the bed last Thanksgiving."

"Give me something great to die for. Please!"

Our hymns were sung in the divine Latin, the Slovak of our native villages, and the English of America.

> Stabat mater dolorosa
> iuxta Crucem lacrimosa,
> dum pendebat Filius.
>
> S'nami Boh, s'nami Boh!
> Razumejte jazyci
> I pokarjajtesja, i pokarjajtesja
> Jako s'nami Boh,
> Jako s'nami Boh
>
> Holy God, we praise thy name;
> Lord of all, we bow before Thee.
> All on earth thy scepter claim,
> All in heav'n above adore Thee.
> Infinite, thy vast domain,
> Everlasting is thy reign;
> Infinite, thy vast domain,
> Everlasting is thy reign.

There were novenas, stations of the cross, Christmas pageants as we moved through the mandala of the church year. There was but a narrow gate to heaven. Because of our many hours of prayer and ritual each week, we would be granted entrance, while the weak-willed so-called Christians—what a sadly anemic word, I thought—and especially those stiff-necked Jews, would be turned aside to burn forever.

"Let us pray for heretics and schismatics . . . to call them back to our holy Mother the Catholic and Apostolic Church. . . . Let us pray for the Jews. May the Lord our God tear the veil from their hearts. . . . Let us pray also for the pagans . . . May they give up their idols and be converted."

2

A VISION

IT WAS A TORRID, HUMID, AUGUST DAY IN 1945 when my mother told me to put on my best clothes, as we were going "downtown." She dressed in her best cotton dress, glistening with starch that kept its smooth surface unfazed as we walked up Forest, across East 116th Street, and finally, just before the imposing St. Luke's Hospital where I had been born some seven years before, down a set of wooden stairs. A bright yellow train with a red roof stopped before us, and soon we were off, at what seemed like breathtaking speed. This was Cleveland Rapid Transit, the "Rappy," hurtling us toward this downtown I had never seen before.

I knelt on the empty seat across from my mother, peering out the window as buildings and overpasses whizzed by. I looked across at her and she smiled, a wonderful mother's smile from a woman who rarely allowed herself such an outward display of emotion. And then, for some fateful reason, my eyes traced down over her dress, the ample chest, the thin belt struggling to define a midsection that had yielded seven of us, her thick cotton hose, her sturdy ankles, and finally her shoes, well-buffed black lace-up shoes with heavy, thick heels. My eyes moved slowly to the right, to the sight of an entirely different female form. Had they not, my life might easily have taken another course.

I started at midcalf, each so slender and encased in such sheer nylon that the pale flesh took on a new and radiant life, shimmering in the rays of the midmorning sun. The ankles were angular, sculpted; light danced about them, further accentuating their sensuous curves, proclaiming the audacity of an unfatted bone to come so close to the surface. And the shoes. Elegant patent-leather pumps with a low heel, so delicate and proportionally fashioned, shoes that seemed more like form-fitting gloves than utilitarian foot coverings. My eyes flashed back to my mother's legs and shoes. Then, almost as if they had been shocked, back to those pumps, those ankles, and up, ever so slowly, to the two shafts of fleshly perfection. My eyes ventured no higher than the woman's two exquisitely conformed knees that almost, but not quite, touched each other, a tantalizing fraction of an inch apart. There was no need to look further. I was breathless, my mouth dry. I had seen enough for one day.

We emerged from the bowels of the Terminal Tower into the blinding sunlight and the calamity of downtown. Cars were stopped, honking their horns; rolls of toilet paper streamed down from the buildings along Euclid Avenue. My mother held my hand tightly as I gawked at people kissing, toasting each other with paper cups they filled from tall green bottles of champagne. They formed little circles and danced around and around, stumbling, falling, always laughing. I was beginning to realize that this war of blue and gold stars had ended. To celebrate this special day, we went to the Forum Cafeteria on Ninth Street. As we slowly pushed our trays along the smooth chrome tubes, I was confronted with an array of amazing foods I had never seen before. Quivering bowls of Jell-O in a dizzying array of colors. French fried, not only mashed, potatoes. Chocolate meringue pie, its tufts perfectly bronzed. All just an arm's length away.

I rested dreamily on my mother's arm on the way home, but it was not the war's end or those delicacies that floated through my mind as I traveled back to my secure, small world. I closed my eyes. Those legs, those shoes! I was too young for lust. But not for questioning. What kind of person could this be? Where did she live? Was her house like mine?

∞

In second grade, I received my first Holy Communion in a wool blue suit so scratchy that I had to wear my pajama bottoms underneath to stave off the itching. In sixth grade, an unsmiling, somewhat distracted Bishop Edward Hoban placed a dripping cross of oil upon my forehead, confirming me as "Louis," a name carefully chosen, my homage to Cleveland Indians' player-manager Lou Boudreau. In later grades, Sister Leah and Sister Augustine found my knuckles with their rulers and Sister Florentine my heart with the spiritual and corporal works of mercy, which I could repeat from memory and tried diligently to practice in my daily life. Clothe the naked. Oh, if only I could have found such a person. Shelter the homeless. I would have given my own bed. Bury the dead. I just never saw any as I walked up and down Forest Avenue to and from St. Benedict's school.

Instead of saintly actions, I stole pennies from the change I was supposed to bring home from Bill's, the little grocery store up the street, and bought candy. I even stole some when he was behind the counter. I peed down the furnace grate in my bedroom one summer night after drinking plenty of soda at a cousin's wedding, too lazy or too afraid to go back downstairs through the scary, dark attic. That winter, when the heat came up, my sin was revealed. I lied about doing my homework, shoveling snow, sweeping the front walk. I always had a full laundry list to report each Saturday at Confession. After all, I had only to look at the cross to see what real sacrifice meant. I was trying to please God, and I was failing most of the time. I secretly reveled in the stinging pain when my mother would slap my face for a smart remark. I deserved that, and more.

If those marvelous ankles and shoes offered a sliver-thin peek into another world, a world apart from the one my family knew here in America and my people had known for centuries, then a green plastic box twelve inches long, six inches wide, and no more than six inches high flung open the window. My Admiral clock radio, a Christmas present in my eighth-grade year, was a magic carpet on which I could soar out my second-floor bedroom window to exotic places of new and forbidden sounds. This was not Fibber Magee and Molly or the Grand Ole Opry or a Gabriel Heater newscast I had heard from the wooden-cased radio downstairs as I sat there with my father. Not The Shadow or Jack Armstrong, All American Boy. No, this was Moondog Allen Freed, the howl of werewolves at midnight heralding his throaty voice. "Ladies and gentlemen . . . the latest from the Penguins." *Earth Angel, Earth Angel, will you be mine, my darling dear, love you all the time.* "Now, mister lovebird out there, is this your song tonight." *I Got a Woman, way cross town, she's good to me. . . .* "And you sweet thang out there, this one's for you, a new one heading to the top of the charts called 'You're So Fine.'"

> Baby you're so fine
> Oh I'm so glad you're mine
> Baby you're so fine, oh
> Baby you're so fine
> Oh how I love you baby
> Baby you're so fine

My St. Benedict's classmates were humming Patti Page tunes, and here I was, listening to music that sounded as if it had been recorded in some-body's garage—some of which had been—with a beat that didn't so much set my polished oxfords to tapping as my groin to pulsing. The beat, the rhythm, was so primitive, so in sync with whatever was coming alive in my young body. Etta James, Chuck Willis, Clyde McPhatter, Big Joe Turner, Ruth Brown, B. B. King. This was "black" music—therefore, in my world, bad music, sinful music. I kept the radio low, and when my brothers were asleep in the beds across the room, I would creep over and slip from beneath their beds one of the tattered magazines they had brought back from a trip to Chicago. In the dim light of the street lamp, I could see mountainous breasts, eyes outlined in mascara, black garter belts. No, I would not do what George Pezo demonstrated with a grin on his face as he massaged his huge penis and spattered my whitewashed basement wall with a wad of mucus. No, I had to be strong. My impure thoughts were already enough for Saturday Confession, and I knew Father Louis or Father Michael would howl through the screen loud enough for the entire church to know what I had done.

Eighth-grade graduation was nearing, and I was finally allowed to attend a Catholic Youth Organization (CYO) canteen on a Thursday night in May 1952. I tamed my cowlicky hair with my sister's Jergen's hand lotion, paid my fifteen cents, and slipped into our parish hall. The air was moist with teenage sweat and suffused with the dime-store perfume the girls had clandestinely splashed on themselves after they left home.

As I scanned the dimly lit dance floor, I saw her, one hand poised saucily on her hip. Her white sweater seemed etched on her body. Her legs were apart, stretching the already tight skirt even tighter. Her bobby socks were swollen white blobs just above her penny loafers. The rotating globe overhead sent quivery beams of colored light across the floor, revealing her, then concealing, revealing. I felt as if I could pass out at any minute. I finally got up the nerve. No, not to dance with her. I could never be that bold, although we had learned the box step in Miss Minch's gym class. I finally got up the nerve to look directly at her.

And she looked right back at me. Was that a smile? The light, the light! I couldn't tell. I felt a pain rising low in my groin, the same wonderful pain I could feel, listening to that music after midnight in the quiet of my bedroom. I turned away immediately. Was it showing?

Where had my innocence gone? Was this any way for a budding saint to be?

3

HIGH SCHOOL

The Man in the Ten-Way Suit

IN REALITY, IT WAS BUT AN UNREMARKABLE, STOLID, three-story neoclassical building, but as I approached Cathedral Latin School on a dreamy, sun-dappled September morning in 1952, I peered up at its limestone facade in sheer awe. I was struck both with its magnificence and with the audacity that had brought me here. All five foot two inches of me passed beneath the school motto etched boldly over what seemed like a soaring arched door for the world to see and for us to live out: "Opere et Veritate." In deed and in truth. I was at once humbled to accept such a mandate and to join the long line of illustrious Latin men who had gone before me, yet not quite sure I was up to the challenge. Cathedral Latin was founded in 1916 out of the downtown diocesan cathedral to provide the initial schooling for future priests and to reinforce the Catholic faith in the sons of immigrants, many of whom, like my own father, had never even graduated from grade school. This, the premier Catholic high school on Cleveland's East Side, was my choice rather than the more working-class Benedictine High School, just a few blocks from my home. I still don't know what propelled me out of my own neighborhood, but it would be the first of many forays into uncharted waters.

Internally, I may have had my misgivings, but nattily attired in my checkered trousers and my reversible vest, I felt perfectly presentable. This, combination number three of my ten-way suit, that ingenious $40 investment in my future I had made at the May Company for my grade-school graduation, was my ticket and crafty disguise for the passage out of Forest Avenue and St. Benedict's parish. Such astonishing possibilities! A pair of blue trousers and a checkered jacket stood in readiness at the rear of my attic closet. Blue trousers, blue vest. Blue trousers, checkered

vest. Checkered jacket, checkered trousers. I was surely ready for anything in the days ahead.

When I walked into that school building, I found a Catholic environment so totally alien to me that I don't think I so much as uttered a word
to any of the other boys in the first weeks of school. Engulfed in such
rarefied air, I found myself overwhelmed with a strange narcosis. I surely
said nothing about it at home. What could I say? How could I explain
to my mother and father, brothers and sisters that there was a world
outside St. Benedict's? There was a Catholicism that went beyond the
rote answers to the Baltimore Catechism. A Catholicism that even in
the 1950s invited at least a modicum of discussion and was not offended
by questions, at least those properly phrased. This Catholicism transcended not only our ethnic group—embracing Irish, Italian, Polish, German—but economics as well. Some of the fathers of my classmates
actually wore to work each day what my father reserved for Sunday use
only. I saw them as they dropped their sons off at school at a time when
my father had already been pounding nails for an hour. They laughed so
easily; they seemed in no hurry; worries were for others, not them.

At Cathedral Latin, there was none of the coarseness of the overweight,
dull-eyed parish priests of St. Benedict's, the only representatives of the
male religious life I'd then witnessed. These Marianist priests and brothers carried books and magazines in their arms, and had obviously read
them. They talked about world affairs and Senator Joseph McCarthy,
new treatments for cancer, and banished European theologians who
would later emerge as the true lights of the Second Vatican Council.
Thomas Aquinas, neo-scholasticism, apologetics. Latin phrases succinctly
summarized their points and rolled easily off their tongues. I went from
class to class, fascinated with the echo of my heels resounding from the
polished marble hallways, as if magically, mystically, my steps, my very
self were being magnified by the place. I sat attentively in my alphabeti-
cally assigned seat and did my homework as if it were a divine summons.
I don't remember ever being so happy in my life.

I and my ten-way suit had negotiated Cleveland Transit bus route 107
so adroitly, so successfully. I was on my way—to where and to do what
I didn't have the slightest idea.

oo

Midway through my freshman year, a tall priest with sunken eyes came
into my religion class. He was a Maryknoll missionary just back from
China, a place of dysentery, hepatitis, dengue fever, malaria. He stood

before us, his beautifully sculpted and anointed hands clasped in front of him, offering his ailments as negligible sacrifices for the love of Christ, yet—to me—they were valiant combat ribbons that normal mortals might never be worthy to wear. He had been beaten, tortured, and imprisoned, all because of his passion to convert the hordes of heathen Chinese who otherwise would never know that Catholicism provided the only true path to God.

On the first Sunday of each month, he would gather a group of us to play basketball and to hear more of his stories. He actually talked very little of his suffering, but more about such moments as seeing the amazed look on a ten-year-old boy's face when the priest told him that there was a power far beyond his village that watched over him every day, loved him, and wanted him to be part of his family on earth. Or the baptism of a ninety-year-old man and his four-month-old great-great-granddaughter on the same day. And of both dying of cholera the next. He talked almost romantically of what power the Beatitudes possessed, of St. John's admonition to love always and everyone, of the dignity of washing another's feet, and of how a few loaves and fishes could indeed feed thousands. Those once disembodied words of scripture—served in dollops at Sunday Mass at St. Benedict's and then, through the sadly suspicious minds of our priests, turned into scathing indictments of our miserable Slovak selves—took on new meaning. The Christ I had known on the cross, contorted in agony for my sins, came down to walk along the shores of the Galilee and sit with his friends and smile at the children who were brought to him.

The Maryknoll priest was a painfully shy man—I could tell that by the way he never could look directly at us—but there was a certain confidence, along with goodness, kindness, and a quiet intelligence, that radiated from that emaciated body. He had to admit—when we asked for the number of conversions he had made—that he had not actually been that successful. Some would sow, others would reap, he said. His objective was not success. His objective was simply to do his best, with God's help, in every circumstance.

Sitting on the gym bleachers one Sunday, looking at the priest, backlit by the afternoon sun and almost radiant before us, I realized I had not experienced such a man before. And that I wanted to be just like him. These priests who had gone to China were heroic. I wanted to do something heroic in my life. I had been given a whole new economy of life, and it made perfect sense.

Even as I so admired this man and wanted to be just like him, I wouldn't admit to myself that I had been attending a vocation group and was signaling my interest in becoming a Maryknoll priest. When asked what I did on those Sundays at Cathedral Latin, I told my mother and father that it was a school meeting, and because the very word "meeting" had such an alien and exotic sound to them, they questioned me no further. I had no close friends, so there was no one who was privy to the details of my small life. I prayed on my knees each night that I would hear God's call, yet had I been asked directly, I would have vehemently denied any interest in becoming a priest. This thorough mental bifurcation prepared me well for a Thursday night at the CYO canteen and a life hardly compatible with that of a celibate soldier of Christ.

∞

Steam rose from the hissing radiators that flanked the dance floor; the air was thick with the suppression of young lust; you could almost sense it just walking through the doors. It was a volatile combination, ignitable at the slightest stare, nod, or smile. Overhead, the ball of tiny mirrors lazily spun on its axis, sending shivering beams of colored lights into the damp darkness. At the weekly CYO canteen, the hope was that good Catholic boys and girls would chastely meet each other, dance without actually touching more than the palms of their hands, and eventually go on to present their virginal selves to each other in marriage. There were those boys—Joe Semancik, Joe Kolenic, Paul Forgach, Bob Estvander, and others—who seemed to have gotten that message. And girls like Marilyn Ungarsky, Mary Jo Sotak, Martha Balash, and Joanne Kovats, who were models of youthful Catholic purity. But, of course, those were not the girls who made the hair on the back of my neck bristle, who caused my mouth to turn dry just looking at them.

So one Thursday night, there stood my temptress, staring right at me from the dim shadows directly across the floor, daring me with her parted lips to stride across the floor and ask her to dance. She was fast, that much I knew from her "reputation"—ah, that damning word. She went to public school, already marking her as off-limits. Not even Catholic. A gypsy, so the word had it; whatever "gypsy" meant I didn't know, but I knew it was forbidden. I had to—I must—resist this "direct occasion of sin" that Brother Behringer had so carefully covered in religion class, a direct occasion clearly demarcated by the outer reaches of those ample breasts, straining beneath what appeared to be her single white sweater, and by the smooth expanse of her tight skirt, stretched ever more tautly as she impatiently shifted her weight, spreading her legs still further apart. For weeks I had seen her and knew that she had seen me, but my resolve had been strong enough to yank me by the collar and out the door, saving me from a sure mortal sin. But this night, my heart was beating, faster and faster; sweat rose on my forehead and in my armpits. This was the moment of anguish for me, as I was assaulted by the sound of two drum-beats: one, the call to Catholic excellence and sacrifice, a moral pounding in my head; the other, a throbbing between my legs that I just knew would so easily be satisfied moments after I slowly gyrated my pelvis against hers, a poor imitation of actually dancing, but enough to keep the ever-watchful sisters at bay.

"Hey, you were at Cathedral Latin last Sunday, weren't you?" I wheeled around. It was the sandy-haired kid from Our Lady of Peace, a neighboring parish, who went to Benedictine High School and attended the Maryknoll meetings. It was obviously his first time at the canteen. He was a good, solid kid, more open than most. We had had a long discussion about how we each felt the presence of God in the Eucharist and what that must be like for the priest who actually is changing the bread and wine into the Body and Blood of Christ. I stared at him. "Naw, must have been somebody else. Gotta go."

I turned my back to him and chose the sweet sinfulness of those breasts, those thighs, mumbling something into her ear as we cast off on our slow and easy slide into hell to the tune of the Penguins' song—oddly enough, with an ersatz religious theme—"Earth Angel." St. Peter had done only half as well when the cock crowed thrice for him. The Maryknoller and priesthood were far away.

OO

I was standing by my locker, now in September of my sophomore year, wearing combination eight of my ten-way suit, carrying a creditable average in everything but geometry, a subject so mysterious that—without the grace of alphabetical seating and Richard Winnicki—I might still be in that class to this day. My Cathedral Latin days were continuing to be just this side of blissful. I had tried out for the basketball team, but with my limited height and ability, that was not to be my pathway to one of the letters with interlocking C and L. Seeing a boy with a quill on his letter, I discovered that the school newspaper was an alternate path for someone who was better pecking at keys than blocking and tackling boys twice my size.

With no more than that, a writer was launched.

I had made a few new friends, and I was thinking that finally, finally, I had crossed the great divide from Forest Avenue to this area, known as

University Circle. That illusion was shattered that September morning as I was getting some books out of my locker. I heard the voices behind me, barely audible, speaking in that sotto voce used so deftly by adolescents to both reveal and mask their cruelty. "Wonderboy. Wondersuit. Look, today I'm blue and checked. Blue and blue tomorrow. Stand by for our favorite: checked and checked coming up!" I turned to face my Greek chorus. Before me were the rightful occupiers of Cathedral Latin's pantheon, boys I had watched and secretly wanted to be exactly like. Their hair was short and flawlessly parted, their shoulders thrown back with that sense of entitlement I so admired and could never hope to ape. Their penny loafers were shined, chinos starched, the sleeves of letter sweaters pushed midway up their forearms. Captain of the golf team; sodality president; yearbook editor; king of the Purple and Gold Ball, our biggest social event and one I was certainly not worthy to attend. Their smug smiles ripened into demonic grins. They didn't need to whisper anymore; the entire corridor was in on the good fun. "Tune in tomorrow to see what Wonderhunky will wear. It's a bird, it's a plane, it's Wonderhunky and his magic suit!" They burst into laughter that spread in resounding waves down the hall.

I closed my locker slowly. I walked down the hallway to the bathroom. I went inside one of the stalls and pressed my forehead to the cool metal. How could I have been so foolish to think I could be just like them? I was, and would always be, from Forest Avenue.

4

COMING HOME,
LEAVING HOME

I SAT FACING A WARMING BOTTLE OF COTTON CLUB CHERRY SODA. Tomas's
Café, two blocks from my house, on the corner of Forest Avenue and East
116th Street, was doing a booming business, as it did every Friday afternoon. This was payday for the men of my neighborhood. On the jukebox
was a polka; on the bar, thick shot glasses, bottles of Erin Brew, and piles
of bills and change. Voices thick with alcohol and the easy camaraderie of
this wonderful sanctuary from work and wife rose up to swirl beneath the
water-stained tin ceiling with the smoke from twenty-five-cent R. G. Dunn
cigars, forming the kind of magical air a workingman—choked all week
by mill grime and sawdust, lorded over by the clean-handed bosses—
yearned all week long to breathe.

A teenage boy from my background had only to look at these happy
faces and to inhale deeply to understand that this is what life was really
all about. That this was what the men of my lineage had done for centuries. As if to confirm the sheer opulence of it all, my father ordered me
another cherry soda, even though the one before me was still half full.
And another bag of potato chips. He casually flipped me a dime for the
jukebox. What else could I possibly ever want?

When the Maryknoll priest called a few times after my hallway massacre, I told him I was sick. Then he stopped calling. My magnificent suit of
many colors and guises was soon rotting in a dump someplace, sliced to
ribbons with a kitchen knife. I was now wearing the sweaters given to my
father on one of his many part-time jobs, this one at a local knitting mill.
They were unsalable seconds, with pulled threads and strange colors like
lime green and a sickly yellow, but whatever they were, they were not
that foolish suit. As my hair began to creep over my ears, more Jergen's

Lotion from my sister's humble shelf in the medicine cabinet provided its discipline. No, I would not be like the clean-cut boys with penny loafers. I could never be one of them, in their insufferable smugness.

I had new role models: tough Italian kids from Murray Hill, with their swagger and glistening pompadours, body hair, and bravado; their pointed shoes; their trousers, with white stitching down the side, swooping down to thirteen inches at the cuff, the absolute minimum if you expected to actually get your foot past. With fathers in jail for running numbers and other American avocations that in their native Sicily would be regarded as perfectly legitimate. Their snarling, angry faces—this I could bring off. This was the real me. Marlon Brando in *The Wild One,* Holden Caulfield in *Catcher in the Rye,* and yes, I convinced myself, the rebel without a cause, James Dean. Alienation was in the air as the sleepy 1950s were preparing a way to the tumultuous 1960s, but of course I knew nothing about the cultural upheavals that were afoot. All I knew for sure was the profound distance—in fact, the ever-widening chasm, even after my valiant efforts to fit in—between me and the rest of the world. There was a new pop star, Elvis Presley, but he looked like a veritable choirboy compared to what I became.

The gypsy girl liked the new me just fine. She ran her fingers through the smooth, Jergen's-tamed "fenders" that met in the back of my head in a perfect DA, "duck's ass." She played with the casual curls that tumbled onto my pimpled forehead. My clothes, my sullenness, my inability to express anything beyond a grunt were perfect. And no longer was there any hesitation on Thursday night, no moral dissection. I followed her home, pinned her against the garbage cans in the alley behind the tenement where she lived near the Cleveland Transit car barns off Woodland Avenue, and plunged my tongue so deep into her mouth that it ached. Yes, I would have a woman like this, who would melt with my passion. A real woman, none of those fancy Beaumont or Marymount girls in carefully pleated plaid skirts and oversize cotton blouses. Tight sweater, real woman. I could be perennially angry with the unjust world. I'd get a job down at one of the steel mills in the Flats along the Cuyahoga River, work like an animal all week long and then live like royalty, if only for those few glorious hours on Friday afternoon. Steady work, that was always the highest priority in my family. School? Nobody was pushing this. Who needed it? I would have a house of my own someday on Forest Avenue. Why had I ever thought life could be—should be—anything else? This is exactly who I was and would always be. I was my father's son, the latest in a long line of Slovak serfs who would work hard, sing loud, and drink well and long. Keep your head down; don't reach beyond your grasp, because surely you will fail.

At school, I seemed to find new ways to get into trouble. Raining down chalk dust on an unsuspecting novice Marianist substitute teacher; gouging the gym floor with the heel taps that now marked me as one of the hoods; stuffing an oozing, rotten tomato into the principal's mail slot. It was a rare week that went by when I didn't have to stay for detention hall.

Following one of these after-school incarcerations late in my junior year, I was swaggering down the hallway when I saw Brother Adolph Kalt coming out of the library. He was an old man, fifty years a Marianist, hunched over, with terrifyingly bad breath, a virtual blizzard of dandruff on the shoulders of his black suit jacket, but with that kind of supernal smile both the holy and mad possess. He was motioning to me, but I swaggered on, perversely proud that I had just spent the last hour of my life writing some inane sentence of self-indictment over and over again. He stood his ground, and I couldn't avoid him. He gestured for me to come into the library and, after peering up and down the corridor as if he wanted no one to know we would be there alone, he came inside, shut and locked the door. "You're in a lot of trouble around here," were his words, which I expected to be followed by a few more lashes for good measure. "So was he." His smile was at once generous and questioning, an offering and a request he was not sure I could understand. He reached out to the bookshelf, withdrew a book in a dark blue binding, and pressed it into my reluctant hands.

"Merton was kind of a wild guy too, when he was young," he chuckled, perhaps remembering a moment in the book, "but he turned out all right after all. Maybe there's some hope for you. Now off with you."

My face to the world did not dramatically change in the weeks and months ahead, and neither did my wardrobe, but for some reason I stopped getting in so much trouble. Was it that I didn't want to be held after school when all I wanted to do was get home and up to my room to read a few more pages of *The Seven Storey Mountain*? And then move on to the next, *The Sign of Jonas,* and after that, *The Waters of Siloe* and *Seeds of Contemplation* and *No Man Is an Island.* There was something in the writings of Thomas Merton I had never encountered before in the lives of the saints I had so ardently read. There were no sanctimonious paeans to God, no once-and-for-all, life-altering conversion experiences. Merton continually confessed his sinfulness, his conflicts, his desire to be and do good, and his ultimate failure in both. His parallel lives. (Like mine!) And what was even more appealing was the way he spoke about his relationship with God. It was an uneven and unpredictable love affair, but both sides were committed to its ups and downs. Merton's thirst for God rose up from those pages, fueled by passion not piety, the unflagging desire to understand his place before God. And here he was, a man of my own time, a bon vivant who lived a dissolute life in England, even made a girl pregnant, came to Columbia University and then turned his back on a budding literary life to join the Trappists, the most austere order of the Catholic Church. I began to have this fantasy that I would, on the spur of the moment, go to see him. He was at a monastery in Kentucky, just one state south. I would ask him how he prayed, how he could forgive himself when he sinned or failed. I would ask him how he knew what do with his life, what it felt like—in those fleeting moments of total abandonment and awareness—to be close to God. And then I would ask him what I should do with my life, what path I should take. I vowed, if that day ever came, to do exactly what he told me.

OO

One of the innovations at Cathedral Latin in my senior year was to appoint Brother Kenneth Sommer—who taught religion and, as a former football player, was known to make his displeasure with rowdy students known by putting their heads as far through the mesh window of a classroom door as he could—as something called a guidance counselor. We had never heard of such a thing. We were to see him in alphabetical order, so, late in the fall semester when he reached the W's and my turn came, I sauntered into his office, twirled my lotioned curls around my index finger, and plopped into the appointed chair, adopting the very worst posture I could muster.

He opened the small folder in front of him. "Hmmm." I slouched further into my chair as he continued. "Grades a little uneven, but you still made National Honor Society. Three years with the newspaper. Hmmm. And these?" He held up a thick wad of yellow detention sheets. "Your first book?" He plucked a single light green sheet from the folder and ran his finger over its face as if it were Braille. I assumed I was in even more trouble. He scanned the sheet once again and looked up at me squarely, his eyes eerily magnified by his thick glasses. "You know you did pretty well on these IQ tests, Wilkes," he said somewhat incredulously. "You know you could go to college?"

"Been thinking of Republic Steel. Steady work. Good benefits. I hear they're hiring."

"It's up to you, but why not just apply? I'm pretty sure you'd be accepted. Even with all your disciplinary problems, you still managed a pretty good average. Let's see, where should you go?" he said, going back to folder. "You were on the newspaper. You could study journalism. Marquette

University in Milwaukee has a journalism program." It was unthinkable
that he would have recommended other than a Catholic university, and at
the time, Marquette was the only Catholic school in the Midwest that had
a journalism major. I had barely ventured beyond Cleveland's West Side,
and Milwaukee was farther than that. "I can send a letter in for you; it's all
you'd need, I think." I had never known this husky, head-bashing brother—
peering intently at me—to be so concerned about the fate of a student, a
nonathlete at that. Especially one with more than his share of disciplinary
problems at Cathedral Latin, who had distinguished himself in no other
way than by being a small-time and poorly played hood. I didn't ask him to
send in the letter. But neither did I tell him not to.

OO

I'll never know why Shamus (that's what he grandly called himself,
although his real name was simply Jim) Thompson singled me out. But
one day, sitting down at my lunchroom table, glancing to his right and
left, he whispered conspiratorially, "A bunch of us are getting together
for a little fun at my apartment Saturday night. Want to come?" If so,
he told me, keep it quiet and show up around seven. There were four
main crowds at Cathedral Latin: the popular guys; the hoods, of which
I was then classified; the unpopular guys, comprising a broad swath of
eggheads and dullards; and the "fast" crowd. As I began my senior
year, I had only heard rumors about the fast crowd's parties, where
beer was drunk from frosted glasses, not swilled from bottles, and
where mixed drinks—no, not highballs with Seagram's and Seven-Up,
but those excruciatingly adult-sounding drinks like martinis and manhattans—were served along with something called hors d'oeuvres.
Their parties were supposedly held in houses where no parents ever
intruded. I couldn't believe this was happening to me.

On Saturday night, when I rang the doorbell at his parents' apartment
(exciting in itself, as everybody I knew lived in a house), Shamus couldn't
believe that I arrived a half-hour early; neither could he believe what
I was wearing. I thought I was quite fashionable in baggy ice cream
flannels with a drop-loop belt, draped to thirteen-inch cuffs; a one-button
roll blue jacket with white flecks; and a pink Mister B shirt, with its huge,
flared collar the perfect framing for the thick blue wool tie in a Windsor
knot bigger than my fist. "Oh, God," he breathed, taking me in, from my
DA to pointed-toe shoes. He slammed the door and whisked me into his
bedroom. By the time the party started, I had been reincarnated still
again, transformed into a person I could barely recognize. I was wearing

a pair of charcoal gray slacks, a pale blue oxford shirt set off with a
striped rep tie, and a three-button herringbone jacket. The penny loafers
were too big, but small wads of toilet paper filled out the toes. My hair
was rakishly parted on the side and slicked back, making me look (in my
mind's eye) like a jaded Gatsbyesque character who just couldn't be both-
ered with regular haircuts. Ethnic bumpkin turned mobster manqué had
now gone preppy.

Just as Cathedral Latin had introduced me to another way of life, so
too did this group and their parties. None of them appeared to have
parents who ever seemed to be around. Curfew? Really. Shamus had a
very good phony ID, which passed muster even at the state liquor
stores. The Shaker Heights and Cleveland Heights girls who came to
the parties laughed easily and smoked cigarettes. As the night wore on
and lights dimmed, we paired off. The younger sister of one of my Latin
classmates wore perfume so intoxicating and cashmere sweaters so soft
to the touch that I couldn't wait to get her onto a sofa or, if unoccupied,
a bedroom. No one would actually think of having sex; everything was
done fully clothed, but that didn't prevent "getting your rocks off," as
we used to say. I lived for those Saturday nights. There was no future,
but what a wonderful present.

I thought that I had arrived, but of course I was more lost than ever
before, living life at its shallowest. Yet even as I was enshrouded in a fog
of alcohol and perfume and testosterone, God would not leave me to my
own worst instincts. He waited patiently in the wings. I rarely missed
kneeling down before I went to bed and saying my prayers; it was bred
into me. Sometimes I would recite rote prayers I knew, but more and more
often, I found my mind wandering, recapping the day's activities, a sort
of examination of conscience. I was ashamed of my sins and vowed to do
better the next day. I repeated the words of Confession: "I firmly resolve,
with the help of thy grace, to confess my sins, do penance, and to amend
my life. Amen." But the next day dawned, and my best intentions were
so much fragile dew, quickly vaporized. I never missed Sunday Mass, at
times stumbling into St. Benedict's in the morning with a terrific hangover. Or, after our debauchery at Shamus's apartment or in the backseat
of a car parked at the Lover's Lane at Shaker Lake, we would travel
downtown to the 2 AM Mass at St. John's Cathedral. There I was, drunk,
with lipstick smudges on my collar and dried semen on my shorts, praying that God would forgive me and show me the right path for my life.
Caught up in the orbit of Shamus and his merry companions, I was
extremely careful not to let them even glimpse my own life. When they

came to pick me up, I would be waiting on the sidewalk in front of my house, and leap into the car. On the one day I was late and Shamus rang the front door and was royally welcomed in by my mother, I later lied and said she was somebody else, a neighbor.

Lost in this euphoria of newfound friends and a hormonal typhoon that blew uncontrolled upon welcoming shores, I was surprised to find that at least one of that fast crowd also heard another drumbeat beside the steady rhythm of party, party, party. One Friday after school, I ran into Jerry Corsaro, one of the regulars, and talk somehow turned from hangovers and hickeys to *The Seven Storey Mountain,* which I must have mentioned and Jerry had read. We did something totally unpredictable and crazy. Jerry's older sister had a radiant coral pink 1955 Ford convertible, and into its backseat we loaded great quantities of beer and headed south. Top down, we drove. We drank. We played the radio at full blast. Night fell and we drove on, in search of this man who would tell us what to do with lives that—as these hundreds of miles were increasingly convincing us—needed some serious redirection. It was the middle of the night when we turned onto a drive, brilliantly lit by the moonlight (a sign that enlightenment was at hand, we were sure).

"For God Alone" read the sign over the archway leading to the main entrance. My hand reached for the knocker on the heavy wooden door. Once, twice, three times. A bolt was loosened. The door began to open. Just then, a bell high in the abbey church tower sounded, its muffled echo rolling over the knobby hills that surrounded the place. Jerry and I looked at each other with a combination of fright and expectancy. We expected Thomas Merton to appear right then, see our fervor, invite us in for a simple breakfast, and tell us what to do with our lives; we could be on our way home in a couple hours. Instead it was the brother gatekeeper, just awakened from his truncated night's sleep, and his heart was not so strangely warmed by these two reeking, besotted pilgrims.

We slept most of the day and, as best one can in a place where silence reigned, tried to find Merton. We looked into the only occasionally upturned faces of the monks, who wordlessly cleaned the guest quarters and served our meals, but we realized that we did not know what Merton looked like. We had surmised that the man who had written the words that had so inflamed our souls would somehow stand out, be different from all the rest of two hundred monks. From the visitor's loft in the rear of the high-ceilinged, unadorned, and impossibly elongated abbey church—characteristic of the elegant intent of Cistercian architecture to focus everything on the simple stone altar—I peered down on the long rows of tonsured heads standing before their choir stalls. They all seemed lost in another world, a world at once appealing in its simplicity and obvious sanctity, yet alien from my own tiny universe.

It was here that Merton, who first arrived as a jaded, lonesome, directionless pilgrim just as I was, had famously written a line I could quote word for word: "As soon as I got inside, I knew I was home where I never had been or would be a stranger." I yearned for such a home, for certitude and peace. But I knew that jumping into the Ford convertible for a visit was a very far cry from making this kind of statement with my young life. Finally I got up the courage to ask the priest who was in charge of the weekend retreatants—a group we were swept into—and he smiled. "Father Louis?" Oh, yes, he's here someplace," he said as he kindly added my request, one of perhaps hundreds he received, to meet the great man.

Perhaps I actually saw Merton during that visit in 1956; I do not know. But he would walk with me through life, and we would meet again and again on the pages of his books in the years to come and in a very special way many years later.

∞

My final days in Cleveland saw the good fortune of a college acceptance and the worst event of my young life.

In the week that I was going down to the steel mills to apply for work, I received an astonishing letter in the mail, advising me that I had been accepted into a college to which I couldn't remember submitting an application and that I had never seen. As of September, I would be in the incoming freshman class at Marquette University; my intended major, journalism.

Then came the day that would forever divide my life into a before and after: May 1, 1956.

My mother had been having medical problems. Her skin had turned a jaundiced yellow. A woman who had always had boundless energy, then fifty-six years old, who had raised seven children while working another twenty to thirty hours a week outside the house, had shrunken inside a shell of constant fatigue. The diagnosis was possible cirrhosis of the liver, which is usually brought on by hepatitis or excessive drinking. A third, less-known reason is malnutrition. It is entirely possible that my mother had for years been starving herself to feed her children.

She had an appointment with a liver specialist in Akron, forty miles south of Cleveland, and so that my father wouldn't have to take a day off from work, I was designated to drive her. Nearing Akron, I was on a three-lane brick highway behind a slow-moving car. I was always a young man in a hurry—to what and for what I most often didn't know—and that morning was testimony to my impatience. I looked ahead to see that the middle lane was clear, and pulled out to pass. Just as I did, a pickup truck coming in the opposite direction did the same thing. A novice driver, I slammed on the brakes, trying to get back behind the slow-moving car. We started to skid.

Next I knew, I was spitting out cinders mixed with the blood oozing out of the gash on my head and dribbling down my cheek. I wanted to stand up, to see what had happened. The ambulance attendant convinced me not to. I was rushed to Akron General Hospital, where the liver specialist had his office and where we had been going. I had only a superficial cut on my head, from contact with the steering wheel. A few stitches later, the bleeding had stopped. My mother had not fared as well. I had hit the pickup truck head on. When I looked at the car some days later, there was a perfect, crazed circle on the right windshield, where her head had made contact. She had died instantly.

My brothers and sisters arrived at the hospital, and it was Frances, who suffered through life with a hydrocephalic child and years of alcoholism before she would die at an even younger age than my mother had, who took my hand at the bedside and said, "Honey, nobody blames you; just know that. It wasn't your fault. It wasn't anybody's fault. It just happened."

When my father came into the room, they stood back. His eyes were red with tears. He was in his work clothes, a thin layer of sawdust a mantle upon his shoulders. He exhaled, his chest collapsing, as if it would be his last breath. He looked at me, then down at the floor. He rubbed his calloused hands together. The room was silent. "That's a fine graduation present," was all he could say in his grief.

OO

How could a seventeen-year-old boy, the unwilling instrument of his mother's death, go on from that moment, leave home in a few months, and travel to a strange, faraway city he knew nothing about, where he knew not a single person? But perhaps it was exactly what I had to do. There was no longer a place for me in Cleveland—not only because of what had happened to my mother but because of what was continuing to happen to me. I had been moving away to another kind of life since the ride on the Rapid Transit, since leaving the neighborhood to go across town to another high school, since reading of Thomas Merton's hunger to know God. There was an incontrovertible force pushing me away from a place that had given me such a firm grounding yet would, I sensed, eventually extract its due, holding me fast.

So, on a September morning, I stood with my father deep in the bowels of Cleveland's Terminal Tower as a mighty Nickel Plate Road steam engine hissed and trembled in its real and metaphysical readiness to take its cargo of dreamers and pragmatists first to destinations stamped on their tickets—but then where? All my belongings were packed in a single large cardboard box, which rested between us. In it, I had a new pair of white buckskin shoes, three fresh pairs of Wigwam woolen socks, some shirts, sweaters, khaki trousers, underwear, a heavy winter coat, and my beloved clock radio. The Cleveland Trust banker's check in my pocket, representing all my savings from my *Plain Dealer* paper route and caddying at the Pepper Pike Country Club, was in the amount of $450. The conductor called for all aboard.

"Good luck, Butch," my father said. He never called me Paul. Since his cry of grief at my bedside, he had never brought up the accident again. This good man, who had worked so hard all his life and who could not understand where I was going or why, was wise and generous enough not to stand in my way. And not to add to the burden he knew I was already bearing.

5

COLLEGE

Red Arrow Park

SHE SMILED WARMLY AS SHE INFORMED ME MY DREAM WAS OVER.

No more than two weeks into my first semester at Marquette, I was informed by the frizzy-haired woman behind the glass cashier's window in Brooks Memorial Union that the account into which I had entrusted every penny I had on the face of the earth was empty. I couldn't believe it, but there were the ever-diminishing numbers. After $250 had been taken out for tuition, the balance of the $450 had quickly evaporated. I stood there, stunned, speechless. Behind me was one of those bouncy, bubbly Irish-Catholic girls from Oak Park (weren't they all from Oak Park?). *"Hihowareyahowwasyoursummer?"* she blurted out to the equally bouncy, bubbly girl alongside her. She could barely stay anchored in her saddle shoes as she waited to cash the weekly $20 check from home that financed the good life for her and—I was finding out—so many others like her. Of course, such mundane items as tuition, food, and lodging had been paid in advance. This was "spending money," the "allowance."

The dream that I had been living—and actually finding quite to my liking—was a game with higher stakes than I had anticipated. I had asked to be dealt in, but I no longer could meet the ante.

During my first weeks at Marquette, I enjoyed strolling around the campus in my white bucks and Wigwam socks, moving effortlessly from class to class, considering which of the extracurricular activities I would join, what fraternity had my kind of guys. The 1950s were a blissfully cookie-cutter age; all you had to do to excel was to conform. If you looked and sounded exactly like everybody else, you were somebody. It suited me just fine; no one knew anything about me or where I had come from. I could pass for another upwardly mobile kid from a Catholic high school, now on his path to a bachelor's degree and the Montgomery Ward training program or some other equally high calling. I would marry a nice Catholic girl—a certified virgin for sure—and settle down in one of those three-bedroom split-level homes with attached garage that were the ultimate American dream.

I adroitly fabricated a new persona and began to envision quite clearly my place in the world as an educated, thinking, middle-class college student. When other students said their fathers were "in" real estate or insurance or manufacturing, suddenly Paul Wilkes Sr., a workaday carpenter, was "in" construction. I hadn't been raised in the Slovak ghetto of St. Benedict's parish, but in "the Shaker Square area," which, although it was only eight-tenths of a mile away from our proletariat crossroads of East 116th and Buckeye Road, could just as well have been on another planet. I talked about summer vacations I had never taken, food I had never tasted, cars never driven, a circle of friends I never had. It was a thin and fragile—a much too thin and fragile—patina of deceit.

I soon realized that the economics of college life for someone like me were brutal. This was not a case of having to get a little part-time job to buy life's niceties or to pay for a spring break visit to the beach at Fort Lauderdale. This was about the primitive need for shelter and food. I had just turned eighteen years old, and I was on my own. The early days of my "Student Social Calendar" are filled with notations of college mixers, visits to women's dorm open houses, a picnic, and a "Variety Show." Then the boxes go blank, except for where I proclaimed how drunk I got, followed the next day by the triumphal hangover I had earned.

In the afternoons, as my fellow students drank cherry Cokes and listened to Pat Boone in the student union, reliving the weekend past and planning the next, I got on the bus, traveling to another Milwaukee that few of them knew, or cared to know. It was the Milwaukee of grit and belching chimneys, sweat and steel-toed boots. In one of my classes, I was reading Zola's *Germinal,* and I realized that was exactly the world I was entering. A common laborer with no skills, I was offering my back and my hands to any bidder.

There was no clamoring for the likes of me, so I took the lowest-paying jobs, stocking shelves at a Wells Street grocery store for minimum wage, $1.00 an hour; emptying bedpans and mopping floors as an orderly at St. Joseph's Hospital for $1.25; running a drill press at Milwaukee Electric Tool, hour after hour, efficiently turning out the same casing, my mind anaesthetized with the dullness. But for $1.60 an hour, I wasn't complaining. With strips of leather lashed to the palms of my hands to prevent them from being shredded by the razor-sharp edges of fifty-pound stacks of thin-gauge steel, I would graduate to loading the mighty machines at American Can Company. Each afternoon, I would leave campus dressed like the others, but in my canvas bag I carried the mufti of another man.

Working twenty or thirty, even at times a full forty hours a week at poor-paying jobs, I barely had enough to live on. Tuition, books, rent. It seemed that just when I was getting ahead, I was laid off. Last hired, first fired. So I bought five-pound cans of peanut butter and made meals of it, slathered on outdated bread that sold for half price. When I stopped for my one hot meal of the day at the White Castle restaurant on Wells Street, I ordered one of their miserably thin hamburgers and a bowl of soup, which came with unlimited packets of saltines. I drank water because it was free. My father had always extolled the virtue of a man working with his hands, but shift after shift, week after week, my rage grew deeper and darker. There was no song in this worker's soul. I knew now so intimately why his Friday afternoons at Tomas's Café were so sweet.

This was the era of the Angry Young Men in Europe, and they had a soul brother in Milwaukee. I wanted life not to be this kind of joyless struggle. I wanted someone somehow to understand me, share my burden, but no one did. I wanted to fall in love; I wanted perfumed hands to soothe my sweating brow and my bleeding palms. I was angry at a world that seemed oblivious to my simple needs, at other students who seemingly had it so much easier, and at those bubbly, carefree girls from Oak Park. I looked at them as they bounced and babbled their way across campus, hoping desperately for their eyes to meet mine, for that magical connection to be made, but they looked right by me, through me. When I did have that rare chance to speak to them—about an assignment or upcoming test—I said stupid, boorish things that pushed them even further away.

There was one girl, and one girl only, among the thousands at Marquette, who I was sure could make everything right and erase all that pain and rage with the first touch. She embodied such perfection that when I merely saw her walking across campus I flushed. Her name was Judy O'Reilly. I found out that much from the college newspaper, on whose pages she regularly appeared. With matched sweater sets and perfect makeup and posture, blessed with a perennial, glowing smile, she represented the Ideal Catholic Girl. Miss Judy O'Reilly was a sorority girl, queen of the dances, on the dean's list. And just the way she walked, with those tight little steps, her books cradled in her arm, melted me. How I wanted to go up to her and say that even though I was just a working-class kid from the East Side of Cleveland and she was obviously from a much better home, I loved her desperately, knew that she was perfect for me, wanted to marry her and go off into that three-bedroom, split-level life together.

But I was a phantom and she was a fantasy. I never so much as said a word to her in four years. Although I looked her way many times, she never saw me.

Meanwhile, on the educational front, the ostensible reason I was here in the first place, I was taking a normal sixteen-hour academic load and doing terribly. After work, when I got to the library to study, I fell asleep. I gobbled down No-Doz tablets as if they were popcorn. As I regularly fell asleep in most of my classes, I tried to sit in the back so that no one would see. Had I not wallowed in my alienation—and self-pity—I might have gotten a reasonably good education, for Marquette actually had some of the top Jesuits in America. My anger poisoned me; I had no one to turn to who might set my way straight.

What was it that had turned me into this kind of person? Was it the morning of May 1 that had forever set me on another path, one of guilt and remorse and yearning to be embraced by the mother I no longer had, and whom I had mostly ignored during those rebellious high school days? Was it the ethnic chip-on-my-shoulder mentality that working-class men often used as their shield against rejection? My own self-doubt that I could go to college, graduate, and go to a life that was different from that of the blue-collar men of Forest Avenue and St. Benedict's parish? It was all of these; each played its own part in the dissonant symphony of those years.

There was no one I could tell of my agonies, so I tried to tell God.

I stayed after Mass on Sunday to pray, and often during the week in Gesu Church, a few blocks from Red Arrow Park, which marked the downtown edge of the campus. With the wind screaming up Wisconsin Avenue from Lake Michigan and my frozen soul aching in my chest, I stopped in for visits at odd hours of the day and night. It was a gorgeous Gothic church, filled on Sundays with students and parishioners. On weekdays it was a dark and quiet place, and, in the same pew just off the main aisle on the right side, I knelt, head bowed, hopeful that God would answer a prayer I could not even clearly make. I wanted Gesu to enfold me. There was the lingering hint of incense in the air, but I could not find God in this place. I heard the dull roar of traffic outside, but not God's voice. I looked to the statues of the saints and Mary as they gazed over my head, little different from the Oak Park girls. The bleeding Christ on the cross was a fine work of art, not a man suffering as I was suffering.

I was not alone in my quest to fathom the ways, wiles, and desires of the Divine, for God and Christ were big topics at Marquette. In classes, God was carefully dissected with Aristotelian syllogisms and Thomistic precision, this Catholic God who was finally asserting his rightful place in American religious and cultural life. The one true faith was spreading nicely throughout the land as Catholics established parish outposts in the suburban diaspora, and waves of young Catholics were being schooled to take their rightful place in the world. We were taught that our dogma must be a seamless, unrendable cloth. Protestants talked of a personal relationship with Christ and God, but through the Catholic prism we had an entirely different view. A personal relationship with God? What an embarrassing thought. What absolute folly. We needed to answer every question and quash every doubt definitively with a closely argued fist in the face of those who had disdainfully regarded Catholicism as little more than papist voodoo. Every circumstance could be codified as sinful (and to what degree) and deserving of eternal punishment, or good, meriting celestial reward.

Although I believed in Catholicism down to the smallest cells of my finite self, I was not very good at articulating my faith in the discipline of apologetics, the rigorous arena of holy argumentation then very much in vogue. The true believer, the one who could count God to be on his or her side in the battle with earthly demons and pervasive Protestantism, was one who could parry and thrust with tightly reasoned, if somewhat predigested and calculating, answers. I could see the logical constructs behind the intricate arguments for Catholicism as having an exclusive key to open heaven's gate, but these did nothing to quench the parched soul I brought into Gesu.

And so I drank elsewhere.

∞

Red Arrow Park, bounded by Tenth and Eleventh streets, Wisconsin and Michigan avenues, was once considered Milwaukee's Hyde Park, where speakers of any persuasion were allowed their platform. In my Marquette years and before it was interred by an expanding freeway system, the park was little more than a few benches strung along the perimeter of an expanse of concrete, punctuated by a few dollops of green space and secreted away from the city by a buffer of low trees. The four-square towers of the law school loomed over the park, but other than their dull, beige-paned windows, there were no unwanted observers.

I spent many Friday and Saturday nights in the park, with the consoling companionship of Blatz beer and Thunderbird wine and an occasional bottle of a cheap whiskey blend. It was even more precious when a major campus event was taking place, so I could read in the school newspaper of the king and queen (at times, My Fair Judy) and all those who had inherited the earth as I drank myself into a stupor. Those fools! I was having a far better time, shivering in the cold, peeing in the bushes. There was a group of us miscreants who gathered in Red Arrow Park, and we were devastatingly funny and cruel as we skewered people on campus whom we knew only by face and reputation—boys with close-cropped hair and a Volkswagen bug and their fraternity table in the Student Union. They didn't know we existed. I hated them.

Of course, had I drunk less and raged less, I could have had a much better four years at Marquette, but I couldn't see that then.

I rented cheap rooms on the edge of the campus in foul-smelling boardinghouses on Kilbourn and Wells and Juneau that reeked of stale urine and dirt and cigarette smoke, but one time, between jobs in my junior year, I didn't even have enough money for the $10 or $12 a week in rent. I was barely passing; my grades in journalism were appalling. I was ready to give up and go back to Cleveland, get a job in a steel mill, and live the life for which I was preordained. Someone mentioned a priest who might let me stay in a room at the back of his office. I looked him up.

Father James McEvoy must have been among the least distinguished Jesuits at Marquette, consigned to being the chaplain for the dental school and given no teaching assignments because he was obviously not on intellectual par with the rest of the religious faculty. He was a short, squat, overweight man who talked too loudly and had the unfortunate habit of hugging students close to a body that was always in need of bathing. But he did have a room (actually a tiny supply closet at the back of his basement office), airless, windowless—and free. At night, I had to slide horizontally onto a folding cot, which stretched beneath a shelf. If I raised my knees, I sent boxes of dental floss and rubber gloves raining down on the coarse woolen Army surplus blanket.

It was not merely that this man provided a place to stay until I could find another job that will forever bind me to him. Across from his office was a small chapel. Although Father McEvoy said Mass there each morning, students could come by at any time during the day to receive Holy Communion. Liturgically, canonically, it was probably illicit, but nonetheless he did it, supplying a sort of walk-in spiritual boost. I was like a starving man at Marquette, grasping for something to sustain me—which, sadly, I too often found in Red Arrow Park. I slowly began to realize that there was at least temporary relief closer by. As I wandered those campus walks, too often lost in despair of where I was going, what I was doing, I always knew I could go over to the dental school chapel for Holy Communion. It was like receiving an airdrop of emergency food supplies into my personal wilderness.

It was a most unlikely spiritual home, this chapel, dimly lit and narrow, its low ceiling blotched with mismatched acoustical tile. But I could kneel or sit in my private sanctuary for as long as I wanted. There I could cry, and I did. There I could doze, and I did. There I felt that God was present, even though no great revelation came in response to my fervent prayers. Rather I experienced a shadow side, a broken God, a humble God, not the God of Gesu Church, not an Oak Park God, grand and perfect and upright. This was a God whose voice was ravished, his throat parched and raw from his own weeping. It was not a God of apologetics and creeds, but a God so exhausted by life's convulsions and pains that he too needed a quiet place to rest.

The young man who pushed through the chapel's swinging doors—built like those on barrooms in Western movies—was not the young man who then went back into the world. If only for a few moments—and I don't know exactly how—I felt God's presence. I felt his love and his concern for me. The rest of my life would usually take over within the hour, the sweet confidence of that presence would fade as the hunger and loneliness returned, but without those moments in that place, I would have been far more lost than I already was.

I perfected the practice of living parallel lives that I had begun in high school. By day I was just another undistinguished, somewhat quiet student. By night I was a factory worker, tough and foulmouthed, making no allusions to his college life, picking up working girls at hamburger joints like Jack Webb's or White Castle, at bars like the Fin 'n Feather, Circle Lounge, and Johnny's Roundup, girls whose hands were as calloused as my own. No Oak Park girls these. No questions asked, no commitments expected.

The third shift at American Can Company ended at 6:48 AM, and by my senior year I had perfected a morning ritual, religiously observed by a select fraternity of blue-collar workers across this land. If I didn't linger after punching out, there was just enough time for a couple shots of Kessler's and a Blatz or two at Johnny's Roundup, across Teutonia Avenue from the plant. It got to a point that all I had to do was walk in, and Billie, the regular early morning bartender, knew what I drank. Then on to my eight o'clock class, the fine mist of machinery oil coating my face, swirls of dirt too deep in my calloused hands for even industrial soaps to liberate. I no longer made any pretense of dressing "collegiate." I came straight from factory to classroom, as much for convenience as to make a fierce statement of independence. I was proud, primevally proud, to be gathering my own food, providing my own shelter. I didn't have to dress for them. They had orange juice on their breath and a Corn Flake on their lips. I smelled of a workingman's aphrodisiac; my breakfast had been a length of beef jerky. I had grease on my knees; they wore starched chinos or plaid kilts. They were there to learn, to prepare for their careers. I just wanted a place to sit down after a night on my feet on the assembly line.

But deep inside, behind all this posturing, was another person, whose face was not contorted in a snarl, whose lips were not quick with profanities. That was the young man longing to feel once again the excitement of hearing a gaunt Maryknoll priest tell of what a life could really be about. A young man searching for Thomas Merton so that the words of his books might be made real in that young man's life. Even a boy kneeling on the furnace grate, understanding pain as the presence of God. I desperately wanted my life to count for something, and I knew nothing about how to achieve that. Instead, I ground myself to bits day after day, night after night. Only those fleeting moments in the basement chapel had any meaning at all.

OO

In June 1960, my father boarded an airplane for the first time in his life and flew to Milwaukee for my graduation. He brought with him a small box, carefully wrapped in sheets of the *Cleveland Plain Dealer,* further protected by many additional interior layers of aluminum foil. But the contents easily triumphed over such flimsy safeguards, for within were huge links of garlic-infused Polish sausage that his friend Frank had cured in his backyard smokehouse. My father had to laugh at how the entire planeload of people quickly sensed his precious cargo. He was not the least bit embarrassed.

I cooked the sausage over my hot plate, and, with some good rye bread with poppy seeds and plenty of Milwaukee beer, we had a great feast the night before my graduation. He was proud of me, I could tell that, this man who went no further than the sixth grade before he took his first job in the coal mines, picking rocks in the breaker. He didn't exactly understand what I had been doing (had he known how anemic an education I had received, he would have had even more reason to wonder why I had spent four years in its pursuit), but he knew that I had stayed the course, completed the job.

We walked around the campus, and I was surprised that I could at least nod to a handful of people, enough to make a creditable witness that I had actually been a student in this place. I motioned to Johnson Hall, where I took philosophy and religion classes that I had barely passed. We mounted the creaky wooden stairs at Copus Hall, the old, rundown mansion that served as the home of the College of Journalism, but there no one knew me. I swung open the doors to the dental school chapel and said I sometimes came to Mass here. We walked through Red Arrow Park. I told my father that I sometimes came here to study. We sat on one of the benches in silence.

I was the last of the College of Journalism graduates to be called up to receive a diploma—by virtue of my last name, and perhaps symbolically because I may have had the poorest grade-point average in the class, 2.34 out of a possible 4.00. Others received awards; my only distinction, unacknowledged on this auspicious day, was as the anchor man on a beer-chugging team that had wrested a trophy from the University of Wisconsin the year before. My father squinted into the Milwaukee sun with blue eyes bloodshot from years of coal and wood dust, set in a face so magnificently lined by the years. He turned to the son standing before him in cap and gown, who had left home four years before with great hopes and a cardboard box. He looked quizzically at the diploma, written in Latin.

"What was it you were studying, Butch?" he asked.

"Journalism, Dad. You know, writing."

"What'ya suppose you'll do with that?"

"I don't have the foggiest idea."

I went back to my third-shift job at American Can Company that very night, as if nothing had changed. Had not a letter from a Cleveland Selective Service board arrived in late summer, who knows how long I would have worked there, or where my life might have gone.

6

AT SEA

COURTESY OF MY NEW EMPLOYER, THE U.S. GOVERNMENT, a complimentary airplane ticket from my "Residence of Record" whisked me to the Providence, Rhode Island, airport and from there to the U.S. Navy's Officer Candidate School (OCS) at Newport. I had never been treated so well in any of my many employments. In the early morning hours of a bitterly cold January night, with a fierce wind howling off nearby Narragansett Bay, I was delivered to the darkened World War II–era Kilo Company barracks.

It was 1961, and the draft was on. If you were classified 1-A, as I was, and chose to wait to be summoned, you would be assigned to the Army, most likely to an infantry unit. Although I didn't know how to swim, in fact was terrified of the water, I volunteered for the Navy. Being a college graduate—though barely—I would serve as an officer.

I was not the model officer candidate, but there was something about the regimented life that felt strangely right to this rebel without a cause. I finally had a purpose. A place. I was provided with clothes, shelter, three square meals a day, and $44 every two weeks. The pay was enough for a Saturday night drunk at the Viking Hotel's Skoal Room in Newport as I tried to convince one of the dark-eyed Portuguese girls—the crucifix-wearing, hard-working textile mill workers we so crassly called the Fall River Debutantes—to come off the dance floor and into the winter's darkness where we could be alone for just a few moments.

The blur of my four years at Marquette behind me, I was now on a trajectory to be an officer and gentleman. All American young men served in those days—except those so sickly or cunning or gay—millions of us around the globe, needed to keep the Communists at bay. Little did any of us expect that, over in a tiny country no one then could easily locate on a map, an insurgency was under way that would draw the next generation of citizen soldiers and sailors into a real war. We were trained for nuclear attacks, antisubmarine maneuvers, and in the secret crypto codes, but we were as much expected to be ambassadors of good will. Friendly American faces aboard huge gray ships with enough firepower to vaporize most countries on a few minutes' notice.

I was a loyal, more or less "my country right or wrong" son of America. Whatever my country would demand of me, the answer was yes. John Kennedy had set the bar: "Ask not . . ." Now that was authentic Catholic thinking, even though Kennedy was hardly a Catholic by the strict standards of the day.

I also had a sense that if I could endure the sixteen weeks of humiliation, I would finally be in the American mainstream. After all, there were guys here from Princeton and Cornell and from obscure Texas schools, and a smattering of those of us who had gone Catholic. It was, finally, the great melting pot. Upon graduation day, I would look exactly the same as everyone else in my double-breasted, gold-buttoned jacket, knife-sharp pleated trousers, and a single ensign's stripe on my sleeve.

My religious life at this point after the very Catholic environment at Marquette, although still strong in practice—to miss Sunday Mass was unthinkable—was lacking in the tactile influences that had so shaped me: that gaunt Maryknoller, Father McEvoy, even the furnace grate on which I offered myself to God. I was now in the service of country, with its own liturgies: raising and lowering the flag; powerful, patriotic songs as hymns.

My company officer called me in during the fourteenth week. He pulled out a folder with my name on it. I was set to appear before the Disenrollment Board. Instead of receiving an ensign's stripe and an officer's commission, I would be shipped off to Great Lakes Naval Training Station and spend my days as an ordinary seaman. Fifty yards of water in the base swimming pool was separating me from realizing my dream. I still hadn't passed the swimming test.

On the last day that I could qualify, I put on my Navy-issue trunks and appeared at the designated corner of the pool. I looked across to the opposite corner, fifty yards away. I made the sign of the cross and eased myself down the ladder. I let go of the ladder and slowly lay back. The Navy was wonderful in its uniformity. There was no quibbling about how the officer candidate would proceed from point A to point B, just that he do so. But I had somehow to make it to the other side. I felt the uncomfortable sensation of water rising to my mouth and nose. My heart was pounding. I started flapping my arms, twitching. I began to move, slowly, almost imperceptibly, but moving nonetheless. After what seemed to be hours, my head bumped against the other side. The swimming instructor shook his head and signed the sheet on his clipboard.

My father had served in World War I in the Panama Canal aboard an oiler, the USS *Brazos,* and he couldn't swim a stroke. My brother Tom joined the Navy during World War II and was assigned shore duty on the West Coast. And on graduation day, May 12, 1961, when the call went out, "Officer candidates, rise," followed in a few minutes by "Officers, seats," the third nonswimming Wilkes joined the fleet.

∞

On a sparkling South Carolina fall day, I strode purposefully through the Charleston Naval Shipyard. I felt like a man in a movie, a powerful destiny awaiting me. I was a man fully prepared for battle, untroubled by the fact that he was in a peacetime Navy. I rounded the corner and saw the ship to which I had miraculously been assigned, the USS *Power* (DD-839). She was a thing of beauty, by any standards, even with patches of orange and beige primer dotting her hull and superstructure. Built in 1945, the *Power* was now in the final stages of a complete overhaul that equipped her with a rocket-launched antisubmarine torpedo that could carry a nuclear warhead, a platform for a drone helicopter, and a bristling array of antennae, for which I would be responsible as the new communications officer.

A salute offered, a salute returned, and Ensign Wilkes was aboard the ship that would take him to at least a taste of war, to an exotic romance, and then at full steam right out of his Catholic Church.

∞

For a kid whose only encounters with water deeper than that in a bathtub were few, I actually took to the open sea. When that last hawser was hoisted from a pier's bollard and the space gradually widened between ship and land, a certain sensation sweeps over not a few of us who have gone down to the sea in ships. Solid ground no longer had any claim on me. I was afloat, and the ship was everything, my universe. Life aboard ship is at once precarious and serene in its exacting limitation. All for the ship; the ship for all.

Each time we sailed from the security and placidity of sheltered East Coast port waters, there was a gradual awakening of this great gray beauty, a sinuousness to the gentle rising and falling of her 390 feet of hardened steel, seemingly supple as she eased over waves slapping at her sides. Yet as we battled a gale in the troubled waters off Cape Hatteras, the ship's keel was unbendable, her axlike bow effortlessly knifing through the huge, boiling waves, diving in, then shuddering in the trough like a woman in love, only to rise up in ecstasy again and again to shake the water off her sleek skin.

On calmer days, I would often go out onto the main deck at sunset and stand there, alone. Except for the rattling of the signal bridge lanyards high overhead and a whistling through the life rafts lashed against the bulkhead, all was quiet. The setting sun surely must have been positioned in other places, but I only remember it off the port stern. That was my time for contemplation, when the work of the day was done, the watch set.

I could now see why Thomas Merton so took to monastic life. Like the regimen of monastic life, that of Navy life placed you exactly where you needed to be at that very moment, told you exactly what was the work at hand and that it would be over at a certain time. And then you would move to the next task, effortlessly. *Reveille. Muster at quarters. All hands turn to. Knock off ship's work. Dinner is served on the mess decks. Taps. All lights out.*

As I spent those quiet times gazing off over the ocean, I began to see (as Merton did upon entering Gethsemane) what a lonesome, needlessly angry, self-pitying soul I had been. Yes, I had worked my way through college—that was something to be proud of—but that degree had come at entirely too great a cost, very little of it financial. But now military discipline was taking over, providing another kind of life prism. It was not quite a religious calling, yet it had many of its attributes: sacrifice; looking out for the common good and the needs of others; living for something admirable, something beyond one's own capabilities or grasp. It was so different from the dizzying options and temptations in college—options I couldn't exercise and temptations to which I often yielded.

I now received a steady paycheck of $222 twice a month, was called "Sir," and, with crypto codes in my keeping and a new pair of Navy-issued sunglasses beneath the glistening bill of my cap, I considered myself quite the accomplished junior officer.

But I had so much to learn. Perhaps the most profound lesson took place one afternoon on our shakedown cruise, the time when a ship is determined ready or not to join the fleet after an extended period in a shipyard. "Mr. Wilkes, report to the bridge," sounded over the PA system. I bounded up the ladder and sharply saluted the captain, Commander Robert Hayes, with a crisp "Yes, sir."

"Mr. Wilkes, remember the capacitor problems with the SLR-21 receiver we had in the yard? I asked you to have a backup on board. The SLR-21 just went down, and we can't get the fleet frequency we need to complete our trial runs. Is that backup capacitor on board?"

"Captain, I sent that request to the supply center weeks ago—"

"Do we have it on board?"

"Captain, I bumped it up to priority just last week, and—"

"Do we have it on board, Mr. Wilkes?"

"Captain, that request is in every supply depot from Key West to Reykjavik, over in Naples, all across the Sixth Fleet, and probably . . ."

The captain just stared at me. The bridge was stonily silent, a crackling over the speaker a reminder of the circuit we weren't on. And I realized that even though I might have learned that "intention equals the act" in some philosophy or theology course at Marquette, such a distinction wasn't going to work in the Navy.

"No, sir, it is not on board."

OO

Although I would never be considered the best officer on board the *Power,* I worked all the harder after that humiliation. The overriding concept was "completed staff work," taking a project from start to finish, without leaving any loose ends. I guess I got better at it, for when the assignments for battle stations (or "general quarters" as it is called in Navy parlance) were announced, I was designated the general quarters officer of the deck. If ever and whenever our ship would go into battle, I would be on the bridge, with the captain and executive officer. And thus I would meet my appointment with destiny—such as it was—in the unfolding drama that came to be called the Cuban Missile Crisis.

It was not long after we had returned to the States in spring 1962, after having been proven battle ready through our readiness training at Guantánamo Bay, Cuba, that one of my radiomen breathlessly ran up to me as we sat pier side in Mayport, Florida, our home port. His hands were shaking as he handed me the clipboard with a huge "Priority" stamp emblazoned on the short message. We were to get under way as soon as our crew could be recalled, and return to a point two hundred miles west-northwest of Cuba and await further orders. We were to have a full complement of fuel, stores, and ammunition aboard.

As the intelligence officer, I knew that the Russians for months had been clearing barren stretches of land on the northern coast of Cuba, and ships had been offloading cargo. It was considered to be Fidel

Castro's response to our aborted Bay of Pigs invasion in April 1961, and was supposedly for defensive purposes only. Now our U-2 spy plane photos showed something else. Huge missile-launching batteries were under construction. We knew that the Russian-built missiles could carry a nuclear warhead, and it became clear that these were offensive weapons, a provocation. Without alarming the entire country—which would later happen during those fourteen tense days in October 1962—President Kennedy during the summer quietly threw up a naval blockade.

Once we arrived at the designated point, we began patrolling a corridor of the Atlantic several hundred miles long. Our orders were to stop—with whatever force was required—any ships en route to Cuba carrying what we suspected might be missiles or parts for those launching sites.

We methodically patrolled in a rectangular pattern—boring work. Then, about noon on the sixth day, I had just taken over the bridge watch when a tiny, shadowy blip appeared on the edge of the radar screen. There had been others; after all, these were international waters. Closer and closer it came; clearer and clearer it painted as the yellow cursor swept over the greenish screen. "Captain," I said as calmly as I could, over the voice-powered intercom. "We have Bogey November at twenty-two miles, heading 080, speed seven knots. Bogey November is closing. Captain, plotting out that course, Bogey November is headed directly for the Cuban mainland. Request permission to investigate." The captain was on the bridge in a few seconds.

We headed straight for the bogey November. With binoculars I finally could make out the outline of a rusting freighter, flying a Yugoslav flag, lumbering along at what was probably its maximum speed. I refocused the binoculars, at first not believing what I was seeing. Long, coffin-shaped crates, too long for the cargo hold, were strapped on deck. They matched the U-2 photos perfectly. Parts for missile launchers and, in bigger, bulkier crates, the missiles themselves.

The boatswain mate's pipe sounded shrilly over the ship's PA system. "General quarters, general quarters, all hands man your battle stations," words we had heard so many times during our training. Then another voice. "This is the captain speaking. This is not a drill. I repeat, this is *not* a drill."

Sailors leaped into gun mounts, scrambled up ladders, disappeared into hatches. We donned life jackets and battle helmets. Six of our most experienced marksmen appeared on deck with high-powered rifles and Thompson submachine guns. Each had a .45 strapped to his waist.

I made a wide sweep and eased our ship into the freighter's wake, then slowly, cautiously slid up alongside. The marksmen raised their weapons chest-high in readiness. The five-inch, .38 caliber gun mounts locked on to the freighter. I ordered the signal bridge to hoist the "K" signal flag, which was the international signal to stop engines. The blinking light from the signal bridge transmitted the same order. We tried to raise the ship on channel 16, the common channel all ships are supposed to monitor. Nothing. Through a bullhorn, Captain Hayes hollered, "Lay to. Lay to immediately. You are suspected of carrying contraband. Stop your engines. Lay to."

Then an eerie silence, nothing. The only sound was the waves slapping lazily against the side of our ship in the twenty-yard gap of choppy water that separated us. There was no sign of life on the freighter, not a single man on deck as it plowed along, oblivious to the bristling arsenal of guns ready to blow it out of the water. We sounded the ship's horn, repeated the signal light message; the captain again took up the bullhorn and hollered still louder. Nothing. No one.

The captain and I looked at each other. To fire or not to fire? Would he be justified and commended with a battle ribbon, or torpedo his career on this beautiful sunny afternoon by firing on an unarmed ship? I'm sure the options and potential outcomes were flying through the mind of this Naval Academy lifer, by nature a cautious man. We heard a squeak across the water and turned back to the freighter to see the wheelhouse door slowly open. A magnificently fat man emerged, shirtless, with a beer bottle in his hand, blinking into the bright Caribbean sun. Then, suddenly focused and completely sober, his head jerked back when he saw what was alongside.

He shrugged his shoulders. A sign of insolence? Defiance? Who could say?

We flashed the message once more, sounded the horn, and the captain called even louder over the bullhorn. The man shrugged again. I could see him better now through the binoculars: tiny, furtive eyes; huge, puffy cheeks. The good Slav that he was, one of my people, was all I could think. He was just doing his job for the boss man and not wanting to get in any trouble. He was to deliver the goods, get his paycheck, and go home to Dubrovnik or Split. I knew him.

The captain was breathing heavily now. He picked up the bullhorn, but I stopped him. "Captain, let me try something." I went out on the wing of the bridge and took off my sunglasses. I locked on him eye to eye, Slav to Slav. He put down his beer bottle and stood there, motionless. I raised my right hand. I passed it in front of my face, and—traversing that channel of understanding between our met eyes—made a sweeping motion, a huge U. Once again. My finger held motionless in the air signaled where we now were; the sweeping U motion told him that he must go back to where he had come from. I had no menace on my face or in my heart. Each of us was simply doing his job.

The fat Yugoslav stood at attention, saluted me briskly, and disappeared back into the wheelhouse. The marksmen on the main deck raised their guns, ready to fire. But as the stern of the freighter swung our way, we all knew that firepower would not be needed to convince him. The ship's wake was a perfect replica of the sweeping motion I had made with my hand.

The captain looked quizzically at me, his path to his fourth bar and command of a deep-draft vessel now secure. "Shall I set the regular watch, sir?" I asked as if it were nothing at all.

∞

On board ship, as we sailed for our half-year deployment with the U.S. Sixth Fleet, I performed well enough as ensign to receive the next half stripe as lieutenant, junior grade, and promotion to operations officer. As we visited Mediterranean ports, I performed even more superbly, if drinking was the measure of the seagoing man. I didn't go to whorehouses—something within me just wouldn't let that happen—or to strip clubs, but in too many of our port visits, I didn't get much farther than three or four blocks inland. There I was, in some of the most exciting, historic ports in the world, and all I could think about was blasting my brain to smithereens in the first bar I could find. Even with the shipboard camaraderie, I guess it was because something was missing at my core. Often at night it would come over me as I lay in my bunk, looking up at the overhead. I felt hollow inside. I might have chalked it up to the fact that I still felt so alone in the world. There was no woman in my life, and, as a vagabond Navy officer, I was unlikely to be able to change that situation anytime soon.

As I would write to my OCS classmate Bill Gould, fellow Catholic and Loyola graduate, who had been assigned to an amphibious landing craft out of San Diego: "if I get tired enough . . . I won't think about the present state of horniness and will not lift the bottle too many times. . . . The Navy life is rewarding at times . . . a drag quite often. . . . The key . . . is getting hitched or so involved in some project or job that you completely lose sight of yourself for the greatness of the other situation. And in losing yourself, you find yourself." It sounded as though a priestly vocation were still at the back of my mind, but I would have denied that vociferously. Only later would I learn of St. Augustine's saying about a heart being restless until it rested in God. All I knew was the restless part. Where this God in whom I could rest would be found I had no idea.

Foolishly, I found a fleeting peace only in drinking myself into a stupor. But in Naples, after a first night devoted to the bars, with a well-earned and colossal hangover, I signed on for a four-day tour up to Rome.

I visited the ancient ruins and monuments, and, of course, I looked forward to seeing the Vatican. After all, I was a lifelong and practicing Catholic—that word *practicing* meaning no more and no less than what was expected at the time: regular Sunday Mass attendance, occasional confession of my sins, and generally not falling into grave sin so that I might gain eternal life. This was not about—in Augustine's view— "resting in God." No, our faith had been codified and routinized for centuries, and no one—least of all I—had any idea that a gathering storm of political, cultural, and religious forces would upend not only my country and the world but the Catholic Church itself. The man carried in a sedan chair into St. Peter's Basilica that morning looked like one of the broadchested Italians I might have seen pouring cement at a Cleveland construction site or reaching for a length of Genoa salami behind a Milwaukee butcher's counter. He was so different from the only pope I had known, the thin, ascetic Pius XII. This was John XXIII, regarded as the interim pope, the compromise pope, really no one's favorite and everyone's third or fourth choice. So pitifully ordinary, not in the least charismatic or exuding holiness as one might expect of St. Peter's successor, he seemed so out of place in his splendid robes, a huge, glistening miter soaring above his chubby face. And yet as the crowd surged forward toward the main aisle, pushing aside the hapless ushers, it was obvious they were not here merely to pay him honor. They wanted to touch him, grab him, devour him if they could. I had never seen such an outpouring of emotion in a church before.

The rush of humanity pushed me forward until I was just a few feet from the red silk rope that secured his passage to the great main altar. Then he passed by, waving his gloved hand in the air, smiling. The pope was smiling! I had never seen such a thing. That smile would be engrained in my mind. What kind of smile was it? What was going through his mind?

7

ONE HOT DAY . . . AND NIGHT

OF ALL THE GODFORSAKEN OUTPOSTS OF THE WORLD, the port of Karachi could certainly hold its own. There, as I peered out the porthole window, were sufferers from elephantiasis (swollen, pinkish-gray legs), leprosy (partial jaw, ear gone, and eye socket hollowed out), tuberculosis (a rasping cough and incredible amounts of phlegm), horrible deformities, mental illness. But on the front page of the *Karachi Dawn* in my hands was a glowing report of the New Pakistan, a thriving democracy after its 1947 independence from Great Britain and partition from India, with stories of economic progress and the conquering of dread diseases. As I looked at that paper and gazed out the window, two things happened: first, I realized that the stories in the *Karachi Dawn* were little more than fairy tales; second, I had actually studied the reporting of fact at Marquette and, given the opportunity, might be capable of coming somewhat closer to the truth.

And there, headed my way on a steamy afternoon through this miasma of wretched humanity, was the woman who would become my wife. She was a Methodist missionary from Nebraska, and our otherwise ineffectual onboard chaplain had preached that morning at her church, Brooks Memorial, and invited the congregation for a tour of the ship. On the tour, in the blistering 110-degree heat, recently recovered from dengue fever and malaria, she grew faint, and was shown to the air-conditioned wardroom, where I happened to be showing the slides from my trip to Rome.

Not that it matters much, but let the record be clear: I did not ask her out. Much too insecure and shy, I was sure this beautiful woman, J.C. by name, would refuse. J.C. offered the third "If there is *anything* I can do

53

for you while you're in Karachi, please let me know," then finally, to the obtuse me, "Dinner tomorrow night? . . . Good; I'll pick you up at six."

My shipmates could not believe that this leggy, lithesome, gorgeous creature in a fine silk dress getting out of a Volkswagen on that sewer of a pier was calling for me. Before dinner, I needed a stop at the Hotel Metropole, and after three throat-closing, head-spinning double Rob Roys, we had dinner with her host family. But we both knew there was more than dinner on the menu that night. She took me to a desolate beach to walk along the Indian Ocean and watch the giant sea turtles, lumbering up to lay eggs. We stopped to sit on one of the low dunes, watching the huge black humps inch back toward the luminous, shimmering water.

She had been raised on a farm in Nebraska, leading the most conventional of lives, but then moved to California where—and I was reading between the lines—she had both lost her way and experienced a profound religious conversion. She came here sponsored by her church to do educational work. I sketched out my own story, but it was obvious that we were both lonely people at sea—I literally, she in a foreign country.

The wind played with long auburn hair spilling over her shoulders. That fabulous sari material rustled sensuously each time she moved on the sand. The moon was full, and two innocents abroad—thousands of miles from home, hormones heated up in the soft, warm night—surely wouldn't let this moment pass, even though I was a sailor soon to ship out. We kissed, and of course I wanted more. Clumsily, we groped at each other. This was still the early 1960s, and, even on that sultry night, we only went so far.

We saw each other every night I was in port. We promised to write. She waved and cried—as did I—as that last hawser left the bollard and the narrow gap between ship and land—fantasy and reality—widened.

Her letters via Fleet Post Office, New York, somehow found me in Ceylon and Somalia and Aden. We continued the romance. It didn't take long: yes, let's get married. I, the lifelong Catholic. She, the Methodist missionary. Somehow we vowed we could work it out. And children. Yes, of course, children. "As many as the stars in the sky," I waxed on in one letter. Being at sea is perhaps the greatest aphrodisiac of all, and the letters were infused with the promise of a magical wedding and a great life to follow.

She was there—on another pier, in another silk dress—when I returned to Mayport, Florida. She meant it. I gulped. Now to this "working it out." My first stop was the base Catholic chaplain. He looked at me as if I were speaking a foreign language. I found the nearest parish, and when I called to make an appointment, the priest asked why. After I explained, he told me to save my time. I knew the answer. No mixed marriages. Keep looking, lieutenant, and find a Catholic next time. Click. On a whim, I called St. John's, the Episcopal cathedral, in Jacksonville and, amazingly, was put right through to the cathedral's dean, who did not play the Telephonic Grand Inquisitor. He would be happy see us the next day. We sat in Dean Robert Parks's book-lined office, staking out our individual claims to Rome and John Wesley. He listened patiently. And? he seemed to be saying. Two good people. In love. Might there not be a middle way, the famous *via media*? And for some reason—after twenty-five years of Catholic living—it made sense.

Six months later, in a church that in years past I would not even so much as entered, I pledged my troth. Two heavy, half-inch gold wedding bands proclaimed that we were deadly serious. We were swooshed under an arch of swords formed by my fellow USS *Power* officers and off to a mints-and-nuts reception at which—to my utter disgrace to this very day—I forbade my father and Aunt Rose (standing in for my mother, her sister) to have anything stronger than the punch provided. The rest of my family had basically boycotted this unholy union, but, God bless him, my father came, along with Aunt Rose, who had borne a child out of wedlock and knew something about public scorn. In keeping with J.C.'s strong Methodist roots (and in deference to her parents, glumly in attendance as their daughter had married one of "them"), alcohol was not going to make an appearance. I frankly don't know what had gotten into me, the virtual port-of-call alcoholic, but suddenly I was a teetotaler.

We attended Episcopal services for a few months, which I found inauthentically faux Catholic, what with all the affected British accents and all, even more lifeless and mannered than the Latin Mass that I thought was part of my DNA. So we migrated to the nearby Methodist church where J.C. had gotten a job, having abandoned both Karachi and Nebraska to be with the man she loved. The minister gave inspiring, thoughtful, cogent sermons, not a strong suit in the Catholic Church of the day. And people actually talked to you after the service. Catholics at the time sensed that getting in and out—in sex and, in this case, Mass—should be done quickly and surgically, with as little human contact as possible. I was now a Methodist.

Everything was in English. And those great Wesley hymns were so easy to learn. To this day, I sing "The Church's One Foundation" with great gusto and not a little nostalgia. But what had happened? The firm cords binding me to the "one true Church" were not as strong as I once believed. I had discovered a coldness in Catholicism that I never knew existed—undergirded by our strict doctrinal stands and the regarding of other Christian traditions as if they were just barely this side of paganism. I wasn't angry with the Catholic Church. I felt more numbed by it. When I had traveled to Rome the year before, in awe I had walked St. Peter's Square, stood before the *Pietà,* and kissed the well-worn bronzed foot of the statue of the first pope, St. Peter. But then I had seen something else, experienced something else. I hadn't yet put the pieces together, but there was an appealing and shocking humanity about Pope John XXIII. I didn't know it, but I had caught my first glimmer of another kind of God and would catch similarly fleeting glimmers during the years ahead. He was a God who would be so present and then capriciously disappear from view. Just like a portly pope passing by, a wise smile on his face.

I didn't know it, but exactly at the time I had been in Rome, the first session of Vatican II was beginning to change the face of the Catholic Church. As I was being married outside a Church that now seemed so cold and lifeless by comparison, the second session of the council had just pronounced that the Mass would henceforth not be in the regal Latin of Rome, but in the babel of people's languages around the world. The altar rail would soon be breached—ripped away—removing what had kept priests and the holy of holies separate from the unwashed and obviously unworthy masses of lay people. Eventually, a total of sixteen council documents would proclaim that the world was not to be avoided as hopelessly sinful and corrupt, but was to be encountered and made holy. And not just by the ordained. But by a new and larger legion, the "priesthood of all believers." The Catholic Church was about to undertake its most dramatic changes in history. And I would not be there to witness them.

I was about to spend ten years as a Protestant. Every so often during those years I would sense an itch I couldn't scratch, a hunger that wasn't satisfied with marvelous preaching and warm hospitality. I pushed such thoughts aside. The God I had been seeking all these years was about to be handily retrofitted.

PART TWO

MAKING IT

8

A YOUNG REPORTER

AFTER THREE YEARS IN THE NAVY, I took my first reporter's job at *The Daily Camera,* a small, family-owned daily newspaper in Boulder, Colorado. My wife and I rented the upper floor of a duplex overlooking the landmark and breathtakingly beautiful Flatirons mountain range. As a member of the First Methodist Church, I was feeling more and more comfortable at its services and less and less and less like a Catholic. Boulder itself was at the epicenter of what would soon be known as the sixties culture. Mind-bending hashish and a cornucopia of pharmaceuticals, in addition to frequent and casual sex, were already being freely enjoyed just blocks from our house and church. In my Corvair (which would later serve as Ralph Nader's *Unsafe at Any Speed* poster child for automobile safety reform), I drove around town in various combinations of my ever-growing polyester wardrobe, wrote a good number of polyester stories, and sat in the first few rows at First Methodist. I continued to convince myself that the tingling I felt at the back of my neck at about the time in the service that Holy Communion would have been distributed—had it been Catholic Mass—was just because my shirt was too tight.

I didn't even know what the word *conservative* implied, but now, looking back, I can see that I was a conservative Catholic. I had joined the staff of a staunchly conservative newspaper, which won a string of Freedoms Foundation awards for its chest-thumping affirmations of America. Which seemed exactly right to me. After all, if you couldn't count on America, what could you believe in? While the *Camera* was extolling the virtues of our nation, my work was at a decidedly lower level, affirming the values of small-town America, covering the installation of Red Cross officers and the appointment of a new sewer commissioner, and writing feature pieces for *Focus,* the *Camera*'s Sunday magazine. I faithfully clipped even the tiniest story I wrote, and my yellowed scrapbook shows a sprinkling of them with a byline, at that time not automatically conferred, but earned.

My editors would have been quite happy with my continuing to write stimulating and heartwarming articles about such earthshaking news as the lady who crocheted the faces of all the presidents into a dazzling set of potholders, but something uncomfortable and unsettling was beginning to stir inside me. I felt it first one day in Green Mountain Cemetery. I had all the facts: promising young Boulder High School graduate who left only a year before, proud to serve his country; a few months in Vietnam, killed in a rocket attack, airlifted out in a body bag, flown to the Denver airport in a copper-colored, government-issue casket. Check, check, check. I was already writing the lead in my head, with "God Bless America" playing in the background. Page one story. Certainly this one would earn a byline.

I happened to catch my reflection in the casket's glassy surface. I saw a guy with a very neat haircut, wearing a Sears wrinkle-proof plaid, polyester jacket, polyester shirt, tie, and trousers—his notepad at the ready. I had to look away. Something was wrong. I couldn't figure it out, but something was terribly, terribly wrong.

It wasn't too long after that experience that I was sitting across a table in a mobile home on the poor side of town with a fine young Mexican American Marine who had made it back, but had been blinded in the right eye by a tiny piece of Vietcong shrapnel. He held it on the tip of his outstretched index finger so that I could get a picture, shrapnel in focus, his face blurred in the background. He was a great kid, and it was a sad story. Again, something was wrong, but even though I might have been good at interviewing other people, I was lousy at interviewing myself.

Vietnam sneaked up on a lot of us in those days. Whatever was taking our country deeper into that conflict, I kept on assuring myself, was necessary. The late John Kennedy and now Lyndon Johnson knew more than I did about the Communist threat to take over the world, and anyhow, having been through the Cuban Missile Crisis, I was sure that we had either to make the other side blink or to bomb them into dust.

My Catholic faith had once been sure and unquestioning, but was now an ever-fading memory. My faith in my country and its leaders was not going to similarly waver. The great fissure that was dividing America was opening, and I knew what side I was on. My writing life was repeatedly taking me to the edge, but I always withdrew, opting for the acceptable, the predictable. As I lay in bed at night, I might see my face reflected in that casket or the tiny piece of shrapnel on that boy's finger, but I shook off these troubling images.

As a citizen I was reluctant even to consider that I needed to change, but as a journalist I began to see that there were better, more interesting stories than those I was grinding out. I made a few forays into waters then uncharted at the *Camera*, not with any kind of ideological agenda or any conscious idea, but more out of instinct. I discovered that there was a married interracial couple on the University of Colorado campus, and I wanted to go beyond the who, what, when, and where and get to the *why*. There was a small group of kids at Boulder High School who were speaking out against the Vietnam War, and although I thoroughly disagreed with them, I knew it was a great story.

I can still see the look on the face of my managing editor as I walked over to his desk with the latest idea, at that time viewed as unsportsman-like, even guerilla journalism. I started ducking the potholder-weaver stories and proposed my own. That earlier realization I had, looking out the porthole in Karachi, that the official view didn't always square with what was happening in real people's lives, was starting to be confirmed. The stories drew some favorable comments and even more angry responses. I was slowly turning into another kind of reporter.

It was about this time that Gay Talese and Tom Wolfe were also going outside the norms of "good" journalism, giving a new texture to the human experience with something that would eventually be called the New Journalism. I couldn't wait for *Esquire* magazine to arrive each month. There was Wolfe tearing along a backcountry dirt road in North Carolina with Junior Johnson, moonshine runner turned racecar driver. There was Talese straddling the beams of the Verrazano-Narrows Bridge with the intrepid American Indian "boomers." I wanted to write like that, so that you could smell the liquor on Johnson's breath, feel the wind tearing at your body suspended on a girder hundreds of feet in the air.

I realized that I needed to learn something about this trade that I had not gotten in the fog of working and drinking and whining my way through college. Graduate school was the answer I came up with. A phone call to Marquette told me not to bother applying to their new graduate school of journalism, as my undergraduate average was too low even to be considered. I applied to six other schools and received a post-card rejection from the University of Wisconsin by return mail. I was obviously not a hot prospect. In my mailbox a few weeks later was a business-size envelope typically used for the single-page letter of rejection. It was from my first choice, Columbia University, which had the best journalism school in the country. My hands shaking ever so slightly and heart thumping, I slowly opened the envelope.

OO

I got out of the car.

That I was in the middle of the George Washington Bridge during morning rush hour on a brilliantly sunny September day meant nothing. I had been planning this for the past two thousand miles. To my left was the winding, northbound Hudson River, shouldered by the sheer bluffs of the Palisades. Off to my right was the magical, gauzy Manhattan skyline, fringed by the soft sweep of Riverside Park along the West Side Highway as it hugged the Hudson's banks. Beyond, the gradually rising tide of buildings that began with humble apartment buildings and slowly ascended to the midtown crescendo. And there I stood—legs spread audaciously apart on the vibrating grating, as cars honked and whizzed by— the conquering hero. A force majeure had arrived, storming in from the West, pulling a U-Haul trailer behind his Corvair.

"New York!" I cupped my hands and bellowed at the skyline. I waited for an answer. "New York, ya hear me?" And, now screaming, "New York: you're going to know about me!"

Where had this display of hubris come from? This Slovak boy from Cleveland, son of parents who went no further than the sixth grade, who himself had barely gotten through college, had a reasonable but hardly sterling Navy career, and now, with two years of experience on a middling daily paper, boldly announcing his arrival in the Writing Capital of the World?

∞

Just rounding the corner on 116th and Broadway and walking onto the Columbia University campus the first day of classes gave me a buzz better than anything I had experienced downing Blatz and Thunderbird in Red Arrow Park, shots and beers at Johnny's Round-up, or the Cuba Libras and other alcoholic exotica in various officer's clubs and fleet bars spanning nearly half the globe. It was now fall 1966, and I was in the very place where Thomas Merton had walked some thirty years before, where Enrico Fermi split the first atom and Franz Boas virtually invented a new field called anthropology, where famous authors and Supreme Court justices, corporate giants, and a future president returned to pay homage to the alma mater that had so profoundly shaped them.

There was something about the way Columbia people walked—quickly and determinedly—as if they were always late for some earthshaking meeting or event. There was that certain look about the students and faculty on the Morningside Heights campus, as if every one of them was thinking great thoughts, having profound insights, and on the verge—just then, as I saw them whisking by!—of acting on them. The air seemed superoxygenated, and each breath automatically added a brain cell or two. Deeper and deeper I gulped in the moist, late-summer air as I hastened my step. I felt this overwhelming compulsion to make a statement. About something. Anything.

With the lush green carpet of grass before Butler Library unfolding on my left, I turned right, striding purposefully toward the journalism school. I paused before the commanding bronze statue of Thomas Jefferson. I was a person used to paying reverence to statues, and although he was not the Sacred Heart, St. Joseph, or the Blessed Virgin, Jefferson was the patron saint of my profession. His chiseled face bid only those of highest principles to enter. I squinted up at Mr. Jefferson, adjusted my tie, threw back my shoulders, and marched through the great bronze doors, the echo of the heels of my genuine shell cordovans on the marble floor in the lobby a rhythmic drumroll.

Not having been shaped and educated at elite schools like Harvard (John Kronenberger), Yale (Phil Smith), or Princeton (Paul Friedman), or even the better Catholic colleges like Notre Dame (Tom Bettag) or Georgetown (Dick Williams), or on a par with the handful of girls (exactly what they were called) in our class who had gone to Smith (Molly Ivins), Brown (Ginny Chappell), and Barnard (Jonnet Steinbaum), I tried not to act like the second-class citizen that I felt in my heart I was. When talk turned to what was playing on Broadway, the background on a major piece in the *Times,* who Iago really represented, or what the confrontation at the Pettus Bridge in Selma foretold, my classmates could have been speaking another language. Where was Selma anyhow? SNCC, SCLC? Hieroglyphics to me. I kept saying to myself that my perseverance and hard work would pay off, but I often found myself with a blank look on my face when conversation turned up one of the gaping holes in my education or simply an elementary lack of awareness of what the hell was going on in America right then.

As a twenty-seven-year-old and a veteran, I was older than most of my class, and I had enlisted in the Navy when military service was a point of pride and a usual rite of passage. The five years between me and my classmates could just as easily have been fifty. I was a classic Middle American, part of the unquestioning Silent Generation, airdropped into a generation that was questioning everything.

For some reason, *Time* magazine hired me as a campus stringer, and when I covered a meeting of the Young Maoists, I thought they would all be Chinese. Students for a Democratic Society organized on a regular basis on the plaza between Butler and Low Memorial libraries, and that seemed reasonable enough. They were democratic, right? Little did I know about the Port Huron Statement and the thrust of radical politics. I was still a conventional, law-abiding, nonactivist member of the class of 1967. But then, one noon hour in the fall, Dick Williams, Phil Smith, and I, walking out past the Jefferson statue, were greeted by a blaring, distorted voice coming over a portable PA system from the plaza. We smiled at each other. Why not? Thomas Jefferson would surely be with us, the true Americans.

The steps of Low Memorial Library provided the ideal vantage point for us, an unlikely trio who had found they shared a common dislike for the shaggy-bearded, smelly protesters who were violating our once-serene campus. This wasn't what we were paying tuition for. Williams, who would go on to write a biography of Newt Gingrich and be a darling of the neoconservatives; Smith, who would work for the *Washington Post* and then go on to far more substantial dollars as a Washington lobbyist and public relations man; and I, who would go on to . . . well, go on. Where the eggs came from I don't know—did we go to one of the little grocery stores on Broadway or Amsterdam? Anyhow, we bravely took up our positions on the steps, and as a ragtag group of a few dozen longhairs, flying the banner of "Vietnam Veterans Against the War," marched by, we reared back.

America's foreign policy changed very quickly just about the time I was leaving the Navy. The *Power*'s sister destroyer, the USS *Maddox*, was supposedly attacked by North Vietnamese patrol boats in the Gulf of Tonkin in 1964. With the Gulf of Tonkin Resolution, America went to war in earnest. The 12,000 U.S. "advisers" mushroomed to 200,000 combat troops in a year, quickly doubled, and by now were over a half million. There were voices to stop the war and bring home the troops, but I was appalled. "Zap the gooks" easily tumbled out of my mouth. After all, this was America. We were always on the right side. These commies in flip-flops and pith helmets had to be taught a lesson. As did the placard-carrying demonstrators chanting, "Hey, hey, LBJ, how many boys did you kill today?"

We flung the eggs and howled with laughter when one splattered on the back or, even better, on the head of one of the protestors. How righteous, how brave, how American we were. Had I been a drinking man, I would have joined Dick and Phil for a beer at the West End, the famed Columbia drinking spot on Broadway and 114th Street. No, I had some journalism ethics to read up on, so I left them to have a quiet Coke in my Columbia University married students apartment in the building over the liquor store on the corner of 112th.

When I got to the apartment, I went to wash up. I looked in the bathroom mirror. It was an oversized mirror, so there was a lot of me to see.

There I was, with my military short hair, Sears plaid jacket, two-blocked tie, and smooth, shaved face. This was the man I'd seen reflected in the bronze casket. But there was something slightly different about him. I was getting to be a better reporter. I would now have to write it as "his smooth, *smug,* shaved face." This was no longer the gritty factory worker coming off the third shift at American Can Company. He was at an Ivy League school. No longer the kid from the East Side of Cleveland who didn't know what side of the plate the fork and knife were to be placed. J.C. had schooled me well. No longer the drunk staggering back to his ship in a port he would soon forget. No longer a little boy kneeling on that grate, praying fervently to a mysterious God. No, what I saw was a domesticated house pet, retooling himself to be acceptable, employable, conventional; to say the right thing at the right time; to be on the popular side of any controversial issue; to keep his elbows off the table and certainly pick up the right fork.

I stared into the mirror, into my own eyes. What would Brother Adolph make of me now? The Maryknoll priest? Thomas Merton? My own father? What did I make of myself?

OO

For class assignments, I wrote a story about the Ambrose lightship that guided ships into New York harbor, covered Mayor John Lindsay's press conferences, told both sides of the city's negotiations with its transit workers, and detailed the election on Long Island, carefully spelling out town names like Patchogue, Mattituck, Cutchogue, and Speonk. But there was another person whom my classmates—and my wife—never knew. I began to walk the Upper West Side alone. I stood at a distance and listened to the old, gray-faced men talking animatedly in Yiddish as they sat together on the benches of Riverside Park. Suddenly, as if the electricity had gone out, they would go silent, gazing down, numbers from a Nazi concentration camp revealed at the cuff of their tattered jackets. I rode the subway to the Cloisters in the Bronx and walked the worn stones of St. Michel-de-Cuxa, the ruined monastery near Prades, Merton's birthplace, where he wandered as a young boy. I listened to the shy young man who sat for hours on the last stool of the Chock full o'Nuts coffee shop across from the journalism school as he told the story over and over about the mother he raped and the baby he killed in a tiny Vietnamese hamlet. I sat on the benches on the Broadway median, yellow cabs blurring by. I don't know why, but I did.

The Summer of Love was about to happen. *Hair* was opening; the Rolling Stones and the Doors were terrifying parents. "Relevance" was

9

THE BIG TIME,
MORE OR LESS

"Last name?"
"Hoffman."
"First name?"
"Dustin."

THE BORED EMERGENCY ROOM CLERK, with requisite impassive face, clacked away in triplicate on her IBM Selectric. The patient sat slumped in the molded plastic chair, his left hand swathed in a bloodstained towel. A wound was a wound was a wound. It was after 10 PM, and other people were waiting. Stabbings, domestic squabbles, gang fights, street rumbles—she dealt with the results. The questions and answers droned on.

So there sat Dustin Hoffman, at the time one of the most famous and sought-after actors in America. And there I sat, right next to him. Hoffman with a gash that would take twelve stitches to mend. I with the story that was about to change my life.

How I had gotten this story was its own story, one that any good journalist—or crass opportunist—would cherish. Hoffman was in Baltimore starring in the pre-Broadway production of *Jimmy Shine,* what turned out to be an instantly forgettable Murray Schisgal play. After journalism school, I had taken a job with the *Baltimore Sun,* and was assigned a feature on this rising star. In the smash hit *The Graduate,* Hoffman had imbued the word "plastics" with the gestalt of the late 1960s popular culture, in two syllables encapsulating everything that was wrong and venal about our Great Land. Meanwhile, he had captured America's heart. Mrs. Robinson was not the only one who couldn't resist his shlumpy presence, bumbling ways, and phlegmy voice. I had first interviewed him in his dressing room after a rehearsal, and when I noticed him picking through all the lush fruit in the basket the theatre had provided, and choosing some sickle pears buried near the bottom, I did what any thinking reporter would do. I noted it, drawing deep meaning from his selecting the most inelegant and least sweet of all the proffered choices. Then I went to the best greengrocer in Baltimore and bought a few pounds in a nicely appointed basket to take him for our second interview, in his hotel room. Perhaps it was the sickle pears that made the difference later on.

Near the end of the first act on opening night at the Morris A. Mechanic Theatre, when the script called for Jimmy Shine to slash a canvas he'd been painting, Hoffman did it with D'Artagnon-like gusto. He went through the rest of the first act and all of the second with his hand in his pocket. When I went backstage after the play, I saw why. Someone had failed to dull the blade, a standard stagecraft precaution. His hand was wrapped in a towel, and his manager was frantic. The entourage raced for the limousine parked outside the stage door. I tried to climb in, but his manager shoved me aside. "No reporters!" I then uttered three words that changed the course of my life.

"Johns. Hopkins. Hospital."

His manager grabbed me by the shirt and yanked me into the backseat. "Get in."

That I didn't actually know where Johns Hopkins Hospital was located was, of course, of some concern. In the nanosecond between the transmission to my brain of the alarmed look on the manager's face, Hoffman's angst-ridden silence, and the sight of the bloody towel, and my lips' blurting out those three words, I had actually made a quite thoughtful decision, drawing on Aristotelian logic and Thomistic Scholasticism, overlaid with the imperatives of the New Journalism. I came to the conclusion that my presence would certainly not exacerbate Hoffman's condition and, although I didn't know where Johns Hopkins Hospital was, I lived in Baltimore and could probably get there quicker than these out-of-towners. Trumping all considered thought was one of the commandments of the New Journalism: Thou Shalt Be Where the Action Is.

"Let me just make sure we're taking the quickest way," I said as we wheeled out onto the street. At the light, I leaped out and asked the cab driver alongside. "Right on Mulberry, left on Broadway. Got it." Minutes later, there we were, pulling up beneath the brightly lit Emergency Room sign. I had saved the day—and probably, I have convinced myself, made that 1.44-mile trip quicker than if they hadn't had this schemer on board.

Hoffman had done the play because he wanted to show that he wasn't a flash in the pan, he confided to me as we sat there in the waiting room, but like the hapless hero of *The Graduate* (as I would eventually write), he had royally screwed up, wounding himself. Of such epic moments are a reporter's life made. I knew I had a story that "had legs," as we say in the trade, legs beyond the beltway that surrounded Baltimore. There was a hot new publication, *New York* magazine, publishing stories by the best of the New Journalism writers, and the next morning I was on the phone and put right through to the editor, Clay Felker. "Have it to me by tomorrow morning. Two thousand words." He hung up. I looked at the telephone in my hand. The dial tone was so much sweet music. Oh, my God, it's happened! The first big break.

I looked for other opportunities to turn local Baltimore stories into pieces for national magazines. Over the next few months, I profiled the aging, alcoholic talk show host Gary Moore, a sort of Lion in Winter piece, and the nation's number-one motorcycle champion, Gary Nixon. *TV Guide* bought a version of the Moore story, and when I queried *Sport* magazine using the hyperventilated zoom-zoom prose in which Tom Wolfe had immortalized Junior Johnson, they wanted the motorcycle star. With three articles appearing in three different national magazines, I felt it was time to get back to New York, which most assuredly still did not know about me. No magazine would hire me full-time with such a thin portfolio, and it was death to go to New York and hang out the "freelance writer" sign, so I swallowed every bit of pride I had and took a job at Harper & Row Publishers. I was to write its quarterly and annual reports and a house organ I named *Footnotes*. When asked what title I preferred, I called myself "editor for special publications," but, of course, I was nothing more than a PR flack. I assured myself that this was only a way station. I hired a very smart young woman, Judy Budding, who couldn't type very well but had gone to Bennington and knew how to answer the phone with great panache, trained her to write most of the reports and the house organ, bought a pensive picture of D. H. Lawrence that hung on my wall, and generally plotted out what to do next. I lusted after the *New York Times Magazine,* the *Atlantic, Life, Look,* and beyond to the absolute pinnacle, the *New Yorker,* but I couldn't even imagine approaching journalism's pantheon as I wrote a string of pieces for *New York,* which at that time was a sort of unwashed, unwelcome, loud, and pushy newcomer nobody had invited.

Harper & Row, in a properly fusty brick-faced building at 49 East Thirty-third Street, was a hallowed place, home to Thornton Wilder and Pearl Buck, with editors like Cass Canfield and Evan Thomas who drank martinis at the Century Club with authors like John Dos Passos and Thomas Wolfe. I experienced nothing of that, being a lowly minion on the dreaded "corporate" side.

I worshipped at another shrine, at 207 East Thirty-second but a few blocks away. In a second-floor walk-up, *New York* magazine was transforming journalism. *New York* today is a compendium of the Ten Best, Five Most, and Fifty Least of just about everything, but in those days, with Jimmy Breslin ripping pages out of a typewriter that his stubby fingers were demolishing, Peter Maas bringing in his sunglass-wearing Mafia buddies, and Gay Talese arriving with precisely crafted (and meticulously typed) pages of symphonic prose, the magazine was a writer's dream. *New York* chided urban stupidities, held up the aching beauty of the Imperial City, and trod the thorny paths of politics, race, gender, and power. Writers wrote in their own voice; there was none of the Cuisinarting into uniform, style-book slurry that other publications demanded. The New Journalism was about what we saw, found, felt, and concluded, all structured within a compelling narrative, an approach considered seditious in the established magazines of the day. The classic way of quoting experts and officials was passing; the participant-observer method employed by anthropologists was emerging as a journalistic form. I was eventually listed on the masthead between Gloria Steinem and Tom Wolfe. Ah, the fate of the alphabet! But I was ready for any cabbie to run me down the first week my sandwiched name appeared. I would have died a happy man, knowing exactly how the lead for the obituary would read. "Paul Wilkes, a contributing writer for *New York* magazine, was struck and killed. . . ."

I'll never forget the night I ran into Tom Wolfe on the East Side as he was browsing in a bookstore for a book on Japanese enamel painting that would spur one of his magnificent digressions in *From Bauhaus to Our House.* I was working on a piece on New York City garbage—where it goes (Staten Island) and why anyone should care. (The city was drowning in it.) I told Wolfe I'd been riding garbage trucks to get a better feel for the story, and he looked on me so tenderly, like a father whose son was finally ready to take over the family business. "Great. Exactly right way to do the story." He had dropped acid with Ken Kesey and the Merry Pranksters, and I was riding a garbage truck out of the Gansevoort Receiving Station, but we were soul brothers. To this day, I wish I had told him about the path to Johns Hopkins Hospital.

∞

J.C. and I eventually bought the lower two floors of a rundown brownstone in Park Slope, Brooklyn, which at the time was considered, like *New York* magazine, beyond the outer reaches of polite society. We were a young married couple in the midst of those disorienting crazy years, with America reeling from a string of assassinations, Nixon's lying and resigning, racial unrest, and the eviscerating of the holy state of matrimony, something a little closer to many homes. Not long after we moved onto Second Street in Brooklyn, a sort of Black Plague swept down the block. On one side, the Ubells' seemingly happy marriage proved poisonous; on the other side, the Bashfords fell victim. Up and down the Park Slope streets, once-healthy marriages were turning toxic and disintegrating, in a matter of days it seemed. But Paul and J.C.? Perfectly fine. Nothing to worry about; in fact, I never much thought about it. I was breathing that rarefied air, a real writer's New York air, dreaming of pieces I would write, clipping snippets of stories so that I could craft better metaphors, descriptions, transitions. We weren't making that much money, but without children, we were living a very comfortable life. I was an up-and-coming writer with a degree from *the* journalism school, a great-looking wife, a few clips of my own. What more could you ask for?

The answer came at a Columbia journalism school function, when a chance meeting with Judy Klemesrud, a daily *Times* reporter, led to an introduction to Gerald Walker, who would eventually be my longtime and beloved editor on the *New York Times Magazine*. He assigned me a piece on New York City detectives; I traded in garbage trucks for an unmarked squad car cruising the Upper East Side. The *Atlantic* saw that article; soon I was lounging at poolside at the home of Masters and Johnson—William Masters and Virginia Johnson, the king and queen of sexual function and dysfunction. *Look* magazine saw that and sent me to interview Ali MacGraw, who cooked up some lamb chops at her apartment; later, on the set for *Love Story* at Harvard Yard, she winked at me just before getting into the MG for that great shot filmed along Storrow Drive. I was in the locker room with basketball stars; on the set with television celebrities; in a restaurant watching the mother of women's liberation, Betty Friedan, attack a mound of steak tartare and tell me about the perils of male domination; at La Grenouille hearing the chef swoon to *Women's Wear Daily*'s John Fairchild about the green beans just flown in from France. It all seemed to be going so well.

I was a great listener. People trusted me, and I seemed to have a knack for getting inside them; unearthing their humanity, their inner fears; connecting in a way, not at all intellectual, but visceral and human, common in the best sense, like my father was able to do with just about anyone who came through our door or pounded nails alongside him. I could find the telling detail, that signature icon of the New Journalism, which in a few words could say so much. The sickle pears in Baltimore. Those ankles on the Rapid Transit in Cleveland. Steak tartare. I didn't have a towering intellect, certainly no family lineage to mine for contacts, but I became more and more proficient at dramatizing who people were by what they did, even more than by what they said. Somehow I could *see* them, stripped of all artifice.

Perhaps that was why I was so masterful at allowing the world to see only those personal significant details that—if I were the reporter—would paint the most favorable portrait of me.

∞

My marriage—like the other aspects of my carefully scripted and ascendant life—could not have looked better. Mr. Compassion, Mrs. Empathy; never a harsh word or raised voice. The 1970s were here with a vengeance, but we were lost in the lull of the 1950s world of Ozzie and Harriet, sans kids. The Wilkeses showed so well, looked so good together, this churchgoing, nondrinking couple. If you were a certain type of self-satisfied cipher in New York, you just loved having them around. So sincere, so pleasant. We wrote those pasty Christmas letters you love to hate about how absolutely ducky our life was. Each year we told you exactly What a Husband and Wife Should Be.

J.C. came from solid Methodist but emotionally distant and frugal Nebraska farm stock. She tried to re-create herself in college as a sophisticated lady, joining a sorority and earning straight A's. Coming from Catholic, working stock, with four years as a college lout, I married her as much for her looks and her missionary aura as for the fact that she knew not only what side of the plate what piece of silverware was to be placed but also how to get soup from bowl to mouth with a minimum of sound. Around the Formica table on Forest Avenue, these were not major concerns.

In a way, we were both continually reinventing ourselves. The flag-draped, My Country Right or Wrong sweethearts fresh from the Navy looked aghast at the excesses in Boulder, becoming, in turn, the wise and proper Columbia University house parents to all those immature, radical twenty-two-year-olds. In a rented Baltimore townhouse, we served quiche and added spinach to our iceberg lettuce salads and thought we were quite the au courant, worldly couple. All of which was preparing us for New York. It wasn't that we were gimlet-eyed climbers, intent on clawing our way to top of any heap we found. It was more innocent than that, but just as insidious.

Assembling and reassembling the ill-fitting pieces that each of us brought to the altar, we somehow wanted it to be perfect, unblemished. Even during those cataclysmic years, when the unspoken bargains that people agreed on to make marriages work began to be articulated and renegotiated, we acted as though nothing were happening. We knew something of the imperfections, the darkness in each other, but our unspoken pact was that we wouldn't, couldn't risk being truly honest. Somehow this might cause the whole fragile structure to collapse, sending it toppling onto our heads, and us back to the lowest points in our former lives. Old college and Navy friends would stop through New York to visit, and I could see by the way they looked at me that they were wondering, *Who the hell is this guy? Do I know him? Did I ever know him?*

There was something else I had lost along the way. Just as J.C. and I were so preoccupied with this perfect image we so masterfully projected, and couldn't honestly face each other, I, at least, couldn't face God seriously either. Dishonesty was a barely perceptible, dull hum in the background of everything we did. Merton had told me about it years before, in *Seeds of Contemplation:*

> We are at liberty to be real, or to be unreal. We may be true or false, the choice is ours. We may wear one mask and now another, and never, if we so desire, appear with our own true face. But we cannot make these choices with impunity. Causes have effects, and if we lie to ourselves and to others, then we cannot expect to find truth and reality whenever we happen to want them.

∞

It might be stretching it a bit to link the honest pursuit of God with the honest enjoyment of good sex, but even as my writing career was taking off, I found I was having trouble with both God and sex. I had gotten so good at fooling myself that I would never have allowed that sex was any kind of barometer. Sex (like my very stylized and desiccated religious and prayer life) was turning into a perfunctory exercise. We grew more and more tentative; I was just happy any time I was able to correctly forward my request for sex, didn't offend by acting too interested in "it," and had touched her in the right places so as not to queer the deal. We choreographed the classic dance of avoidance: going to bed earlier or later, feigning sleep, or stirring up any argument that would preclude later intimacy. Where was that head-pounding passion we knew on the beach in Karachi? The half-life of that kind of pure animal instinct can't be infinite, but did our sex life have to dwindle down to the vibrator we bought in desperation? Like a modern-day sexual shaman, there I was, deftly wielding a battery-powered, penis-shaped hunk of plastic. Like a fool, thinking this was the answer to what proved to be a much bigger question.

Why was it that sex was so perfunctory? For one thing, J.C. hated her body, a rather beautiful body by today's standards, but in the bust-conscious era when she came of age, J.C. looked upon herself as sadly deficient. I never thought that. She wore breast enhancers—"falsies" was the popular term—and each night before bed, she would turn her back to me and embarrassedly take off that duplicitous bra. Perhaps I should have just spun her around, thrown the bra in the wastebasket, and told I loved her exactly the way she was. I think I tried to convey that, but obviously I didn't succeed. As for birth control for that ever-diminishing number of times, there was the pill, which was a waste of money, estrogen, and progestin. Because, after all, we would never allow anything to happen unplanned.

Such as children. Funny how the issue of having children kept being put off—next spring, next year, not right now. How the soaring refrain of "as many as the stars in the sky" faded into the rumble of a two-career life. She wanted to go back to graduate school when we were in Baltimore; in New York, I was about to quit my Harper & Row job and take the leap as a freelance writer. With the women's movement in high gear, she started a women's center to help foster the emerging consciousness of women. I finally got my first book contract. We always had an excuse, but we were kidding ourselves.

Once settled in Brooklyn, we attended Park Slope Methodist Church, and on the surface I was a happy, churchgoing Protestant. It was a good church, with an excellent pastor, Phil West, who was an inspiring civil rights activist. My politics had changed by this time. I was one of the hundreds of thousands of protestors who marched in fall 1971 to protest the Vietnam War, and Richard Nixon, seemingly on his way to reelection. The war was wrong—that wasn't hard to see. Like many of late awareness, I wanted to make a statement.

But that rumbling in my soul, set off each Sunday in church as we sang the final hymn, wouldn't go away. What was wrong with me? There was an altar and stained-glass windows; the God that John Wesley sought was the same God I sought. Wesley, that preacher on horseback, should have been an inspiration: no fancy High Church for him; he went to the common people, the marginalized ethnics of his day. But each Sunday, it was as if a meal were about to be served, but after the tasty hors d'oeuvres of sermon and scripture, I was shown the door. I left hungry, not exactly knowing why. So what do the unsatisfied do? They turn elsewhere. Before I knew it was happening, I was carrying on an affair.

It began innocently enough as I was putting books on the shelf in my tiny office just off the bedroom on the second floor of the newly renovated brownstone. My hand grabbed two paperbacks. Their well-worn spines stared back at me at eye level. I could have neatly replaced them there and gone on, but I didn't. I sat down on the bed, paging through, smiling at the sentences and paragraphs I had underlined. I felt that same kinship I had known when reading of *The Seven Storey Mountain* and *Seeds of Contemplation* in high school and then during the lonely days at Marquette and at sea with the Navy. But when I married, I had put Thomas Merton off-limits, like everything else Catholic. He had been waiting, a life preserver hung in readiness on the bulkhead of my passing years.

In the months ahead, I made forays out to the Community Bookstore, working my way through his many books. *Wisdom of the Desert, The Silent Life, Thoughts in Solitude;* the list went on. I read them one after another in the sanctuary of that windowless office, never tipping my hand by putting his books on the bedside table. This "bum" Merton—I'm sure Brother Adolph would again agree—had turned out pretty well after all. It was only at the back of my mind that Merton had actually died, accidentally electrocuted in Thailand in December 1968. For me, he was still a living, goading presence in my life, that thumping drumbeat behind the smooth, orchestrated Muzak of my life.

And what was Merton saying to me? There was very little, if anything, in his books about Catholicism per se. Nothing about returning to the one true Church. Instead, he was saying that becoming a saint was the only pursuit worthy of any man's life. That you had to give yourself away in order to really find yourself. That you had to give yourself to something bigger than whatever it was that you thought would bring you happiness. You had to give yourself to God, and in turn God would fill that emptiness that St. Augustine talked about when he said, "My heart is restless until it rests in you." This last drumbeat thudded loudest in my brain.

For I was restless. I was writing for fancy magazines, and when the first copies were delivered to the corner newsstand on Seventh Avenue and Second Street, I'd quickly turn to the story and run my finger over my byline, as if it were in Braille. As if only by touching "Paul Wilkes" would it be real; my eyes or memory were not to be trusted. And then that haunting call that writers know so well. *And? What's next?* I would launch off on the next story, or juggle two or three. There were a few stories from those days that actually mattered, but too many followed the exploits of inconsequential people and ephemeral events. This was before the real cult of celebrity was born, but the public still had a healthy appetite to see the bitter fruit at the bottom of everyone's basket.

With page after page of Merton, my life seemed more and more meaningless. I wasn't a bad person. I was a nonperson. My tepid religious commitment, my cauterized relationship with my wife and my God had

10

HOME, AGAIN

BY NOW, MY FATHER WAS SPENDING a lot of time at the Formica breakfast nook table, his lungs so clogged with years of coal dust and sawdust that even a dozen steps across the cracked, maroon linoleum floor to the refrigerator left him gasping for breath. On the worn wooden bench he crafted so many years ago when the table was surrounded with his children, he kept a stack of newspapers and magazines.

"I don't know what the hell he's doing," he would tell anyone, my sister Peggy informed me—whether asked or not—"but I guess Butch is writing about something or another." It appeared he had read my stories, perhaps more than once if the curled edges were any sign. Another would soon be added to the stack, this time with him in it.

As young people of my generation married, they no longer moved in with the parents or into the top floor of a double-decker, but to new, split-level homes with attached garages in the Cleveland suburbs. The blacks who had once been contained downtown were now moving into what had once been the all-white, virtually all-Slovak St. Benedict's parish. "White flight" it would later be called. That was the story I was doing.

But my father wasn't going anywhere. Even though he had signed papers to finally sell 11412 Forest Avenue, he had made no arrangements for where he would live, his intuition telling him that he didn't have to worry about his next home.

He looked more and more like a noble Indian, a wise chief, creases etched deeper into his cheeks and forehead, his skin a fine mahogany, his eyes barely slits amid folds of skin that sagged from the weight of years. I realized how much I cared for him, yet how little time I had spent with him in the second half of my life. Even now I had so little to say to him; our worlds were so different. I just sat across the table in what would be my last hours with him, my feet resting on the heating grate that was the site of my early prayer life, watching his chest rise and fall with each labored breath. I hoped he was proud of me, his only child to go on to college. I was now thirty-four, and one thing I had not given him, which all of his other sons and daughters had, was grandchildren. My sister Marian had eight children, the others a minimum of three, for a total of thirty-two grandsons and granddaughters. If my failure to produce children disappointed him, or if anything I had accomplished filled him with pride, or if his heart still ached from the death of his wife, I would never know. He never told me. It was simply not his way. As a writer, I was constantly making judgments about people; he never did. He was not a man to talk about success or failure, of good or evil, and certainly not about his faith. I know for certain that he never uttered the word "Catholic." That would have been too "fancy" for him. *God, Catholic, morality*— these were just words. He was so much like Merton, after all. If you were yourself, nothing more or less, that was how you were measured in his eyes. What mattered was that if you promised something, you delivered; if you bought good tools, you kept them sharp and rust-free. You didn't grab for more than your fair share, and you had enough sense to go home to bed when you had had enough to drink. His benchmarks for personal excellence were as clear as the lines on his Craftsman ruler hanging on its designated nail in his basement workshop.

Georges Tames, the legendary *Times* photographer who took the famous picture of JFK standing at his desk, back to the camera, that came to be known as "The Loneliest Job," had been assigned to this story. His stories of photographing famous people dazzled my family, but when he picked up the camera, he was not raconteur but worker. He shot perhaps one or two frames for other parts of the story, but he shot many of my father. He recognized greatness and wanted to portray it honestly and well.

oo

A month later, Peggy called to say that my father had died. His heart had simply grown tired of beating for lack of oxygen. The funeral was a simple enough affair, a village funeral really, with his children, grandchildren, and a scattering of neighborhood and parish people, all of them old, in attendance. There was no one from outside our enclave, for he was a man of this place, not of the world. Except for the priest facing the congregation and pronouncing the prayers in English—this much I knew had changed—the funeral mass seemed little different from those I remembered from when I was a Catholic.

"When I was a Catholic." What a haunting sound that had to it. Was it a precious something now irretrievably lost, or merely a stage outgrown— as a growing child's steps are no longer wobbly? I quickly pushed such thoughts away. It was a bit harder as I knelt for the Consecration there at St. Benedict's, where I had first encountered the Christ of mystery and frightening power. It was even harder when the others went forward to receive Holy Communion and I stayed in my pew.

I asked Father Michael, the pastor, if I or someone in the family might say something during the homily, but the answer was a chilly no. St. Benedict's was not about to concede anything to Vatican II even as the parish itself was dying. (It would close ten years later.) But as the casket was wheeled into the vestibule, I don't know what possessed me, but I grabbed one of the handles and jerked the casket to a stop. My father was not going to be buried generically. The funeral director looked alarmed. This was not supposed to be; all was to go smoothly. I tightened my hand on the handle. I began to speak. My voice was firm at the beginning, but not at the end.

I told of a man who waited at that kitchen table, day after day, for us to come by. His pot of chicken soup simmering on the stove every Sunday morning, whether he felt good or not. The shot and a beer set before you. A man who bought dozens of eggs, links of sausage, only so he could give them away. A man who wanted nothing for himself and was only happy when he was last, not first. The vestibule was silent except for soft sobs; they knew exactly what I was talking about. I took my hand off the handle.

After the burial on a low knoll at Calvary Cemetery, next to my mother's grave, all seven of us, our spouses, and the grandchildren came back to the house. I, usually the most talkative of us all, found I had nothing more to say. I climbed the stairs to the attic. There in the back room was the sagging bed where each night my grandmother warmed my side before she rolled over onto her own. I sat on the old mattress, just to hear the familiar wheeze of the springs below. The tree on our front lawn had been cut down, and the harsh light through the front window revealed the thick layer of dust on everything, an aging widower's legacy.

I walked downstairs and out to the chipped and rotting front porch where I once swung in the glider, waiting . . . waiting for something to happen. I stood on its steps where I bounced my rubber ball, a solitary boy hoping to catch a glimpse of that Beaumont girl coming home from school, her knees tantalizingly breaking the pleats of her crisp skirt. In the kitchen I ran my hand over the edge of the tiny, four-burner Maytag stove where my mother had stood, cooking. Meal after meal after meal,

her varicose veins bulging, but she never sat down. There was the bread-
board, so long out of use that cobwebs had sealed it off from the world.
　My mother.
　You never helped with my homework, but you listened to my prayers.
Night after night you sat at that table, as your own eyes drooped with the
fatigue of tending your own house, in addition to the house of another
woman, rich enough to play golf or tennis or bridge, none of which you knew
or cared to know. You allowed me to speak to God out loud. You helped
shape my soul, and now my soul was so hollow. Such a difficult child, I spoke
back to you with so little respect. I was ashamed of you. And I was in such a
hurry on that first day of May 1956, when my youthful inexperience took
your life. I never saw them lay you in the ground. I never could shed tears on
that freshly turned soil as I just did for your husband, my father.
　I slowly descended the steps into the basement. I took an Erin Brew out of
the case in the fruit cellar and stood on the cold cement floor in my father's
tiny work area, his rusting cans of nails on the shelf, short pieces of wood
stuffed into the rafters. "Butch, you'll never know when you'll need a piece
just that size," he would say. He called blacks niggers, Jews kikes, Hungarians hunkies, Italians dagos, but he would work alongside and respect any
man who respected his own tools, who didn't waste a nail or even the smallest piece of wood, who would put in an honest day's work. He knew his
place, and would never aspire or rise to a position of power. He didn't want
dominion over anyone else, understanding in such a profound way how infi-
nitely different each life was, how uniquely each person was composed. He
would have made a terrible reporter. He could never have written those pithy
snap judgments we come up with so blithely. I didn't know what I as a son
had given him, but I realized what he had given me.
　Sitting there, sipping on a warm Erin Brew—my first drink in so many
years—I realized that when I stripped away all the many pretenses
I affected, I was his son after all. I knew for certain that I had his gratitude,
gratitude that I had found work—not bringing buildings back to life, tearing out charred beams and walls as he had done, the work that had eventually killed him—but honest work nonetheless. Yes, I waited to see my
name in the *Times,* or the *Atlantic, Look, Life,* but it was the work itself
that brought a glow to my soul. That I had done it well, honorably, that
I had given nine hours of work for the eight hours for which I was paid.
　I finished the beer and slid the empty back into the carton. The shelves
in the fruit cellar were bare. Once they had been filled with Mason jars of
peaches and tomatoes, green beans and pickles that my mother had put
up. But all that was gone now.

ON THE STREETS

THE SMELL CAME DOWN TWO FLIGHTS TO MEET US. When we climbed the dusty stairs, we found the door to the second floor apartment slightly ajar, and after no one answered our knock, we stepped inside. My feet kept sticking to the floor. It was only after I was halfway across what must have been the living room that I realized this was not just an unwashed floor. I was walking over a layer of human excrement.

Mary Skelly had a wonderful smile on her face and no underwear on her bottom. I can still picture her and smell that place as I did that hot afternoon. The floor was littered with empty gin bottles, half-full soup cans left to rot and rust, cartons from take-out food, battalions of cockroaches greedily policing their perimeters. Old, yellowed newspapers thrust curled, furtive edges to the stained ceiling. Mary's filthy cotton housedress had a skunk-like stripe down the lower part of its back, brown instead of white. But she was smiling so sweetly, so serenely. Gordon's and Gilbey's, Fleishman's and Seagram's—the great houses of working-class gin—had been such warm and obliging hosts, never leaving her alone or without solace. In the corner, what first appeared to be a pile of rags, was her son, Peter. He must have been in his midforties, but it was hard to tell.

The elegant Cleveland lady with the fine, stockinged ankles aboard the Rapid Transit had started me on one path, and now Brooklyn's own Mary Skelly, her bare ankles caked and stained, was about to send me on another.

The Skelly's rent-controlled apartment was one of those classic walk-ups over the storefronts on Seventh Avenue in Brooklyn—then a rich array of meat markets, fish stores, and greengrocers, a hardware store and a newsstand, but today a collection of sushi parlors, high-end coffee bars, patisseries, and boutiques. My companion, a few sticky steps ahead of me, was Father Ronald Petroski, the new assistant at St. Francis Xavier parish at the corner of Sixth and President streets only a few blocks away, who had been alerted by someone in the building. Thus the knock on the door, which opened onto hell.

J.C. and I, good Methodists, were introduced to Father Petroski, but I can't remember how. I certainly wasn't looking to come back to the Catholic Church—in fact had little interest in things Catholic. Father Petroski, a chain-smoker, was charismatic, troubled, and neurotic. But most appealingly, he had an offbeat, infectious sense of humor. He loved to tell of the latest exploits of the dachshund Nikki, who hovered near the face of his mistress—the septuagenarian, homebound Mrs. D'Angelo—as she attempted to quell her palsy and receive the proffered host from Father Petroski. With a swipe of his tongue, "Scccuuuulp," Nikki was sanctified, batting about .500 on the priest's weekly visits. Every time the priest told the latest chapter, he adorned it with details. "Nikki, Nikki, sweeta Nikki, give Father Breoski a chance. Sita down, Nikki, sita down. Thatsa Jesu, Nikki, Jesu Christa." Father Petroski had her Italian accent down perfectly. I just about gagged, laughing so hard. The priest was a rebel who had barely made it through the Brooklyn archdiocesan seminary at Huntington, Long Island, because of his unstinting antiwar and civil rights stands, and he was so unlike the priests of any parish I had ever known as to be almost of another church. Another planet. His tales of tending to the poor and ill of the neighborhood were laced with humor, insanity, and holiness. A young, idealistic priest on the streets of Brooklyn, nails bitten down to the quick, possessed with a love of the unlovely, he was a perfect subject for *Look* magazine. So I began following him on his rounds, and the Skellys came into my life. And they would not soon leave.

Ironically, the story on Brooklyn street priest Father Ronald Petroski never ran. *Look,* a grand, once-fat, general interest magazine, folded under the pressure of the 1970s onslaught of specialized magazines that delivered exactly the right audience for the right product. It was a sign of the times. A lot of "general interests" were fading—marriage, fidelity, having children, trust in authority among them.

I wanted to experience every part of Father Petroski's life, so I attended one of his conventional Masses at St. Francis. I then learned that the priest also conducted a weekly "folk liturgy," a foreign term I dutifully recorded in my reporter's notebook. It was scheduled to begin at ten o'clock, and I arrived at the designated place a few minutes early. I took a seat beneath a basketball hoop at the back of the yawning St. Francis Xavier school gymnasium. Teenagers—the girls wafting clouds of fresh, fruity perfumes, the boys trailing Old Spice aftershave and underarm dampness, all of them madly chewing gum and exuding hormonal vapors—set up the place, more or less. A table at the front, rows of chairs close by; no altar, no pews. There was no familiar odor of incense, just the smell of a recent waxing of the glistening gym floor.

Father Petroski whisked in twenty minutes past the assigned time, a stoneware chalice, loaf of Italian bread, and bottle of Chianti cradled in his arms, a stole flung over his shoulder. Ten minutes later, Mass—and my return to Catholicism—began.

At the Gospel reading, Father Petroski left the table that served as an altar and walked out among the folding chairs, reading the parable of the Good Samaritan.

A man fell victim to robbers as he went down from Jerusalem to Jericho. They stripped and beat him and went off, leaving him half dead. A priest—"One of my crowd," he interjected, "pious, the righteous, we with the blessed hands, we the really good ones, got it?"—*happened to be going down that road, but when he saw him, he passed by on the opposite side.*

Likewise a Levite came to the place—"Levites, they were the temple folks, the regular churchgoers, tending the altar, making sure all the rituals were just perfect, just perfect," he repeated, bitter irony in his voice—*and when he saw him, he passed by on the opposite side.*

But a Samaritan traveler—"this poor schmuck, this foreigner," his voice was rising now, "despised by all the righteous ones, all the churchgoers, looked down on by all the weekly attendees just like you good little Catholic boys and girls"—*who came upon him was moved with compassion at the sight. He approached the victim, poured oil and wine over his wounds, and bandaged them. Then he lifted him up on his own animal, took him to an inn, and cared for him. The next day, he took out two silver coins and gave them to the innkeeper with the instruction, "Take care of him. If you spend more than what I have given you, I shall repay you on my way back."*

He walked briskly back toward the altar. The staccato beat of his loafers against hardwood floor echoed over the hushed gathering. Reaching the front, he slammed the lectionary onto the table, rattling the bottle and chalice. He wheeled around. "Here we sit, week after week, singing 'Weave, weave, weave the sunshine out of the falling rain,' or 'Day by day, day by day, oh Dear Lord three things I pray.' Each Sunday we walk out of here feeling soooo good, soooo holy, and you know what that adds up to, cats and kittens? That adds up to nothing! Nothing, zero, nothing! There's a poor lady rotting up on Seventh Avenue a couple blocks from our little comfort zone. 'Oh, Jesus, sweet Jesus, meek and mild.' Crap, total crap! We're going to hug and kiss at the sign of peace, and who's going to climb those stairs to hug and kiss that woman with shit running down her legs?"

His eyes, rheumy for obvious lack of sleep, searched the still rafters for an answer. There was not a sound. All was silence. My hand was frozen over the notebook.

At the Consecration, Father Petroski extended the loaf of Italian bread in his outstretched right hand and slowly, mesmerizingly, almost tauntingly, passed it in an arc that encompassed everyone in the gym. He did the same with the chalice. The Mass moved on. Although I knew its trajectory, to hear the words in English that were no more than small print italic under the Latin I never mastered in my ill-fated altar boy days was to hear them for the first time. "Lamb of God, you take away the sins of the world, have mercy on us. . . . This is my Body, given for you. . . . Do this in remembrance of me." Then, the impossible barrier that I knew so well: "O, Lord I am not worthy to receive you," followed by the ladder to vault a soul over it, regardless of the height, words that had never quite registered before: "but only say the word and I shall be healed."

A line was forming to take the bread and wine, to receive the Body and Blood of Christ. Before I knew what was happening, I was standing. I set notepad and pen on the folding metal chair behind me.

Moments of conversion are, of course, not the result of rational decisions. There had to be millions of tiny blips of unconnected desires and terrors, admonitions and invitations floating around in my subconscious self right then. And the moments of conversion that are the most exquisite for most of us are not dramatic experiences, vaulting from bad to good, for few of us are Saul on the road to Tarsus or Augustine leaving his sybaritic life behind. We dimly become aware that we are no longer satisfied; something has been clamoring at the back of our mind for attention. Our needs—which we have convinced ourselves had been met—had not been met at all. We had been deluding ourselves. And then, subtly but surely, unconnected experiences coalesce, the unformed is formed, the oily residue of rationalization through which we had been trying to see is suddenly wiped away. We see so clearly after all. Was it not always so, we ask ourselves? Wasn't it always this obvious?

I joined the line of teenagers, their eyes cast down, who looked as if they had aged at least a generation in the last hour. Father Petroski extended the loaf—now ragged and unseemly from so hands taking from it—and I tore off a huge piece. I had not been to Confession in almost ten years. I was using birth control. I was masturbating. I never bought but lustfully looked at *Playboy* and *Penthouse* whenever I could get my sweaty palms on them. I was, for all to see, a Methodist and therefore certainly ineligible to receive. If I had stopped to think, with that crusty piece of bread resting in my palm, and survey my total unworthiness, I surely would have had to return it.

Take, eat, this is my body.

Mother's bread, holy bread, Italian bread, all the good and honest loaves of bread I have ever eaten, all came together in that ounce of bread on a Sunday morning in a Brooklyn parish gymnasium. This was not the tasteless wafer of my younger days. This was food, not ritual; a meal, not a symbol. This was vital food for the journey of my life, sustenance proffered by One who had patiently waited, ready to address the hunger in my soul I didn't even know was there. I ravenously bit into the piece of yeasty bread, as if it might be snatched away at any moment, then a second, a third bite. My throat was both closing in nervousness and opening in expectation. I gulped unceremoniously one final time, and it was finished.

When my turn came, I peered into the cup of wine. Except for that sentimental, warm bottle of Erin Brew in the fruit cellar, I had not had a drink since months before I married and, for some reason, had vowed myself to alcoholic celibacy. After all, J.C. was a Methodist, and Methodists didn't drink. I drank too much and got too rowdy; God forbid this wild beast be set loose.

Take, drink, this is my blood.

There I was, reflected in the Chianti, my face clear, then blurring in the ripples as I cradled the chalice in my hands. It was a modest vintage from obviously not the best year. It tasted perfectly wonderful. A creamy richness, washing over my tongue, its vapors dancing up into my nostrils. I felt a pulsing at the back of my neck, first straining, as if I were lifting weights, then so pleasantly released. Leaving me stronger, tingling.

∞

At first there was religious schizophrenia each Sunday morning. Methodist or Catholic? Methodist *and* Catholic? Then gradually I was drawn more and more to the St. Francis Xavier gymnasium and Father Petroski's folk liturgy. J.C. came with me, at first tentatively. After all, she had been warned by her parents about the Catholic's voodoo worship of idols and blind obeisance to a mere mortal, the pope. In a good part of Protestant America, Catholics weren't even considered Christians. But then, surprisingly, she came with me, more and more enthusiastically each week. Sunday after Sunday—Father Petroski not being a man given to understatement, and who used well theatrical gestures and uncomfortably long hesitations that were both inborn and studied—the musty coverings of the Gospels were peeled back or blatantly ripped asunder to reveal a vibrant, living, caring God in the person of this man called Christ. This Christ was not the Christ of the St. Benedict's altar, of the Baltimore Catechism, of high school religion or college theology courses—places where others more astute than I was may have found him richly alive. My own shell had been too thick, my soul too literal, my mind too regimented to make this breakthrough. Now I could see, after all, that it was the Christ in the sad eyes of that Maryknoll missioner from China, in Brother Adolph's sly grin, in Thomas Merton's poetic reflection.

With Vatican II—and during my decade-long absence—Catholicism had blinked. The "one true Church" admitted there were other paths to God. The assembled bishops of the world had effectively upended the top-down, hierarchy-knows-all model to enfranchise the lowly lay person. The predictable, formulaic march to salvation was now reconfigured as a faith-driven wandering of a pilgrim people. Musty, fusty practices that had been with the Church since the Council of Trent in the sixteenth century were taken from the attic and set out on the curb, discarded. With Father Petroski I could begin to see the dim outlines of something extraordinary, even beyond the new and revolutionary practices—the use of English, the altar ripped off the back wall and set before the people, the more relaxed informal vestments. It was something at once enormously appealing and frightening. Exhilarating and freeing. Demanding. Uncharted. Liberating. Father Petroski kept calling for an all-or-nothing commitment, part his theatrical rhetoric, part gospel reality. A summoning to greatness, a greatness in Christ.

After all, wasn't this exactly what I wanted for my life, what I had first read in *The Seven Storey Mountain* so many years before? That there was no other worthwhile objective in life but to be a saint? But had I pursued that great calling? Had my life showed this? No, it did not. Harddrinking, foulmouthed high school and college student, I hadn't gone on those mission trips to help the less fortunate. I *was* the less fortunate, I had convinced myself. My Navy days, my early newspaper jobs—yes, I had tried to serve my country with honor and to write, when I could, about issues that mattered. But all that was so tepid, so half baked, so lacking the passion and commitment I saw in this priest. I was good, generically good. And so woefully inadequate.

Each night at my bedside—as a Catholic or, for fewer years, as a Methodist—I knelt and examined my conscience, replaying the day, detailing my failings, noting the occasional triumph of will or grace, and praying that the next day would find me a better person. I looked at the gulf that separated me from those who believe enough in God to truly trust him to guide them, provide for them, comfort them. And each night, I drew back in cowardice, a master of equivocation. No, not me. Not yet. I wasn't going to be the Maryknoll priest I once thought was my calling; I would not follow Merton into a monastery. After all, I was married; I had burned those bridges. But I knew—or at least hoped—that there must be a way for me to, no, not be a saint—that would be far too vain, "fancy." But a way to live a life . . . how can I say this? A life in Christ? Still too "fancy"? A life that mattered. A life with Christ beside me. That would do. I just didn't know what that life was, or exactly how I might be able to move close enough to that Christ to live it.

All the rich Catholic education I had received provided the sturdy, if dogmatic, foundation. Years in Protestant churches had given me a new appreciation of the Word of God, the scriptures that before had been so many strands woven into cords to bind and whip me. And now, because of that pudgy, homely Italian I saw carried into St. Peter's Basilica years before, the Catholic Church itself was shaking off centuries of stale and empty practices to reveal the fresh-flowing, living presence of a God among his people. I would not want to say good-bye to the church of the Wesley brothers by simply slamming an ungrateful door. But ultimately there was not enough *there* there. Were ritual, kneeling, and bowing in my DNA? Was apostolic succession, the primacy of a pope? These are the very parts of Catholicism that I would accept yet rail against in the years to come. It was not all the trappings of Catholicism that constituted the "there." It was, quite simply, the Eucharist. The presence of Christ, that powerful intersection of the human and the divine that takes place at every Catholic mass, no matter how well or poorly said. Looking back over my years away from the Church, there was not a Sunday I did not feel that something was lacking, like a perfect smile with a tooth missing.

Soon even those evocative Sunday mornings in the St. Francis Xavier gymnasium were not enough. In the spirit of Vatican II, a group of us organized a small intentional community that met weekly in one another's homes, creating our own evenings of prayer and song and reflection. We were not alone; these "home churches" were cropping up all over the country. Such books as Louis Evely's *That Man Is You,* Malcolm Boyd's *Are You Running with Me, Jesus?,* Henri Nouwen's *The Wounded Healer,* and Merton's own *Seeds of Contemplation* brought an immediacy and poignancy to our attempts to keep our Sunday morning faith alive the rest of the week. Father Petroski was often with us to offer the Eucharist. But when he was not there—and I was very careful in how I introduced this to a group of about a dozen Catholics and Protestants—one of us said the words of blessing over bread and wine. In the spirit of the early church, we did the best we could with what we had at hand. Week after week, we read and pondered the scriptures. For non-Catholic Christians, this was

hardly new. But for the newly awakened Catholics, it was novel and intoxicating. When I was growing up, the unstructured reading and discussion
of the Bible was discouraged, if not forbidden, because of a fear that we
wouldn't fully understand. Our priests had to ladle out a tiny portion from
the lectionary each Sunday and then tell us exactly how to digest it.

I was not alone in this conversion process; it was happening to many
Catholics. The equation was being upended. More and more Catholics
were better and better educated. Many priests were finding that their
seminary education had been pitifully shallow and that their degrees were
but worthless pieces of paper from unaccredited institutions. Their rote
Sunday sermons were no longer sufficient. Catholics were becoming
more inquisitive and assertive, putting behind them the idea of a Sunday
"obligation" or accepting predigested spiritual gruel. Catholics began to
see that this was a faith far deeper than novenas, adoration of the Blessed
Sacrament, and unthinking obedience to even the slightest utterance from
Rome. The drumbeat, week after week, grew stronger. Stop playing
games and mouthing pious phrases. Start living the faith. Vatican II had
exploded the myth of the Church's being the "perfect society," complete
in itself with little need to interact with the rest of the world. There was
a new marching order: go into the world and sanctify it.

My faith life was awakening, and my writing life was taking off. I had
landed a first book contract to conduct a yearlong study of the prototypi-
cal average American family. The rest of my life was handily falling apart.
I was on a collision course that would spew wreckage for years to come.

Pounding headaches that had built in intensity over the past few years
reached such an excruciating point that I became an outpatient at the
headache clinic at Montefiore Hospital in the Bronx. It was the first such
clinic in the world, the virtual Vatican of headaches. I begged for relief.
Tensions at home? I was asked. "Well, yes, my writing does create its
own strains. Surviving as a freelance writer is a high-wire act, but I've
learned to live with that." Tensions in your personal life? "The usual
stuff, nobody's perfect, you know, but generally doing just fine. Got a
great marriage, thank you." Sex? "Sure, sure, as much as I want," I lied,
"when my head isn't pounding," which it was a lot of the time. Fiorinal,
a concoction of two standbys, aspirin and caffeine, and then a handy-
dandy barbiturate, butalbital, banned in many European countries, was
added to the mix. Ergotamine. Nothing helped. I could dodge those
questions at Montefiore because I was so expert in kidding myself about
my life in general, our marriage in particular.

I did have a perfect marriage, in the way that a department store window is perfect. Dustless, unwrinkled, smooth, on display. But on a closer

look, lifeless. Our sex life was now nonexistent. In public we were engaging and—to the undiscerning eye—affectionate. In the privacy of our newly renovated brownstone, there was the chilly, carefully modulated acrimony of two people who no longer trusted each other, afraid that letting out their most intimate, confused thoughts would just provide more ammunition to be used against them by the other. Perfect marriages extract a great price, demanding continuing, superhuman effort to carry on the charade.

"Don't you think you ought to look at your anger, Paul?" J.C. would say on those rare occasions when I actually raised my voice, *her* voice so controlled, so straight from her master's degree in counseling classes at the University of Maryland. It drove me right out of my mind. If I wasn't truly angry before, I was now raging.

"Why do think you have to act like that? Do you need to do that? What do you think you're saying when you . . ." She suggested I go into therapy. I would have sooner walked out onto the Manhattan Bridge and taken a dive into the East River. And remember, I couldn't swim.

OO

The at once liberating and ultimately impossible and debilitating 1970s clarion calls of "Do what you must to be happy" and "Be who YOU are" were in the air. Each of us answered in a different way. J.C. had started her woman's center in a working-class section of Brooklyn, and women who had been trapped in awful marriages saw her as a messiah. I was becoming more involved in Father Petroski's street ministry, taking food to shut-ins, ferrying alcoholics to treatment, standing up at court hearings for hapless tenants about to be evicted. Who could fault such good intentions? The two of us were trying so hard to be good people, yet we were anything but kind to one another. I was coming back from a child abuse hearing, trying to figure out what to do with the three battered kids a junkie father and alcoholic mother had left in their wake, when a song came over the radio.

"It's Too Late" was the title, and Carole King was bemoaning that "something" inside of her had died and she could no longer hide from its awful truth. That was a popular enough theme in the 1970s. People no longer died, "something" passed on, and, as this song wailed from my car speakers, it was because one person in a relationship (marriage, just one of many options and for many a bit too formal at that) was "changing." Oh, this couple had tried, too. But now it was simply too late. "It's too late . . . it's too late . . . it's too late."

I almost tore the knob off the radio, snuffing out Carole King in midsong. What soppy drivel. What painful truth.

In Karachi, in Mayport, had I fallen in love with a person or with the *idea* of marriage? Had I married at what seemed to be the right time in my life, but to the wrong person? To the woman who had once seemed an ideal life partner? We were so much alike. But were we, really, or had we lopped off pieces of ourselves in order to fit snugly, smugly together? Had we failed to "grow together," in the popular parlance? Were we changing in different ways, going in different directions? What had happened? Where did we begin to go wrong? Whose fault was it? All foolish questions; I knew that. Each night I ardently prayed to God to lead me. But I wonder if God was just my front man at a time when I simply wanted out of a marriage that had died.

OO

I stood in front of the padlocked entrance to 219 Sixth Avenue. The storefront's dingy aluminum door had been battered by a series of break-ins, and a thick piece of poorly painted plywood had been crudely nailed into the frame, behind the shattered glass. When I had toured the space the week before, two menacing Puerto Rican men had stopped me. It was their private—read "drinking"—club, and if I took possession, I would answer to them. I handed the landlord $125 in cash, the first month's rent. He gave me the key. Our intentional community had talked and prayed about having a "street presence," where we could leave the comfort of our living rooms and actually serve the poor. Well, here we were.

The place was filled with so much trash, old furniture, and rusting fixtures that it would take weeks to clean, and even then, this foul, dank storefront with windows that didn't open, radiators that didn't heat, outlets that didn't work, and a toilet that wouldn't flush would just barely qualify as habitable. But to me, who lived a half-dozen blocks away in a *House and Garden* townhouse, it was my field of dreams. We used a hot plate in the St. Francis Xavier rectory basement to heat our first pot of soup, little more than some cans of Campbell's supplemented with whatever vegetables the members of our little community had in their refrigerators. We swung open that battered aluminum door and offered the soup and ourselves to whoever walked in.

Christian Help in Park Slope—CHIPS—was born.

I had given myself the chance to live as a saint, the saint I was once again telling myself I wanted to be.

PART THREE

UNMAKING IT

I 2

CHIPS DAYS

ONE AFTERNOON YEARS EARLIER, when we lived on the upper west side, J.C. and I were walking around in Greenwich Village and came upon a craft sale, set up on the fringes of Washington Square Park. She had gone off, and I was absentmindedly wandering among the very 1970s offerings of feathered earrings, bead necklaces, macramé headbands, incense, leather vests, bong pipes, and hemp bracelets when my eye caught something shoved to the back on one of the tables. It was a cross made of hobnails. I stared at it.

I was a Methodist then, and Methodists certainly don't wear their religious beliefs on the outside. I hadn't worn any religious symbols for some time, and I was never an impulse buyer. I furtively glanced around to make sure no one was watching. I snatched the hobnail cross and thrust a couple dollars in the direction of the seller. Embarrassed, not knowing why I bought it or what I would do with it, I consigned the contraband to the back of one of my dresser drawers.

Years later, searching for some warmer socks after a shower on a cold morning, my finger touched something unfamiliar, small, cool, and hard. I took the cross out and cradled it in my hand. In the harsh winter light streaming through my bedroom window, it lay there in my outstretched palm, inert, so much dull metal. I dressed; I was alone. I slowly slipped the cross over my head and looked at myself in mirror—halfway expecting to be confronted by some wild-eyed religious fanatic. It was just me, wearing a blue oxford cloth shirt. And a hobnail cross. I smiled into the mirror. What was wrong with me? It didn't look all that out of place.

I began to wear the cross, not only to CHIPS and to the weekly gatherings of our intentional community but also—at first under my shirt—in my daily life as well. I didn't know what I really wanted for my life. In a single day, I could help a paraplegic onto a bedpan in the morning, have

lunch at a fancy midtown restaurant with a *New York Times* editor, and
that afternoon sit on a bench at the Brooklyn House of Detention with
a young expectant mother whose current boyfriend had tried to dice
her former suitor into small pieces. The hobnail cross was the touchstone
I needed, something to remind me of what wasn't yet a commitment but
an urge—constant, uneasy, uncomfortable—brought into being by a force
I couldn't understand or escape.

Like any Catholic exposed to seventeen years of religious education,
I could recite the words of Matthew's Gospel from memory: "for I was
hungry, and you gave me to eat; I was thirsty, and you gave me drink; I
was a stranger, and you took me in, a prisoner and you visited me." These
mandates had been only words up to now, obviously directed far over my
wretched head. But now the words were embodied in the people who
came to us at CHIPS. It didn't escape me that even though I was wearing
the symbolic nails that held Jesus Christ to the cross, I was no more than
a day tripper into the world of poverty. I could leave misery behind at will,
safe in my clean, warm brownstone. The people I served did not have this
option. They were the crucified ones. They were held fast by virtue of their
birth or skin color or lack of education or balky X and Y chromosomes
that had not been apportioned properly. Their lives were so precarious,
each day a trek in the wilderness, each day a study in survival. There was
never enough money for food *and* heating oil *and* clothes *and* rent. Medical care was occasional and often too late to prevent deeper sickness or
permanent damage to their bodies. Their children had ear infections that
went on painfully for days, while the children of my Park Slope friends
were on amoxicillin and on their way to recovery almost immediately.
"The asthma" was considered so common that if only one member of a
family suffered from it, they considered themselves lucky.

I had no grand plan as each day unfolded. I simply wanted to listen
and respond as best I could, with the limited time, abilities, and resources
I had.

When I was honest enough to face it, I realized that my life—at least
my life after the Navy—had been a parody of conscious living. Connected
with God? Hardly. I had grown so self-satisfied, so sanctimonious. We,
the alleged "pioneers" in Park Slope, had been brave enough to take the
subway to Brooklyn. There, we diligently scraped paint from our wain-
scoting, sanded our hardwood floors, refinished the elegant sliding doors
and put them back on their once-rusty tracks, while valiantly seeking
just the right plaster rosette for the ceiling of the living room or the most
"original" tin ceiling pattern for the kitchen. And only then could we rest
from our punishing labors with a little brie and Carr's Table Wafer

Crackers, a chilled glass of pinot grigio (or, in the Wilkes' abstemious case, lemonade—freshly squeezed, of course). A little plaster dust in our hair, paint on our hands. The struggle of it all!

But, of course, we contributed to our churches, dropped a quarter into the hand—without touching it—of the occasional panhandler, filled out the pledge sheet for the United Way, hated the war in Vietnam, gave to Save the Children and the American Cancer Society. We were good people, really. Tepid, but good. So much salt without any flavor. As I was now beginning to realize, that was simply not enough. For behind discolored doors and rusted gates on President and Berkeley, Fourth, Fifth, Sixth, and Seventh avenues, up those dank stairways on First, Second, and Third streets was the "Other America" Michael Harrington told us about some ten years before in his classic book on poverty. *New York Times* under my arm, I had walked by those houses and buildings so many times on my way to the subway, never once thinking of who was within. I never knew the loneliness, the illness, the sheer want that was so endemic in my otherwise pristine little Park Slope world.

Now I was in and out of those buildings. I opened door after door into hell. My life continued to change, and what I never imagined I would or could do, I did. I went to the Italian greengrocers down on Fifth Avenue, not to buy my romaine or arugula, but to ask for their bruised produce. At the fish market, I collected the carcasses left from the fillets I once bought. The butcher saved bones. The baker gave us leftover bread or, the day after a holiday, the delicacy whose moment had passed. On February 15, the cakes shaped like Valentine hearts were ours; on Easter Monday, a flock of coconut-encrusted lambs. We scavenged dented cans, smashed cartons, items whose sell date had passed, making them no longer salable to the likes of me. Leftover food for leftover people. The biblical crumbs off the table. These were the makings of our soup, of the bags of groceries we gave to anyone who came to our door.

Some of the first CHIPS volunteers asked if we shouldn't have some criteria, to make sure the people were *truly* needy. My response came out of a place in me I didn't know existed, with a clarity I might not have had, had I thought about my words for an instant: "Just that they come to us, literally begging, says enough. Let's not humiliate them further. I didn't see Christ applying a means test. We're not going to either." Perhaps it was no more than a throwback to the unadorned faith of my parents, that God would provide, that he was watching out for the little ones, the poor ones, the needy ones. It was the rekindling of a fire I didn't even know was part of me. It was an immigrant's faith: marginalized families, though unwanted and looked down upon, knew they were embraced and held precious by a God that transcends the immediate.

At first I was sheepish and tentative about begging from local merchants, but soon that melted away as something welled up within me. I am a reporter, used to marshalling facts, yet it was something I could never quite understand or explain, even today. It was a power that I had never experienced before. "Ask and you shall receive." Yes, that was exactly what was happening. Bolder and bolder, I asked and—amazingly, but true to scripture—I received. I went to the local toy store, and the employees emptied out a storeroom of toys that had fallen out of favor, providing us with boxes of little presents we could give to the kids who came with their bedraggled parents, who patiently thumbed through our racks of donated clothes. The dry cleaners gave us the clothes never picked up. I asked anyone who would listen to clean out closets and bring castoffs to CHIPS. If bell-bottom trousers or fuchsia blouses or herringbone vests or wide collars were the rage last year, they were our stock-in-trade this year. If someone needed a stove, one miraculously appeared. Money for a bus ticket or gas bill. Just the right sympathetic case worker to cut through the bureaucratic red tape. Again and again. Improbably. Predictably.

CHIPS was scheduled to be open only a few afternoons a week and on Saturday mornings, but I found myself turning the key in the door more and more frequently, a glass door now, replaced by one of our "clients," who was a very good handyman when he wasn't on a binge. The walls were painted with a rainbow of donated colors and within was a motley assortment of cast-off chairs, a desk, shelving for canned goods, racks for clothes, and an old refrigerator that sounded like a sputtering Piper Cub taking off. All in all, a pretty ragtag place. But to me it was home, and each time I opened that door, I felt the power once more.

With a certain single-minded tenacity I took on whatever was at hand. The neighborhood kids came running in one afternoon and led me to Eddie. He was sitting on the curb at Fourth and Sackett, sobbing, drunk, with urine-stained trousers, a filthy shirt, one shoe, no socks, and thoughts of suicide. He was off his Antabuse, he mumbled, and certain to be fired from his job. He took out a picture of an elegantly dressed Manhattan doorman who bore just enough resemblance to the man before me to convince me they were one and the same. I put on my best sports jacket and crisply ironed trousers and convinced his boss to give him another chance, meanwhile finding Eddie a rehabilitation program that his insurance would cover. I visited him weekly, bringing along his favorite chocolate chip cookies.

Angel, a cherubic Hispanic man, hobbled in one day and, in broken English, told of a leg that never mended properly after an automobile accident. I overlooked the minor fact that he had also gained forty pounds from eating nonstop while recuperating in front of his television set. Ed Mohler, one of the intentional community members and a cofounder of CHIPS, was a pediatric orthopedic surgeon, and through his efforts, we got Angel into Kings County Hospital for a repeat surgery.

And then there was Anthony, the supreme challenge. Anthony, ten years old, was an engaging but otherwise feral creature whose mother in Mexico had sent him via a one-way ticket to a father in America who couldn't control him. Anthony was living on the streets, hustling outside gay bars in Brooklyn Heights for change and doing God knows what for larger currency. I knew that if I didn't get him into a good group home, the kid was going to be found floating in the Gowanus Canal. I took him into my own home for a while and then, through a combination of tenacity, grace, and prayer, we found a spot for him in an exclusive summer camp—free—and then in the best residential home in Westchester County for troubled youth, which I was initially told had a nine-month waiting list. How it all worked, I still don't know. I stopped questioning.

There was no problem too great, no person outside our "catchment area"—that wonderful bureaucratic deflection I heard over and over. CHIPS was open to any problem, any person, any time. I readily gave out my home phone number, and when a call came in the middle of the night, I didn't hesitate to respond.

As I prayed each Tuesday night with the members of our tiny community, my head buried in my hands, words began to spill out of my mouth that had only been vague, unformed thoughts. "Lead me, Lord, take command of my life. Shape me into that person you want me to become. Let me hear your call and not run away. Let me live like you. Let me be willing to make the sacrifices and not count the cost. To serve those who society has discarded, those who need love. To be a voice for those who have none."

I didn't quite know what to make of this abrupt change in my life. I was sometimes embarrassed by my own thoughts, mortified by my words. I was not priest or social worker. I was a childless, married man. I had no credentials, no official sanction, no special training. Nothing. *Who the hell do you think you are, Mr. Paul Wilkes?* I asked myself more than once. *What exactly are you up to? Who put you in charge of the poor of Park Slope?* I never had a good answer. I was only an ordinary, cradle Catholic shaped by a Council of Trent absolutism and taught to be a lowly, obedient serf in this great kingdom. I had left this seemingly monolithic, unchanging, and unchangeable Church, only to find that in my absence, through the Second Vatican Council, I had been crowned as part of the royal family, one of the "people of God," each of whom had been duly appointed to sanctify the world. And that I had been given the option to model a life on Christ.

I was living a strange mix of what were once discrete and mutually exclusive vocations: marriage—and a very middle-class marriage at that, complete with a country home on a Pennsylvania lake and frequent trips abroad—and an ever-stronger calling to live and work with the poor in a life of voluntary poverty. *Voluntary poverty*. This term had leaped out at me from the pages of the *Catholic Worker*, a monthly newspaper that had fallen into my hands. And I had just as quickly suppressed this concept. Too much, too great a commitment. But I couldn't get it out of my mind. The best I could do was to view myself as a strange hybrid, a sort of contemplative and unauthorized monk, one who lived in the world, who happened to be married and to earn his daily bread as a writer, yet whose real "work" was at CHIPS. It certainly was confusing, but I couldn't go back to what I had been. I didn't really know what lay ahead.

I was then in my midthirties, and I found myself believing more and more that I could go through the rest of my life without recognition and acclaim. The hollow feeling on seeing my byline in even the best publications was evidence enough of how shallow the writing life had become. My foolish shouts on the George Washington Bridge that New York would someday know about me were so far behind me now. Power? Influence? I had never known these benchmarks of New York life, so nothing would be lost there. Material goods? These never mattered that much; I'd come from so little that I could live that way again.

As for my marriage, sexual intimacy had imperceptibly ebbed so much that we never spoke of it. Nor did we speak of having children. We were now almost like shadowboxers, afraid of any sort of contact, afraid it might be taken as a sign that we'd be obliged to go further. After being derailed so many times between first touch or kiss and making love, I had become chary and tentative. And unsure. It was I who was doing something wrong, I was sure. Sex was so excruciatingly complicated to transact that both sides had given up in exhaustion, and negotiations had simply broken down.

But I was married, and I had promised "for better, for worse." If my faith meant anything to me, I couldn't let this slip away. I prayed fervently as I lay in that king-size bed night after night, watching the slits of a night sky through our shuttered window. After all, Heloise and Abelard, once passionate and sinful lovers, had eventually embraced celibacy and become saints. Why could we not live some variation on that theme? But, this wasn't "we," I knew. It was I. I could see the look in J.C.'s eyes as I spent more and more time at CHIPS and on the streets. Was this the man she married? Was he going mad?

∞

CHIPS was now a year old, and I wanted to find out how other, similar places were doing, so I invited a group of young men and women who had settled in a rundown area of the Bronx to work with the poor. I prepared a nice dinner, and as we sat on antique café chairs at the round oak table in the kitchen of the brownstone, I listened to their stories of drug addicts and alcoholics, abused wives and neglected children, bureaucratic nightmares. But they had gone the next step: they had embraced voluntary poverty. The people of the Bronx Storefront Community lived where they worked; they had no safe haven. They were dressed in cast-off clothes and bore that stale, musty odor that is one of the natural by-products of being poor. I was fascinated by them. They seemed happy and fulfilled, not pious or preachy, more like Catholic Special Forces troops that took on any challenge that came their way. CHIPS was nothing compared to BSC. Their smell was a badge that I wanted to wear; their stories were ones that I wanted to live.

We went into the living room, with its wall of bookshelves, comfortable designer sofa and matching chairs, freshly lacquered parquet floor. I kept the lights low, so low we could hardly see each other. I was embarrassed by the contrast between the relative opulence of my house and the cockroach-infested Bronx apartment where I had visited them some weeks before. As the evening went on, I finally couldn't hold back. I told them how guilty I felt about living in such luxury. I should be living as they were. They looked at me and were quiet. I waited.

"You're nuts," said Mike, one of them. "Just enjoy it. We live in a shit hole."

PRESENT

THE BRONX STOREFRONT COMMUNITY AND CHIPS were part of a very informal network called the Catholic Worker movement, which was started on New York's Bowery in 1933. The founders were an unlikely pair: Dorothy Day, an ex-Communist, anarchist, radical journalist, and unwed mother who had embraced Catholicism; and Peter Maurin, a French-born itinerant preacher and philosopher. At the height of the Depression, they had a vision to create a newspaper that would promote Catholic social teaching, meanwhile founding "houses of hospitality" where the poor would be treated with dignity. Through the Catholic Worker, which began at a penny a copy and has that price to this day, the movement rapidly spread. People flocked to the Bowery and started houses in other cities to live with the poor, in radical and religious poverty.

If one were to draw a flowchart of twentieth-century Catholic social activism, the Catholic Worker house would be a way station for thousands upon thousands of lay Catholics who wanted to apply gospel values to overcome real-world injustices. Unionists, civil rights workers, community organizers, idealistic college students, priests, and nuns came to the Worker to see the gospel lived out. And so I was just the latest in a long line in fall 1973 when I took the F train from a very clean Brooklyn station, got off at the Broadway-Lafayette stop, which reeked of urine and garbage, and made my way over to 36 East First Street.

Even though it may have been one of the more famous addresses in Catholic America, 36 East First was very much in keeping with the Worker. It was a pitiful-looking former storefront, with panes of glass shielded by rusting, heavy grates. The paint was peeling, the front door appeared ready to come off its hinges. On the sidewalk in front were a motley lineup of street people, to polite society the dregs of humanity, but here Christ's precious ones. This was a time before such drugs as crack, heroin, and cocaine had thundered onto the scene, and marijuana was a middle-class recreation, so most of the people standing in front and those who had already gathered for the talk were alcoholic or mentally ill, often both.

I walked inside. The air was dizzyingly hot and rank. The din was deafening. I timidly stood off to the side and looked around. Is this what I wanted for my life? That was the direction it was going. Either I was going to jump off this fast-moving spiritual freight train now, or I was going to be sped to places I might not want to go. I had idealized the Worker life, Worker houses, and CHIPS, but the brutal reality was here before me. A woman with huge, ulcerous sores on her swollen legs. A man with layers of shower curtains, like so many plastic petals, cascading off his shoulders. An emaciated couple in their forties, hollow-eyed, sitting facing the wall, hand in bony hand. I shook my head as if to shake off what was going through my mind right then. I had to remember: my work was not to be a social worker, to "solve" their problems. I was to be the face of Christ to them. We had talked about this often in our intentional community.

A man bellowed something I couldn't understand. Over the heads of people, I could see a stool sailing across the room. It crashed into the wall. "You spineless sonofabitch, I told you not to use my cup. Do you hear me!" Pandemonium broke out. The screaming spread; shoving fights were breaking out all around me. I looked to see how far I was from the door.

"Bill, you stop it right now, or you've got to go!" It was a woman's stern voice above the noise.

I could see her better now as she made her way through the crowded room. She was a small woman, with angular cheekbones set in a scowling face. Her gray hair was coiled on top of her head. She was wearing a simple cotton flowered dress that almost fit her. Although it was unmercifully hot, she was wearing a sweater. Bill limply dropped his head and listened as she scolded him. I recognized her, and when she came back my way, I impulsively reached out my hand. Dorothy Day took it and immediately introduced me to the night's speaker—a Dr. Miller, who was writing a history of the Worker—as if she would prefer not to have any attention paid to her and was actually annoyed by it. Overhead, the blinking fluorescent lights cast a yellowish tint. I stared at her at close range for just another instant, and behind that scowl I saw something I will never forget.

There was a certain fierceness about her, certainly in keeping with her beliefs, which she had written about for so many years on the pages of the *Catholic Worker*. A holy fierceness. She never rhapsodized about her work with the poor. It required and called forth, she maintained, "a harsh and dreadful love," Dostoyevsky's famous line in *The Brothers Karamazov*. I knew the line well. And I knew its context, which came uncomfortably close to summing me up. A wealthy woman comes to the monk Zosima, waxing on about her dream of a life of loving service to others. She will live in holy poverty as a Sister of Mercy; such a wonderful thought brings tears to her eyes. But then it crosses her mind: the poor will probably not thank her for her great sacrifice; they'll complain that the soup isn't hot enough, the bread not fresh enough, the bed too hard, and the covers too thin. She confesses she couldn't bear such ingratitude, to which the wise monk replies with that resounding line: "Love in practice is a harsh and dreadful thing compared to love in dreams." There would be no stage lights to enhance the face of the poor, only pitiful, hand-me-down fixtures that never worked right. No sweet odor of grace, but their ripe smell. No applause for work well done, just howls and screams.

So what was it I saw in Dorothy Day that night? I can only describe it this way: she was *present*.

It was not about grand or dramatic presence. Dorothy Day was there, slightly stooped by her seventy-six years, standing solidly on the pockmarked floor, entirely, completely present to that moment in that place. Alert, aware, with an unspoken understanding that even as she had nothing at all to say to me, there was nothing that needed to be said just then. The room might grow quieter or louder, Bill might lash out again or not; whatever the needs of the moment, she would face them. For she was confident that she was not standing there alone.

Dorothy Day disappeared into the crowd, and I leaned against a wall. I didn't know what the days ahead would bring—if I could be loving in the face of ingratitude, patient when attacked, kind when others were unkind to me. As for living a harsh and dreadful love, that was something I would leave for another day. I didn't know what I could be in life.

But, looking at her that night, I knew one thing for sure. I wanted to be *present*.

∞

I sat, head down, trying to be present to this moment. It was a Sunday morning, not long after my evening at the Worker, in the St. Francis Xavier gym. All was still as Father Petroski's voice echoed through the vast space with the Gospel reading.

Now someone approached him and said, "Teacher, what good must I do to gain eternal life?" He answered him, "Why do you ask me about the good? There is only One who is good. If you wish to enter into life, keep the commandments."

He asked him, "Which ones?" And Jesus replied, "'You shall not kill; you shall not commit adultery; you shall not steal; you shall not bear false witness; honor your father and your mother'; and 'you shall love your neighbor as yourself.'"

The young man said to him, "All of these I have observed. What do I still lack?" Jesus looked at him and loved him. "One thing you lack," he said. "Go, sell everything you have and give to the poor, and you will have treasure in heaven. Then come, follow me."

Father Petroski paused—as he often did in readings like this one—in a way that asked for a response. His eyes searched the iron girders overhead, then the faces—our faces—before him. He continued, his voice lower.

When the young man heard this statement, he went away sad, for he had many possessions.

I couldn't breathe.

I4

THE PILGRIMAGE

I SQUINTED UP AT THE FLICKERING MAZE OF YELLOW NUMBERS on the poorly lit board high overhead. At first I had a hard time picking it out: *Short Line 801. Yes, that was it. Or was it?*

I always arrived just in time for planes and trains, cavalierly stepping on board just as the door closed. Today I was an hour early, the sign of a man unsure of his destination or, in my case, of a man who needed TIME to reconsider going at all. I set myself and my knapsack down on one of the long, wooden benches clustered at the center of the main concourse. Passing in front of me was a blur of fast-walking commuters, streaming toward their working day. Those of us "on the bench" were of a different breed, not in much of a hurry. On my right was a snoring man, whose head was resting on a huge bundle. On my left, a woman was in animated conversation. With herself.

New York's Port Authority bus terminal is an urban colossus, the world's busiest bus station, covering four city blocks, 1.5 million square feet embracing passengers, stores, buses, and subway trains, while allowing plenty of room for con men, pickpockets, male and female prostitutes, the homeless, and various lowlifes spilling over from the tawdry porno shops, peep shows, and bars rimming Times Square only a few blocks away. Every morning, Port Authority inhales a hundred thousand people as they stream into this hulking, sprawling edifice, their quick steps rapping out a determined rhythm, a murmured song to the bustling city itself. Nine or ten hours later, these people are exhaled, exhausted and stale, to retreat to their homes for the night.

The dreamers arrive at Port Authority in much smaller numbers and at less predictable times throughout the day. They walk much more slowly, for they don't yet understand the city's pace. Young girls who will be Broadway stars come with both terror and anticipation on their bright

faces. Young men with patchy beards and a guitar case jauntily slung over
a shoulder, the next Bob Dylan. Writers, of course, come to New York.
After all, this is the place to "make it," to be a star. Why else come?

Those dreamers have a far different look on their faces when they
depart Port Authority. They are leaving because they weren't quite as
good or as strong as they thought they were back in Topeka or Houston
or Atlanta. The city has broken them. And they most probably will never
return. Their look is blank, expressionless, somewhat like the face I saw
in the men's room mirror just before boarding the 801 for Olean.

I could identify with them. I too was leaving New York a broken man.

For a young writer, I actually hadn't fared all that badly. I had a couple
of published books, another about to be completed, bylines in the *Atlantic*,
the *New York Times Magazine, Look, Life, New York*, the *Nation*. Not a
stratospheric resume, but certainly respectable. Some would say, a bright
future before him.

I wasn't broken by the city. I had—at my own request—been broken
by God.

My life had been shattered by a God who had stealthily stalked me for
years, but who then, when I lowered my sanctimonious, protective, rationalizing shield, saw his opportunity. He struck, and struck decisively.
This was not the distant God I prayed to first in Cleveland, then in
Milwaukee, at sea, in Boulder and Baltimore. Not an imperious God,
friendly God, or compassionate God. Certainly not Merton's God of
"mercy within mercy within mercy." No, this was a far more calculating
and jealous God. This was a God demanding everything, brooking no
compromise. He had waited for me to put a leg onto the big stage of
New York and then, as the lights were going up, he threw out the scenery,
the script, the plot. Instead, he shoved a new and improvisational story
into my hands, a new vision of what it is to be a human being. How did
I respond? I dumbly had the audacity to ask this God to direct that story. I
told him I wanted to live as he had lived, to have the faith of a mustard
seed, to be a lily of the field, the bird without a nest, the traveler not
knowing where he would next lay his head.

He listened to my pleas. He answered my prayers.

On those Sunday mornings in the St. Francis Xavier gymnasium and in
fetid apartments, he allowed me that passing glimpse of his face that
scripture at once promises and warns about. And my entire life had gone
to hell. Here I was, thirty-five years old, wearing jeans and flannel shirt,
a knapsack at my feet, about to embark on a journey to hastily found
destinations. I didn't know what else to do. I was paralyzed. I couldn't
keep going on as I was, my marriage a tortured pas de deux, the distant

rumbling in my soul now a deafening roar. In the past few weeks there
had been a senseless, horrible death that put me over the edge. My head
pounded. I couldn't sleep. I couldn't think. I couldn't pray. I couldn't
write. I could hardly complete a spoken sentence. I needed to cut loose
from everything familiar. I needed time and space to think.

As I sat there in Port Authority, I hid my face behind the morning's
Times. Had one of my editors, briefcase in hand, bustling in from his
New Jersey or Westchester home, come across this knapsack-bearing,
almost middle-aged hippie, so sadly late for the revolution, I don't know
what excuse I could have conjured up. I had a car; what was I doing taking a bus? And where exactly was I going? I didn't exactly know. For
how long? Well . . .

Once on the bus, we whisked through the cool darkness of the Lincoln
Tunnel before bursting into the brilliant sunlight, hustling past the hazy
New Jersey skyline dotted with the belching smoke of refineries, and
finally turning onto the Palisades Parkway. It was a lovely, clear day. The
leaves on the great oaks lining the road were a vibrant, emerald green.
The outcroppings of rock were as majestic as they were unexpected. If
you forgot that you were speeding along on a ribbon of asphalt, it was
hard to realize that you were just minutes from the city. Looking through
the window of the speeding bus, I saw no sign that man had yet intruded.
I was just minutes from my former life, yet already in another world.

It would be a sort of pilgrimage, I'd decided, the archetypical remedy
for the restless, questioning soul. I had the addresses of some houses of
prayer and monasteries in the Northeast and a religious community of lay
men and women up in Canada. I hoped that in one of them I would find
an answer to the question I was not capable of clearly asking. None of the
places was near any major city, but somehow I hadn't factored that in to
my hastily conjured travel plans. Still, I knew I had to leave the convenience of a car behind, denying myself an easy escape or quick return. It
had been only a few days before that I had told J.C. that I had to get away
and do it now. I was surprised when she quickly agreed to the non-plan of
a man she knew planned out everything in his life.

After a phone call from the bus station at my intended first stop, I was
picked up by a sixtyish man wearing a windbreaker and a pair of badly
wrinkled khakis. It was a short, mostly quiet ride to the monastery of
which he was a member. Once within the cool, dark chapel, I felt
I could finally breathe easier. I sat there for an hour, sending a tirade of
fervent prayers sailing heavenward in rapid succession. A bell rang, as
if to stop me cold. The monk who had picked me up at the bus station,
his work clothes now covered with a long white choir gown, filed in

with his brother monks. Their voices rose and fell in Gregorian chant. On that day, it was a strange, sterile sound, more a reflection of my state of mind than of the genius of St. Gregory. Monks of his day were largely illiterate men, so Gregory wrote simply in neumes, notes sung on a single syllable, with no meter at all, the chant's rhythm—when there was one—gathered up like small bouquets of two or three notes. Anyone could learn to chant.

After the monks filed out, I lingered in the chapel, already picturing myself as one of their number. (Mind you, I had been there no more than a few hours and didn't even like Gregorian chant.) I had found The Answer. I would spend my days in the timeless cadence of this monastery's life, lost to the world, in the arms of God. I would be the simplest of them all, obedient, eyes cast down, taking the lowest place at the table, doing the most menial work.

It was love at first sight. I spent the afternoon in mystical rapture, lazing in the library, sensuously running my hand over the spines of books— Thomas a Kempis, Origen, Julian of Norwich, Augustine, John of the Cross. Over the years that I would be here as a humble friar, I would read them all. I fantasized that I would live as they had lived. What a blessing that the revelation would come on the first day of my pilgrimage. I had underestimated God. He was mercy within mercy within mercy after all.

I walked into the kitchen as one of the monks was preparing supper. He dumped powdered mashed potatoes into boiling water. He slapped slices of cold boiled ham onto a serving plate. The lettuce was iceberg. He roughly hacked the heads in halves, then quarters, then eighths and dumped the pieces into a wooden bowl, some spilling onto the floor. I said hello, and he nodded. He was wearing a white T-shirt, stained brown beneath his arms, and an apron that gave evidence of the last few community meals. At the sound of a bell, we filed into the refectory, which once must have seated at least fifty or sixty men. Now there were fewer than a dozen.

The conversation was not about Origen or Augustine, but about the "silly old bitch" who had come to them earlier that week, claiming she had had a vision of the Virgin. "Imagine, this poor thing"; one of the monks mimicked the guest, his bulging eyes tracing an arc at the upper reaches of his lids. "I said, 'Honey, if the Virgin is appearing around these parts, at least she could tell us about it.'" There was a monk or two who sat quietly, eating. The rest of the small community howled with laughter.

I tried to shake my reporter's snap assessment of the place. But my more considered impression was not wrong. It was a sad place, filled with too many misanthropic men with nowhere to go. There was something toxic in the air. Not that being gay, which a good number of them were, was the issue. Looking back, there had been a devoted teacher at Cathedral Latin who enjoyed tucking his hand into the back pockets of the boys and giving a squeeze; effeminate priests at Marquette who were great professors and spiritual mentors. Father Petroski was most likely gay, and he had profoundly changed my life. But here, in this kind of enclosed life, the gay overtones and gay humor were corrosive, undermining the kind of esprit de corps needed to bond a group of men. Years later, studies would definitively show that a greater percentage of gays stayed behind in the post–Vatican II exodus from religious life that was now under way. For some, religious life would remain a calling; for others, a safe haven, a secure escape.

The same silent friar with the same wrinkled khakis took me back to the bus station a week after he had picked me up. I thanked him, and he mumbled a reply. He reached across for the door handle, slammed the door shut, and was gone, back to that sad place. I would travel on, undaunted and totally confused.

During that first week, the weather had cooled; an early frost glistened on the ground. I headed further north. The trees were tinged with the first blushes of autumn as I rode through the foothills of the Catskills. I read, I slept, I stared out the window. I felt like an impetuous fool. But the hum of the wheels was strangely comforting. I kept telling myself: my journey was just beginning.

15

NOT PRESENT

THERE WERE SO MANY REASONS BEHIND THIS TRIP, but really it was Mary Skelly.

Besides being a hangout for kids, CHIPS had turned into a crisis intervention center where Brooklyn's poor could go with a rumor, concern, or problem and not get tangled up with the police or the welfare system. So when we heard that Peter Skelly was wandering the streets, looking more disoriented than usual, I made a note of it. Things were pure chaos on most days, so I kept transferring Peter's name to the next day's list of things to do. I was taken with my own busyness; the holy one was in such demand. Finally, a couple weeks later, I made time to pay a visit to that second floor walk-up.

The apartment door again was partially open, and the smell was truly breathtaking, but of a different vintage than I remembered from my first visit. My shoes made that sickening sound on the feces-covered floor, but even that sound was different, more muffled. I rounded the corner that demarcated the living room, the chipped wall's surface filthy with brown, smudged handprints. I saw her bare feet first. Then the rest of Mary Skelly.

The rats that had been gnawing on what little flesh she had left on her face skittered away. Her eyes seemed to be moving, but as I drew closer, I could see that a swarm of maggots had taken up residence. Her feces- and urine-stained cotton dress lay slack over a body that was little more than an assortment of bones. It was like looking at a poorly exposed x-ray; all the ribs showed clearly. Only a slight rise showed her hips. Nothing else. Peter was asleep in the corner, not twenty feet away.

She had been dead for days; that much was obvious. And Peter, her loyal son and drinking companion, was not about to leave his mother alone even now, only foraying out to replenish his liquor supply. He was not about to have this sick and tortured relationship ended by something as inconvenient as death. Somehow, in his confused mind, this too, would pass. Mother would awaken from another stupor, and they would go on as before.

Except for the drone of buzzing flies, all was still. Why didn't I come right away? Mary, you were little more than a bothersome note that I pushed from day to day. To say I felt a failure would be letting myself off too lightly. I looked down at what was left of Mary Skelly. "I'm sorry, Mary. I'm so sorry," was all I could say.

I had been a part of their lives. But in some way, I was not *present* in their lives. That was the true sin. I had not lived a harsh and dreadful love, but a love stingily apportioned, at my convenience. They were names on a list, another "case" to be worked on. I looked over at Peter. What *I* felt was unimportant right now; I sensed that. Peter was in no condition to do much of anything, but I knew I somehow had to get him in good enough shape to properly bury his mother. He had always been on the margins. This, he must do. I vowed that—for him. Then I called the police.

There was a no-nonsense Irish landlady in Park Slope named Mrs. Linehan, who took in pensioners and the disabled as a business, and I prevailed upon her—not so subtly citing the Beatitudes—to waive the usual fee and help Peter Skelly get somewhat sober and cleaned up so that he could participate in the funeral. A few days later, Peter, the flaking skin from a face ravaged by a drinker's psoriasis fluttering softly onto the shoulders of an ill-fitting suit, his skinny neck rising startlingly out of a white shirt two sizes too big, his hands trembling with the DTs, stood in the first pew of the cavernous St. Francis Xavier Church. A handful of mourners, hastily gathered from our CHIPS family, stood behind him. Father Petroski told of a fine cut of a woman and her loyal son, with her until the end, an end he charitably didn't spell out. Peter put his trembling hand on the coffin as it was wheeled to the back of the church. We drove Peter out to the cemetery on Long Island, lowered Mary into the ground, and kept on driving to an alcohol rehab center further out on the island. I helped Peter out of his suit—which I promised Mrs. Linehan would be hers after this use—and into a pair of lime green hospital pajamas.

"Peter, you did her proud," I said.

OO

The Benedictines at Mount Saviour Monastery, a group of some forty hard-muscled, tough guys, resembled a Marine battalion ready to take the next hill. Twenty years before, four Benedictines had come to these forested, rolling hills at Pine City, outside Elmira, New York, with a vision of early monastic egalitarianism that was then foreign to American Benedictines. Certainly foreign to the only Benedictines I had known, my parish priests in Cleveland who lived in feudal splendor amid their subjects. Here at Mount Saviour, my next step, priest and lay brother would share equally in physical labor and spend equal time at prayer. This was Benedict's original *ora et labora,* which had been largely eroded by modern conveniences and thinking.

.I wanted to take this monastic experience in much smaller bites than I had done with my first experience, so when it was mentioned at breakfast that monastic guests could help out around the farm, I quickly volunteered. I worked with Brother Bruno, who was possessed of such happiness, goodness, and simplicity that he seemed to embody the monastic ideal. Even as he methodically shoveled manure alongside his abbot Father Martin, Brother Bruno was grinning like a kid who was having more fun than was legal.

I wanted so badly to talk to a monk—any monk—about the confusion in my life. Hadn't some of them known confusion before coming here? Did they sometimes doubt they were in the right place? Did God make his will known? How? When? Except for our work periods, when we were advised to maintain a "custody of the tongue," the guests were kept apart from the community. It was just as well. I probably would have babbled about "a special calling" or something like that. Today, after spending time at many monasteries, I know this kind of person so well. They radiate undifferentiated introspection and an unappealing, manic fervor. Monks are wise to run from them.

I spent many hours sitting before the Blessed Sacrament altar in the stark, octagonal chapel. Behind the altar was a fifteenth-century Flemish triptych of the Crucifixion. Here I found a quiet beyond quietness. I wanted to rest in the presence of God, to be as close to his physical presence as I could even as he remained so elusive. I was struggling so hard to understand and to discern what he wanted of my life. Sometimes I would pray, other times fall asleep, not yet used to the monastic day that began before dawn. But most of the time I was reading, both there and in my small room. Was it the word "Desert" in *Letters from the Desert* by Charles de Foucauld that caught my eye in the guest house library, or did a monk recommend it? Whatever the case, I devoured the book and wanted to know more about this man.

I moved on to *Seeds of the Desert,* by René Voillaume, who started the order modeled on de Foucauld's life called the Little Brothers of Jesus. My days on that pilgrimage are often a blur, but my virtual hours with de Foucauld at Tamanrasset in Algeria are as clear as a slide show. I can still see the face of this hollow-eyed dreamer, for whom a Trappist monastery was not demanding enough. I can feel the day's blistering heat and the night's numbing cold inside his humble hut among the nomadic Tuareg in the Sahara's trackless waste. I can see the gun pressed to his skull, the finger at the trigger, a willing lamb of God about to be butchered by the very people he came to help. The wretched of the earth; de Foucauld would have nothing less. And for his devotion, they killed him. He died with not a single follower.

It is sometimes hard for those outside the Catholic tradition to understand our fascination with such people. But this was what we were raised on, the suckling milk of Mother Church, the stories of those who cast all reason aside to live—and, if required, to die—as Christ did, loving whomever God had called them to serve. Not that far from Mount Saviour, up the St. Lawrence River, Isaac Jogues felt called to bring Christ to the Iroquois, and they peeled his skin back, hacked off his fingers, burned him with hot coals, and finally bludgeoned him to death with a tomahawk. Damien went to serve the wretched lepers on Molokai, one day at Mass happily proclaiming to the colony "we lepers" after he had contracted the disease. He died the death he had invited. Saints like these were our spiritual heroes and adventurers extraordinaire, without a drop of pious sentimentality about them. They stood fearlessly against time and place with a purity of vision that brooked no compromise. And, to me, they lived lives that truly mattered.

When the predictable hangover came over me after such flights of intoxication, I groggily took stock. I was a married man, a writer, the founder of a tiny little upstart Brooklyn storefront that could close tomorrow. A fool on a fool's errand with a knapsack slung over his shoulder containing a change of clothes, plenty of Fiorinal, some American Express Travelers Cheques, and a Rand-McNally road atlas. What was I thinking about? At the end of this trip, I would be back in Brooklyn, back to my normal life. Where was all this heading?

I bid my Benedictine companions of a week good-bye with a tender and good feeling about them. Although it had crossed my mind that this could be a permanent place for me, that feeling quickly faded. No, I was not called to be a Benedictine monk. I was married. I headed further north, into Canada, to Madonna House in Combermere, Ontario, a professed community of lay men and women, who also ran houses of hospitality like CHIPS. As I rode on a bus through a sleepless night, I felt more and more energized by the thought: a lay person committed to a life of poverty and service. Yes. This is what I should be doing with my life. My path to God was about to be revealed, I was sure.

One of the Mount Saviour monks, hearing that I was going up into Canada, mentioned that I should look up Tony Walsh, a lay man who years ago had started a house of hospitality in Montreal and had recently visited Mount Saviour. But I was so eager to get to Madonna House, sure it would be the template for the rest of my life, that I headed northwest another 250 miles.

OO

As I would find out many times in life, the seemingly "perfect" solution or answer to my prayers never is. Madonna House was another example showing me that God is a God of indirection, not prediction. Founded by a contemporary of Dorothy Day, Catherine de Hueck, who claimed Russian aristocratic lineage and insisted she be called the Baroness de Hueck, Madonna House was located on a farm in the rolling hills of the Madawaska Valley in rural Ontario. It was an intriguing concept: a mixed lay community that took vows of poverty, chastity, and . . . apparently, obedience to the B, as she was reverentially referred to. I am the master of rash judgments, and as I sat through Madonna House lunches, with the Baroness punctuating the meal by ringing a bell every time she had a thought to share—and with immediate silence descending as she spoke—it just felt very (invoking that great 1970s word) weird. The young men and women, staff members as they were called, seemed so humorless and driven. Driven I could go for; humorless implied that something else was wrong either with the place or with these folks. I couldn't forget Brother Bruno's smiling face or the many pictures of Thomas Merton, looking as if he too was having a great time. Before he went into the Trappists, Merton had worked up in Harlem at the Baroness's Freedom House, and he wrote about it in glowing terms in *The Seven Storey Mountain*. I felt as though I were betraying him when I left after a week. But I couldn't get away fast enough. Tony Walsh—it was time to meet this Tony Walsh.

OO

Three bus rides later, I arrived in Montreal and went to the Benedict Labre House, a squat, two-story Catholic Worker house of hospitality in a rundown neighborhood at 308 Young Street. Tony Walsh had founded Labre House two decades earlier and had some years before handed it over to younger leaders. It was named after the saint who, like de Foucauld, had lived a life of prayer and bodily mortification, sleeping on the ground more often than in a bed, eating whatever was put before him, but meeting everyone with a simplicity, grace, and gentleness that immediately embraced them. Tony was waiting for me the first evening at a small Indian restaurant on St. Catherine Street. He was in his midsixties then, with thick glasses that magnified his eyes, and a way of chuckling as he tucked in his chin that gave him the look of a little boy who knew he should be more serious about life, but simply couldn't bring it off. He didn't seem the least bit like his patron, Benedict Labre, or de Foucauld, as he dove into the spicy samosas, raita, and lamb curry. I introduced my impressions of Madonna House gingerly, but found that Tony agreed completely about the fussiness and too-serious piety of the place. Not his cup of tea, he admitted. I liked him immediately.

Although he had never married, our lives were not that dissimilar—at least when it came to our rocky and winding spiritual paths. He had known some success as a teacher on a marginalized, poor Indian reservation, but something inside him made him uncomfortably aware that even this was not enough. "I just kept getting the feeling to go deeper, deeper; and I didn't much understand what 'deeper' meant," he said with that characteristic chuckle. After years of painful soul searching and—if my diagnosis over an excellent dessert of coconut-ginger hung yogurt can be trusted—a nervous breakdown, he started Labre House. He now was a full-time itinerant, speaking where he was asked, staying for as long as it seemed useful, a spiritual director charting paths for confused searchers like me. Tony had that engaging ability to talk about the most serious subjects and never sound very serious at all. Everything he did was "small potatoes." He spoke of God as if God were a trusted and understanding friend. Living a life of voluntary poverty in service to the poor was a most desirable and attractive career path. His conviction showed in his dancing, mirthful eyes.

I didn't have to explain much to Tony; he could read between the lines. He knew exactly what had brought me to start CHIPS. He understood the conflict I was feeling between my comfortable middle-class life and the demands of life with the poor. My sentences that rambled into nothingness and my obviously contorted face (only years later would he tell me about his first impressions) were outward signs of an inward struggle.

"Don't force it," he said. "Go down and see Mark; he's a good person to talk to."

When told that Mark was Father Mark Delary at a Trappist monastery in central Massachusetts, I looked at Tony quizzically. Trappists were the silent ones; they didn't speak to anybody. What little plans I had laid for this trip certainly did not include the Trappists, who I still imagined living the life Thomas Merton had written about in *The Seven Storey Mountain*. "That's changing; stop down there," he said airily, as if the monastery were just down the block.

OO

Buses are the perfect means of transportation for the spiritual pilgrim. In most cases, as in the spiritual life, you can't quite get *there* from *here*. You are taken places you don't necessarily want to go. Not only does the trip take longer than you want it to, but you constantly wonder whether or not you'll ever get to your destination and, not occasionally, why you are going at all. What would have been a short drive had I brought my car turned out to be a multiday trek, zigzagging my way through eastern Canada, New York, Vermont—with a short stop to hear the famous melodic monks at Weston Priory—and on to Massachusetts. I found myself standing on a windswept hill, peering through the morning mist at the imposing fieldstone walls of St. Joseph's Abbey, just outside the small town of Spencer.

The monks of St. Joseph's, I found, were hardly living the medieval life of Thomas Merton's Gethsemane. In fact, they were being led to the very cutting edge of the Human Potential Movement. The abbot, Thomas Keating, had gone on pilgrimage to the Esalen Institute—the Vatican of New Age thinking in Big Sur, California—which posited that our capacities were unlimited and needed to be unleashed from conventional thinking. After Vatican II, Keating had brought "facilitators" to the once silent halls to reorient his monks to the use of dialogue both with each other and their interior selves, and Zen roshis to teach the wisdom and practice of Eastern monasticism.

Certain distinct smells stay with you, bringing back vivid memories. I can close my eyes and recall the smell of the small sitting room in the retreat house at Spencer, an amalgam of distant food being cooked, clean cotton sheets, mortar between the fieldstones, and whatever wax dully glistened on the hardwood floor. Father Mark and I sat there for what would be the first of many meetings over the years. I don't even know if we had gotten to our chairs before I started. I wanted to live fully, I blurted out. To do the will of God. To give myself to the poor. I had started the storefront. I wanted to be there twenty-four hours a day to give food to the hungry and hope to the desperate. I wanted to give my life to something so that when it came time to die, I would know that I had at least tried to live a life that mattered. My marriage was a desert. I wanted . . .

He was a strange-looking man, a physician who had entered the Trappists some thirty years before. He looked like Jiminy Cricket, with a longish, insectlike oval face and yellowing buck teeth that shot out past his lips when he smiled. It was chilly in the room, which was amazingly elegant for a Trappist monastery, containing the paneling from a French mansion that had been bequeathed to the order. Father Mark pulled his black cowl up over his balding head. He listened to my ranting for a good while, then drew his hands from beneath the black scapular he wore over a long-sleeved white tunic. He looked intently at me, as if all that I had said had made perfect sense and that he saw clearly what my next step should be. I awaited the call, the call to greatness in service, the call to voluntary poverty, the monastic life, the marginalized life, a life of a castoff, with castoffs, the itinerant. Any call.

"What are you reading these days," he said in a flat voice.

What was I reading? "Everything by and about de Foucauld, John of the Cross, just finished *Cloud of Unknowing*."

"No, no, outside that," he countered. "Novels? Nonfiction?"

I stared back blankly.

He was a great fan of Flannery O'Connor and Annie Dillard, neither of whom resonated with me. But, of course, that didn't matter. As the seasoned spiritual director he was, he knew the emotional roller coaster I was on and that although my intentions were admirable, my brain was overloaded with the steep climbs and quick drops. The latest experience or thought or religious book held The Answer. If I only prayed or fasted more, I would know it. I sat there, my elbows on my knees. I stared down at my hands, fingers intertwined. My knuckles were turning white.

"You realize that what you do is also important."

"Writing?" It was as if I were naming the most venal, profane occupation a man could have. "Father, writing just doesn't matter anymore. At one time, I wanted it so bad I could taste it. That's changed. I don't hear the call of the gospel in a *New York Times* story on the latest headline-grabber."

"Don't push this too hard," he said, strangely echoing Tony Walsh's words. "When the roshi was here last year, he reminded us that the Buddha told the seeker: don't seek 'it.' Let 'it' find you. As for looking for this thing we call 'God,' Lin Chi said, 'If you meet the Buddha on the road, kill him.' If I had an answer for you, you'd have to kill me." He laughed, closing his eyes, running his tongue over those buck teeth. "I wish it were easier. Only when we look back on our lives does it make any sense. We just have to keep slouching toward Bethlehem." He also liked Joan Didion. He tucked his hands back under his black scapular and stood up to leave.

I stayed for a week, and although I wanted to see Father Mark daily, he rationed the visits, wisely knowing that his words or mine were but a very small part of what was happening. I rose with the monks at 3 AM and went to bed when they did, at 8 PM. I walked the monastery hills. I read. I slept. I listened to Alexander Scourby's magnificent reading of the New Testament during our noonday meals. As one of the monks took me back to the bus station in Spencer, I peered out the window, onto Route 37. The trees were bare now. What was alive at the beginning of my trip was no more. And new life would not emerge for some time. I headed back to Brooklyn and what I had left behind.

16

THE SOFA

BRIAN GAY'S REAL ESTATE OFFICE ON SEVENTH AVENUE had a slightly sinister air to it: a blousy, chain-smoking secretary at the front and Brian lurking somewhere in an inner room, engaged in other pursuits, beneath legal radar, my journalistic mind presupposed. It was a dusty place, with heavy oak office furniture firmly rooted in the 1920s. On being summoned, Brian would appear in the front, a slick-haired Irishman with a pasted-on grin, ready to be of service, providing the service did not take an extraordinary amount of time and for which he would be reasonably remunerated (preferably in cash).

Brian had sold the young, enterprising Wilkes couple their brownstone some five years before, the alleged "owner" being a fleshy-faced young man who smelled faintly of alcohol, whose last name was also, and not coincidentally, Gay. Brian was turning over the property, little doubt about it, having bought it a short time before from who knows what unsuspecting widow or older couple who were unaware that their neighborhood was now growing in popularity and price. J.C. and I had bought in partnership with Lou and Jane Gropp with the agreement that we would have the lower two floors, the Gropps the upper two.

My business this day fulfilled the first of Brian's requirements: it would take no more than a few minutes. His notary fee was $3, about the cost of a shrimp salad sandwich and a soft drink at Herzog's, the delicatessen across Seventh Avenue. With three quick sweeps of a pen—which he asked for as soon as I had lifted it from the third copy—it was finished. He applied an embossed stamp.

I was now both homeless and penniless.

∞

When I arrived back in Brooklyn after my two-month pilgrimage—a hollow-eyed man fifteen pounds thinner, with a weather-beaten, stained backpack slung over my shoulder—it was obvious that the marriage was at an end. I could call this sad moment many things, all of which and none of which were accurate. Could it have been simply an anomaly of the era, a result of the 1970s, when "being who you REALLY want to be" was enshrined as both a birthright and a cornerstone of mental health? A case of Divorce Black Plague that had swept along Second Street, infecting the Ubells on one side and Bashfords on the other, sending those long-term marriages into the dumpster? (Had I forgotten to put blood on my lintel so that the sword would pass my house?) Or was it the realization that this strange thing called love had simply slipped away in the course of our programmed life? This was the most likely answer, but a pretty shaky reason.

All of that was in the background now. Front and center was the call. Which brought up the most troubling possibility of all: was "the call" just an excuse that justified my ending what I had promised would be a life together "until death us do part"? I didn't know then, and I don't know now. But I know I was suffocating in my own self-involved life, and I wanted to breathe again. And, ever so slightly but surely, the earth had shifted beneath me. I simply could not go on as if nothing had happened.

The short document I signed that cloudy, dismal morning at Brian Gay Realty was a legal separation, which in two years would yield, according to the benevolent laws of the State of New York, a "no-fault" divorce. My fault? Not really. Hers? Not hers, either. "Something" had undone our marriage. However I wanted to define "something," the State of New York left up to me. The separation agreement also stipulated how our worldly possessions would be divided.

This was simple. I took the story of the rich young man literally. I gave away everything I had.

Two days after I had told J.C. that our marriage was lost, she handed me the document, a bit surprising in its speedy preparation. Still, I didn't consult a lawyer or have anyone else read over the document. I didn't even read it myself. That would have been cheating, a sign that I wasn't really serious about the new life I was about to lead and the old one I was leaving behind.

Moving day was not a pretty picture. Too many precious things were simply thrown away. Topping the list were my Navy uniforms with the stripe and a half indicating my rank as lieutenant, junior grade. How I would have liked to have my own sons—little did I know that there would be such a thing many years ahead—just to be able to touch the flecks of green and know that the sea's salt had seasoned not only those stripes but their father as well. Books, notes, college and high school mementos. That precious Cathedral Latin letter sweater with quill. A few cardboard boxes and a battered suitcase were all the worldly possessions I now needed to worry about.

∞

Face down, the smell of stale beer lingered in my nostrils. A cloud of sweat—old, musty, private parts sweat—enveloped me. Something slightly lumpy, very old, and very fried was under my cheek. A smooth patch on the tufted pillow of the sofa, already worn to a glossy patina by years of use and abuse, had that familiar smell. Semen? I sat bolt upright. I spat out cat hairs that had clung to my lips during a fitful night's sleep. The first light of morning filtered through the slit between the stained curtains, hanging limply on a rod bowed at the middle.

It was Christmas morning, 1974, and there I was, sleeping on a filthy sofa in a third-floor walk-up. Gary Mesacar and Fred Melton were two Union Theological Seminary students, who had once stood in awe of the *New York Times Magazine* writer who had started a Brooklyn soup kitchen. They were not that surprised when he made a request: a bed for a homeless person. When told who it was, there was only a mercifully slight hesitation before they said yes. It was more shock than reluctance.

I had vowed to be a lily of the field, unconcerned with anything material. I succeeded brilliantly and biblically. I did not have so much as a place to lay my head when I signed that separation agreement. I trusted that God would provide me a place to stay, and through the goodness of these two seminarians, he had.

I awoke early that Christmas morning to an empty apartment. Gary and Fred had both left the city to be with their families. I boiled some water for a cup of instant coffee and took it and a piece of outdated Entenmann's pecan roll to the front window. The rising sun cast dirty shards of ochre-tinged light down Seventh Street, glancing off a rear-view mirror here, burnishing the remains of a shattered wine bottle there, tiny sparks of life on an otherwise drab city street. The trees were bare, sidewalks silent. Lashed fast to a front door, a single evergreen wreath with flashing colored lights struggled to pierce the gloom. I was alone with thoughts of Christmas Present—or so I deluded myself.

Christmas Present was simple enough: an about-to-be-divorced man finally was living the life to which he had always aspired. He was alone, homeless, trusting in God, feeling at once profoundly sad on this festive day, yet alive with a sense of purpose he had never experienced before. On balance, Christmas Present found me, in my eyes, in pretty good shape.

Outside my dingy surroundings, the war in Vietnam continued to deteriorate into the morass that history would eventually document. Even as President Ford tried to put the best face on a war he had inherited from Richard Nixon, now five months gone in disgrace over his paranoiac Watergate fiasco, the North Vietnamese were massing their troops. By May, they would take Saigon and send Americans and South Vietnamese frantically scampering up a ladder to board the last helicopter out.

On the domestic front, other battles raged. Betty Friedan, whom I had profiled for the New York Times a few years before, had indeed mothered a revolution, and women were finding they no longer were an appendage to their men, but independent souls, capable of earning their own living and charting their own path—often without a husband. J.C. would now join their ever-increasing number.

As for the Catholic Church, Pope Paul VI had devolved into a sad, Hamlet-like pontiff, his 1968 encyclical affirming the strict prohibition of diaphragms, the pill, condoms, coitus interruptus, and other ingenious forms of birth control that Catholics worldwide nevertheless still used. Humanae Vitae signaled a watershed moment, after which papal pronouncements would never again command the unquestioning obedience that Catholics had once rendered.

In my reverie, images of Christmas Past skittered though my mind as I made a second, then third cup of coffee. A little boy in Cleveland, at midnight Mass, singing not "Silent Night" in English but "Noc Ticha" in Slovak, a language he once knew, but couldn't run from quickly enough. An ensign on the bridge of USS Power, squinting into the brilliant sunset in Guantánamo Bay. With crossed swords and applause, the young lieutenant and his bride walking beneath the arch of honor to a new life.

What of Christmas Future? I envisioned year after seamless year of work with the poor, the unloved, society's dregs. Nothing held me back now; I was totally, completely theirs. I would be, as Tony Walsh said, "a man for others." No possessions to weigh me down, no personal wants to put before their needs, no ties to bind me to any one person, so that I could serve many. I saw myself as a man once somewhat known to the world who would now be lost to normal human pursuits and accomplishments, going deeper and deeper into the mystery of God, taken on paths he could not then imagine, but on which he would never be alone.

But if my life was so on track now, why did I find myself crying as I looked out over Seventh Street and ahead to the rest of my life? Was my bliss so overwhelming?

17

80 WINTHROP

IT IS AMAZING HOW SOMEONE WITH A CIRCLE OF FRIENDS, a home, a promising career—all the elements of what we call a life—could so quickly fall off the face of the earth. To be reincarnated only blocks away, where the conventions, courtesies, and usual amenities of middle-class life suddenly were gone. These were strange days. Did I turn my back on the Park Slope friends when they saw me? Or did they conveniently look away, avoiding eye contact as you do when you see a madman raving to himself? I certainly must have been an embarrassment to them, this once well-dressed fellow who now wore tattered, ill-fitting castoffs and a pitiful parka with a faux-fur hood liner, which I bought at a discount army surplus store in down-town Brooklyn, lest I use one of our donated coats. Made in Jamaica. $19.95. Useless against cold winter winds. Shivering, I just put on another sweater beneath, then another, the more tattered the better. Layer by layer, I was taking on the uniform of the people who came to me for help.

∞

The Friday night "clarification of thought" meetings at the Catholic Worker—with speakers on various social justice and spirituality topics— served as an ingathering of a certain, mostly Catholic tribe, not the overtly religious ones or those working in Church institutions and none of the hierarchy, but nuns for sure, a priest now and again. The life and witness of Dorothy Day and the Worker had implanted something they could not erase from their minds, and they wanted to be around to hear the stories and stir the embers of their own consciences to live a more intentional life.

∞

I knew I couldn't stay at Gary and Fred's. The Bronx Storefront Community members offered me a bed. I was getting to know more of the Worker people—Frank Donovan, Geoff Gneuhs, Jane Sammon—and I could stay there. But I wanted to live in the Brooklyn neighborhood, close to CHIPS. "Jacques might have a place for you," Frank Donovan mentioned, directing me to a short, balding man who was listening intently to an animated woman with the aluminum pie plate lashed perkily atop her head. She told him: Did Jacques realize that we all were in danger? You could never tell when the rays would strike; therefore constant vigilance was of utmost importance. It was all she could do to keep the rays from entering her brain. Jacques Travers, pensively resting his cheek in the palm of his hand—a look I would grow to know and love—took in every word with a serious expression that bid her to continue her diatribe, which she did with even greater gusto and volume.

Jacques, I would later find out, had been living an aimless and dissolute life in France, and on a trip to Rome was so disgusted with himself that he was ready to commit suicide. He came upon an American priest, Pierre Conway, who, after hearing his story, handed him one of Dorothy Day's books. This reminded me of my chance meeting with Tony Walsh in Montreal. The idea of sharing his life with the poor, as she had done, so completely transfixed and transformed Jacques that within the year, he was on his way to America. He supported himself teaching introductory French at Brooklyn College, at low pay, decidedly not on the tenure track, meanwhile devoting whatever he earned to the small community at—and he stated the address as if it were at heaven's gate—80 Winthrop.

Jacques was a tiny man, with an impish, smooth, virtually unwrinkled boyish face, although he was probably then in his early fifties. I had known and would come to know many good people, many holy people. Jacques was neither. He was a saint. The true saint is never merely good or holy; there is an entirely different dimension to these individuals. They see God in everyone. It is not forced or a conceit; it is so natural as to be barely discernable. There is really no overt piety about them, nothing that marks them. It is only when you draw back and look into yourself that you know they have something you do not, and will not ever, have.

When Jacques greeted me, with my suitcase and cardboard boxes, at the door of Apartment 4-D, 80 Winthrop Street, in the Flatbush section of Brooklyn, it was as if I were being ushered into an elegant suite at the Plaza. He showed me around proudly, never apologizing for the chipped paint or peeling linoleum, but pointing out the spindly plants that grasped for the tiny bit of sunlight filtered through a grimy window that looked out on the apartment building just feet away. He proudly introduced his

companions: Donald, a pale-faced man of about thirty, who said nothing
at all, but who, at Jacques' bidding, extended a hand that lay limply in my
own as I tried to shake it. Freddie, described as a fine sea captain, wore a
stocking cap and, after wiping his mouth with the cloth that he was also
using to dry the dishes, smiled through his toothless mouth. I was then
ushered into the Professor's room, where a wizened man lay at a strange
angle in a Barcalounger. I would learn their stories soon enough, I was
sure. Their fall from independent to dependent living might not have been
as precipitous or chosen as mine—most had been on a long, slow slide over
the tenuous edges of accepted society—but here we were, together, none
asking the other how we had come to live together.

   Donald and Freddie shared a bedroom, and I didn't note where Jacques
slept. He brought me into a tiny room barely wide enough for the single
bed that was to be mine. A colorful throw covered the blankets, two of
them, actually, electric blankets minus the electric, but neatly smoothed
in place. The throw, Jacques noted offhandedly, had been knitted by
Dorothy Day over thousands of miles of Greyhound travel. I now had a
home; I now could devote myself to the work to which I felt called.

OO

I never had the discipline or inclination to keep a diary, but we did keep a
log at CHIPS so that we could follow up on our guests, as we called them.
And today, as I leaf through those early pages of CHIPS history, I know
that something very good was being born. We prevented the poor and disabled from being evicted. We secured jobs where none were to be found.
We rescued battered wives and children from abusive husbands and fathers.
There was a spirit among us outcasts—whether by choice or by fate—that
our common destiny was just that: common. It is strange how, once you
get past the smell and the many conflicting and sad stories—a good
percentage of them true—there is a certain comfort in being with the poor.
Pretenses, posturing, preening—the triad of New York literary life—had
no place. You just could, as the lingo went, "get down to it."

   A small coterie of people helped out at CHIPS. There was Mary,
a glum, depressed teenager whose physician father once told her she was
an abortion who lived. She would lie for hours on our sagging sofa, only
to rise up magnificently to take a pregnant woman to Methodist Hospital
up on Seventh Avenue or to soothe frightened children who appeared,
suddenly homeless. Anne Enright, her neck caved in from a cancer operation, swathed her disfigurement with elegant silk scarves, and with equal
panache served humble bowls of soup and outdated cookies as if she

were a Park Avenue socialite. Clyde Forman, a black man who battled alcoholism and triumphed most of the time, took on the street toughs with a firmness and compassion that either frightened or melted them. Sheila Hanks, a professional social worker, now a bit at sea in her new role as a full-time mother, brought her tiny Amanda into a place that most mothers would have shunned, and applied her knowledge of the intricacies of the social welfare system to work magic for hopeless lives. Janine Lachs, who survived the Holocaust, wanted to do something for those who were currently bearing society's yellow stars.

Day after exhausting day as I fell into that bed at 80 Winthrop, I had the sense that I was finally on track; I was clearly following the dream that had come in and out of focus for much of my adult life. I was living an ordained life—not ordained by ecclesial power, to be sure, but in a sense consecrated. Obedience may have been lacking, as there was no one to be obedient to, but poverty and chastity were mine. Both were easy. I had nothing, so there was no concern about earning, preserving, enhancing. My sex life had become so desiccated that I never much thought about the fact that I was a thirty-seven-year-old heterosexual who might be expected to have the normal urges. Yes, of course, I could see that certain hips were more finely shaped than others, that a well-tailored silk blouse could caress a woman's body beautifully, that the bouncing ends of a well-turned page boy haircut had an undeniable allure. But all that was behind me now. I quickly cauterized such thoughts, preventing them from going any further.

In the midst of the city, there was a monastic rhythm to my life, *ora et labora*. The *ora* began before sunrise at my bedside before going to the tiny church of Holy Cross over on Church Avenue for early Mass. Then to *labora* at CHIPS to take on whatever came through the door. I was a man on a mission. I was disciplined; my prayer life punctuated the day. I rarely raised my voice; I gave myself selflessly to the poor.

"Do not give to the poor expecting to get their gratitude so that you can feel good about yourself. If you do, your giving will be thin and short-lived, and that is not what the poor need; it will only impoverish them further. Give only if you have something to give; give only if you are someone for whom giving is its own reward." Dorothy Day's words encapsulated exactly what was going on in my life. Or so I was convincing myself.

When I came home to 80 Winthrop, I looked upon it as the true testing ground for my faith. Stale, damp, airless, permeated by the unmistakable stench of cockroach feces. Each time I walked through the door, I held my breath. Then, when my lungs could take it no longer, I gasped, hoping that by overloading the system, my sense of smell would be short-circuited, knocked out of commission.

For Jacques, it was a happy little household, a frame of mind—or soul—that I struggled to achieve. Donald, a former Green Beret, loaded with many milligrams of Thorazine, walked about like a zombie, the last firefight in Vietnam running a continuous loop in his mind. The Professor, who refused to rest in an actual bed for fear that doing so meant he was dying, cadged bits of toast and English muffin into recesses of the Barcalounger, providing a steady food supply not only for the cockroaches but for the mice that eagerly visited him when he lapsed into sleep. He was indignant when I changed his urine-soaked pads, glaring at me with eyes at once alert and distant. Freddie, an otherwise good-natured man, mumbled incessantly, his monologues like verbal Muzak. No dish or glass in our battered kitchen cabinets matched, most of them were chipped. The refrigerator needed cleaning; the stove was crusted with the memories of many meals.

I hated myself for even noticing such things. But then I would come upon Jacques, sitting quietly on the sofa that he changed to and from a bed when everyone was asleep so as not to call attention to himself, reading St. Thomas's *Summa Theologica* in the original Latin. And I would know I was living a truly extraordinary life with an extraordinary man. Or, on a shopping trip with Jacques when money was especially low and I reached for the gallon jug of rotgut Gallo only to have him say, "Oh, no, Paaaul, we must have a wonderful wine tonight. Theees Cabernet Sauvignon!" His joie de vivre, his mellifluous French accent, his sense of beauty and of the importance—in the midst of our poverty—of a good glass of wine, made me see that there was a brighter path than the one I was trudging along. "*Cher* Paaaul, we can be poor of pocket, but we can never let our spirits be poor." Coming from Jacques, it was never an admonition, only encouragement.

OO

Holy Cross parish is set in what was once a blue-collar Flatbush neighborhood of Irish plumbers and policemen and transit workers. It is now a sad area in the midst of urban decay, with a rusting refrigerator teetering over a Church Avenue gutter clogged with paper and garbage, where poor West Indians, Haitians, and Mexicans struggle for their first American toehold. When I was there, it had become predominately black and was called a "transitional neighborhood," but of course the transition had long since passed, and its fate was obvious. To passersby or to those who once lived here and knew the neighborhood in a previous life, it was considered a very dangerous place. Holy Cross, once open all day, was locked securely except for Mass times.

For me, Holy Cross in Brooklyn was what Corpus Christi on the Upper West Side of Manhattan was to Thomas Merton, a place that as much found him as he found it. It was a sanctuary where a weary soul finds rest from the world and tries to pray. A place where he (and I) sought not only God's solace but his insight and direction for our lives. There are five frescoes over the altar at Holy Cross, depicting Christ's first visit to the temple, when he was separated from his parents, the Last Supper, Crucifixion, resurrection and ascension. And beneath the frescoes, at the top of its soaring altar screen, is a stark, bronze crucifix. This was the symbol of the God I had first known when I looked up the altar at St. Benedict's, a God who was distant, powerful, and cold, who I could speak of and to only in hushed tones, if at all. An irritable, unappeasable crucified God, who tallied my many sins each night and could present me with a bill of lading that would surely ship me directly to hell.

But that was not the God to whom I now prayed. There was another God behind, beyond, within this one, a battlefield hero, unbidden, but who willingly and without ever questioning the cost or my worth had volunteered his life so that mine could be spared. He was a God whose once impenetrable shroud had been torn asunder by the revolutionary words of Vatican II. I was invited to come closer, to feast at the table of his Eucharist and drink the blood he willingly shed. For he was my friend, my life's companion. He was all I ever needed. And what could I do but love him and try, in some small way, to return a portion of the life he had first given me?

Mine was a strange case of spiritual schizophrenia; I was at once feeling the rising power of God within me, his presence so palpable, and yet also sensing my utter inadequacy as I looked across what continued to be, day in and day out, an unbridgeable chasm. I worked so hard to love the Professor, Donald, and Freddie. I could see their humanity, their great struggles to be whole. I could see they had not been treated kindly by life. But something was missing. My affection for them did not come naturally, as it did for Jacques. It was a supreme effort, all the time.

I lingered after Mass most days with my lengthy prayer list. I wanted each petition to be phrased with different wording, as if I were writing a story and didn't want to bore God with repetition. I prayed to this new, more immanent God that Angel's leg would heal, that Peter Skelly would stop drinking, that Donald would wake up from his posttraumatic miasma and smile for once. Only at the end did I mention myself. And each time

I felt selfish and weak. After all, I was finally living the life I had always hoped to, a life for others. A life where my needs simply didn't matter in the face of the grinding poverty and disease and desperation of my people. I felt so blessed to be at 80 Winthrop where I could share on a daily basis the life of the poor, the mentally ill, the marginalized. And to have CHIPS, which for the past three years had provided me with a passport into people's lives, so that I might be trusted with their agony. Not many people get this opportunity; I knew that well.

> Lord my God, I call for help by day;
> I cry at night before you.
> Let my prayer come into your presence.
> O turn your ear to my cry . . .
> I am reckoned as one in the tomb;
> I have reached the end of my strength . . .
> You have taken away my friends
> And made me hateful in their sight.

The words of Psalm 88 pierced my soul with their searing awareness; I found my heart pounding, both in my own agony and the fleeting bliss I could feel at the same time. I tried to shrug off my inner conflicts as just a symptom of a stage I had to go through. Didn't de Foucauld and John of the Cross and Theresa of Avila go through their desert experiences before they truly encountered the power and the surety of the God, the Christ they sought? Didn't Thérèse of Lisieux have a crisis of faith on her very deathbed?

My life was to be intentional, purposeful, biblical. If I presumed to live a Christlike life, I had to be ready to suffer my agony in the garden, the small daily crucifixions, the abandonment of friends, society's scorn. My mind took me places, both to heights of insight and to forlorn depths I had never experienced before.

There was something, though, that I noticed by their absence. My headaches had completely gone away.

∞

I saved up $600 from a small monthly payment I was receiving from the Navy and bought a 1964 Volkswagen bus, aptly painted red, white, and blue by the young hippie who had been its previous owner. I drove to hospitals and detox centers and the back doors of supermarkets and bakeries and butcher shops. I was quite a sight, I'm sure, in this rusting, belching VW that I always parked on an incline because it could be turned over with a little push when the starter balked, which it often did. Every so often, I would just keep driving and end up four hours later on Massachusetts Route 37 outside St. Joseph's Abbey, where, exhausted, I would sleep for a good part of the days I was there, see Father Mark, and drive back to Brooklyn.

Although I thought I was articulating fairly well and rationally my search for God in service to others, I never found Father Mark especially enthusiastic about the direction my life was taking. He kept saying that the writing life was also a worthy vocation and that I shouldn't be pushing so hard to—what was the word he used?—"optimize" my calling. I listened patiently, but I was not about to weaken in my resolve. He obviously didn't understand.

There was another, unlikely, voice in my life in those days, a Jewish woman about my age named Barbara Koltuv. J.C. had maintained that I needed professional help, and reminded me at predicable moments (an outburst, a sulking mood), "Shouldn't you take a look at that?" Her words, in that deadpan, practiced, Therapy 101 voice infuriated me and made me vow that I didn't need to and never would "take a look at that." Which makes it all the more remarkable that within the week after I separated, no longer nudged into the world of analysis, I began to make phone calls to find a therapist. I sensed I was going through the most tumultuous period of my life. Down deep, I realized I needed help. Badly.

I knew about as much about the basics of analysis as any New Yorker, surrounded as we were by analysands extolling the virtue of the approach of whomever they were seeing. I first visited the office of a Freudian psychiatrist. He stared mutely at me. I knew I had to bring the chalk, but this was too blank a slate to write on. I contacted the Jungian Institute, remembering that Jung saw the need and place of the transcendent, whereas Freud thought the whole business of God was so much voodoo and superstition. So, once and then twice a week, I traveled to Dr. Koltuv's elegant apartment overlooking Washington Square Park at 2 Park Avenue.

Too much detail about one's therapy (mine would last four years) isn't usually of interest to anyone else, but one point came quickly clear: Barbara Koltuv also was not encouraging about my path to sainthood, goodness, holiness, the Christlike life. "Where are you in this? Don't gloss that over. What did that feel like?" she would interrupt me occasionally during that first year, which was a lot of my talking and her listening. Feel like? How stupid. What could be a worse barometer of the intentional, spiritual life? Feelings were exactly what the saints didn't pay much attention to. But for some unknown reason (thank you, God) I stayed with Dr. Koltuv, even though I never felt that this outwardly secular Jew had much of a clue as to what this cradle Catholic was talking about.

∞

Some friends from my former life did eventually find me, and I could tell by their tone of voice on the phone or when they saw me at CHIPS that they believed I had completely lost it. Barry Jagoda, a successful NBC producer who would go on to serve in the Carter White House, came by 80 Winthrop one evening, just as I was going out to the garbage chute with a sodden lump of the Professor's diapers. I slipped one hand out from beneath and Barry, without hesitating, shook it. Of such moments are casual relationships transformed into deep, lasting friendships. We sat on a couple of threadbare overstuffed chairs in the dimly lit living room, with Freddie mumbling in the kitchen, the Professor ranting in his room, and Donald marching patrol duty in the long hallway. Our talk was of Columbia classmates ascending the media ladder. Tom Bettag was on his way to becoming the producer of Dan Rather's *Nightly News* on CBS. Mollie Ivins had put her sweater sets and pearls aside, reclaimed her Texas roots and boots, and was a nationally known columnist. Paul Friedman was about to produce the *Today* show. Paul Branzburg, our Harvard Law graduate, had, at twenty-eight, won a Pulitzer Prize with the *Louisville Courier-Journal*. And then there was Richard Stone, who, in the midst of a successful run of front-page stories at the *Wall Street Journal*, had gone to the roof of his West Side apartment building and jumped.

"Go figure," Barry said.

"Depressed. Was he depressed, Barry?"

"We're all depressed. We just don't jump off buildings."

"Right. Right."

I was saying "right," but I knew something was very wrong.

∞

"I'm sorry, could you speak up?" My hand paused over the logbook at CHIPS, ready to document the incoming need. There was a lot of noise in the background, typical, and I couldn't hear well.

"You're from what? You want to do what? Sure, sure, I'll be here all day, anytime."

"Vhat vas that?" Janine asked, in that marvelous Austrian accent.

"*Newsweek*. Somebody selling subscriptions, I think. I didn't think they went door-to-door. Couldn't hear her."

18

THE SCENT OF A WOMAN

THE YELLOW CAB LURCHED TO A STOP IN FRONT OF CHIPS. After disgorging its fare, the cab squealed away from the curb even more quickly, its "Off Duty" sign dispelling any question that it wanted further business in this Brooklyn neighborhood. It was a rare enough sight; our area was served by gypsy cabs, if any at all, and certainly not the mainstream Yellow fleet. And equally rare was the passenger the cab had brought us. She stood there, a huge bag slung over her shoulder. Not that people with bags—often containing everything they owned—were strangers to us. But this was a bag of supple Italian leather. The woman started toward our door, her perfectly coiffed black hair swept back from a meticulously confected face anchored by etched, smoldering eyes and lipstick that traced the contours of her delicate lips. From the tips of her fingers, with blazing crimson nails, surgically tapered, to the tips of her toes, encased in $300 worth of Ferragamo pumps, this was not our usual visitor. And when she came through the door . . . the perfume, oh god the perfume. People like this never—I mean never—came to CHIPS.

In the year before the founding of CHIPS and then during its first year of operation, I had been researching and writing my first major book, which followed a statistically average 1970s family through a year of their life. Lippincott was to publish the book, which I had almost forgotten about. Although "You are there" portraits are quite ordinary today, it was then a relatively new form, immersion journalism, whereby the writer simply stayed with a subject for an extended period of time and wove a narrative around real-life events. For me, the subject was a Long Island family: foreman father, at-home mother, perky older daughter starting college, sullen teenaged son drifting aimlessly after high school, and angelic twelve-year-old younger daughter. The Neumeyers, as I would call them to protect their identity, had graciously and bravely opened their lives to me, and the resulting book chronicled their quest to live—and not quite realize—the American dream. I traveled the Long Island Expressway into a world that was as alien as if I had gone to another country or planet. Here was married life, with children, something I knew nothing about. Even as my own marriage was deteriorating, I said nothing about my life, as they told me everything about theirs. I never took a note in front of them. I never expressed an opinion of my own throughout that year, but eagerly listened to theirs. I was the perfect reporter and companion, always interested in everything they did, the smallest details of their lives—lives, I would eventually write, that had more to do with Greek tragedy than American triumphalism. The children hated the programmed suburban life their parents had worked so hard to provide them after leaving a tiny apartment in a bustling Bronx neighborhood years before.

As I was to find out, *Newsweek* was not interested in my subscription. The magazine had prepared a lengthy review of the book, *Trying Out the Dream: A Year in the Life of an American Family*. The stylish woman who had emerged from the taxi bearing this amazing scent was Jill Kremetz, the famous photographer, come to take the accompanying author portrait.

When I look at the proof sheets of that photo session today, all I can do is weep for this pitiful creature. Frame after frame reveal a man contorted in a scoliotic posture, with rings beneath his hollow eyes like swollen charcoal smudges, set off by a complexion as sallow as parchment. His unwashed hair lays lank on his head, accenting a wretched haircut. Even though it was a dark, moody winter's day, he squints as if looking into a glaring light. When he tries to smile, he grimaces as if in pain. When he attempts to look pensive, he looks drawn. When he tries to strike an authorial pose, he appears dazed. My brain was urging me to convey certain expected emotions. My soul, more honest, balked at such commands. And my face reflected soul, not brain. That pitiful Jamaican-made parka looked as cheap and useless as it truly was. Frame after frame: leaning on a table, against the door jam, seated, walking on Sixth Avenue, gesturing . . . something was very, very wrong with this man. Anyone could see that.

"By the way, congratulations," she said with a smile that I was to wrongly interpret. She came closer with her 50 mm Leitz lens.

"I know . . . I guess . . . *Newsweek* is a pretty big deal," I said, somewhat sheepishly, not used to such smiles.

"And the Literary Guild. Very impressive."

"The what?"

When I was working for the *Baltimore Sun,* I dreamed of someday writing for a national magazine, any national magazine. When I got to New York and began to write for smaller national magazines, I read the *New York Times Magazine* with awe, at once hoping yet never really believing that I would someday casually walk up to a newsstand and open the Sunday magazine to see my name on the index page. But to see my name on the spine of a book? To have it reviewed by one of the biggest and most important magazines in America? Selected by a prestigious book club? The young writer who had stopped his car on the George Washington Bridge some ten years before and brashly bellowed out his challenge to the dusky Manhattan skyline had achieved them all. And here I was, unshaven, in castoff clothes, acutely embarrassed by all the attention.

I don't know what got into me, standing there in front of CHIPS, the madman of Sixth Avenue, Mr. Voluntary Poverty, Mr. Voluntary Celibacy. It must have been the perfume. Or the sheer closeness of a female's body. Or the third day of a mind-numbing fast I was observing. I fumbled, but I asked Miss Jill Kremetz for a date, something I never was very good at, and a skill I hadn't practiced for many years. She let me down gently. "Paul, that would be sooo wonderful, but . . ." she was very much in love with her man. Who just happened to be Kurt Vonnegut. Whom she would eventually capture in marriage. She had her eyes on the prize and was not one to waver or tarry, certainly not with the likes of me.

∞

I didn't think much about the photography session after that day, except to be strangely happy with the rejection. I was looking for signs in those days, and this was a sure indication that sweet perfume, a lady's wan smile, and her elegant shoes were little more than passing temptations. Which had to be faced (this far I had come in my therapy) and then soundly rejected (Dr. Koltuv might not have agreed entirely here) if I were to live the life to which I felt called. Women were not part of my life anymore. The vanity of writing was behind me now, just as it had been for Thomas Merton when he entered the Trappists. That he eventually went on to write forty books was a piece of information I was conveniently overlooking. I had read many of Merton's books since receiving *The Seven Storey Mountain* from Brother Adolph's hand. But he was Thomas Merton, a spiritual master. I was not. I would keep my promise. My writing life was over. My new life was with the poor, being poor, living poor, a life with Christ. That was what God wanted of me.

CHIPS was by now both mystifying various city social service agencies and becoming known as a refuge of last resort in our part of Brooklyn. When social workers, priests, and nuns didn't know where to turn, they turned to us. When neighborhood people knew of a family put out on the street, they came to us. We started an overnight shelter, which at the beginning was the usual gathering of drunks, addicts, and the deinstitutionalized mentally ill. On a bitter cold February night, the first mother and baby showed up at our door, presaging what would be a more common plight in the years ahead. A couple of old bedspreads were nailed into the ceiling, providing as much dignity and privacy as we could afford this modern-day Madonna and Child.

I was sleeping half of my nights at CHIPS now. Getting everyone settled was often difficult—fights, epileptic seizures, drug withdrawal, psychotic outbursts—*Catch-22* had nothing on CHIPS. But then the storm would calm, as if the Lord were there in the boat. The gentle breathing of the young mother, the snoring of men whose nasal passages were ravaged by cocaine, the sudden cry from a storm-tossed mind, the whimper of a baby. Ultimately, all sweet sounds in the peaceable kingdom we were trying so hard to create.

I had read Thomas Merton's famous meditation in the fire tower, and I thought about it as I lay awake on my cot one night, the tiny, crowded room finally quiet. With all the difficulties of this new life, what a fortunate man I was to be able to share my life so intimately with these, God's ambassadors. There was a mystical dignity about the poor, a clarity I had never experienced before through the many, blurring lenses easily summoned in a middle-class life. I hadn't understood this quality in the early days of CHIPS, but now, living at 80 Winthrop with Donald and Freddie and the Professor, spending nights here with an ever-changing group of the homeless, there were moments of blinding grace that sometimes astounded me. The homeless mother tenderly tucking in her tiny baby boy beneath those threadbare blankets. The way the schizophrenic, Roger, carefully folded his jacket into a neat square and placed it under his cot. Morris, who had spent decades on the street, his many layers of clothing suddenly transformed into so many petals of a flower, in so many muted shades; his swollen legs finally allowed horizontal rest; his chapped, gnarled hands folded over his bloated body like an innocent schoolboy. Even the bare forty-watt bulb that shone over the entrance to our wretched bathroom glowed with a radiant warmth, the Christmas star.

"God has given me the sense, the need—I don't know how to put it—an instinct for the Absolute . . . an extremely rare gift of which I have been aware from my childhood." I read the words of Leon Bloy by that faint light, and I knew exactly what he was talking about. Bloy, along with de Foucauld, Dorothy Day, Francis of Assisi, and Peter Claver, all were granted a clearer and clearer vision of where their energies should be focused, what they had to pursue, how they had to live. Bloy, a Frenchman, was one of the great beacons by which the Catholic Worker movement was guided, a man of great inconsistencies, "his flirtations with piety alternating with crude rebellion," as one biographer would put it. I had no idea how prescient those words were that night.

Something had been planted in me, something that continually stalked me, which put me at unease when my life was devoted only to myself, my needs, status, acclaim. The Hound of Heaven, relentlessly pursuing. And now I was beginning to sense what a life with God, with his chosen ones, the poor, could be, and I understood what Bloy had found: "it involves an insatiable and ravenous hunger for what the earth does not contain and its effect upon its possessor is an unbounded loneliness."

Dorothy Day talked of the "long loneliness" of her life, of Dostoyevsky's "harsh and dreadful love," the unadorned love for the poor that selfishly demanded everything of a person. Finally, finally, I had a hint of what this life could be. It was transcendent at times, and at others excruciatingly barren. At once so sure, and then so much folly. Spiritual and holy, vain and self-righteous. The sentiments collided like bumper cars in an amusement park, impacting with a dull thud, rattling the teeth, mind, and best of intentions, before erratically veering off. I stared up at the ceiling, a history of overflowing sinks and toilets from the floor above written on the stained acoustical tiles. In the dim light, I gazed out over my flock, their bodies heaving gently under the tatters of blankets.

> *Feed the hungry.*
> *Give drink to the thirsty.*
> *Clothe the naked.*
> *Shelter the homeless.*
> *Visit the sick.*
> *Visit those in prison.*
> *Bury the dead.*

I could recite the corporal works of mercy from a child's memory of the Baltimore Catechism. In my own simple way, I was now trying my best to live these seven mandates for which we will have to give account at the Last Judgment. "Lord, when did we see you," as the Gospel of Matthew asks. Oh, I saw them now: I saw them so clearly. Not that I saw Christ in them. I was not that good a person; I was not Jacques. But I saw my father and mother with their six children sleeping in that airless attic. I saw the retarded children I went to school with at St. Benedict's. I saw the encephalitic child my sister Francis bore, whose name also was Paul. I saw the look of hopelessness on Peter Skelly's scab-ridden face. I saw the faces peering through the thick glass at Kings County Hospital, Building K, the psychiatric ward. No, not Christ, but those marginalized by birth or fate.

I turned back to Leon Bloy just as the light went out. We hadn't paid our electric bill, and the city made good on its threat. So much for altruism. This corporal work of mercy had to be ransomed by hard, cold cash in the morning. Another bump in the road to supposed holiness. I had to smile. More purification. I rolled over and fell deeply asleep.

OO

Who was it that brought the March 24, 1975, *Newsweek* into CHIPS? I glanced at the review, winced at the pathetic picture, not believing that I could look so gaunt, so miserable. Surely this wasn't me. I was the rescuing angel, the happy, fulfilled servant of the poor. Clyde, Janine, and Anne were terribly excited about the review, showing it to everyone who came in. Our homeless guests glanced at the magazine, then at me, not quite putting the two together. When someone they knew had a picture in a publication, it was usually a mug shot.

Newsweek's circulation at the time was around three million. At least one of those copies found its way to an eighteenth-floor corner office at 90 Park Avenue, just a few blocks from where I had worked at Harper & Row. A second phone call came into CHIPS that was *not* from or about someone in need. This time it was from the powers that be at Westinghouse Broadcasting. Would Wednesday at ten be convenient for Mr. Wilkes? Anne Enright, the volunteer who in her real life was an executive secretary, took the call with great aplomb, affecting—or was this my imagination?—just the slightest hint of a British accent. She wrote the appointment on the back of the only piece of paper at hand, still another notice from the New York Sanitation Department that we were putting too much garbage at the curb.

I had not worn a suit in many years, and when I went to my small closet at 80 Winthrop, there, in a protective bag, pushed to the back, was a blue suit I had bought not long after my discharge from the Navy over a decade before. It looked perfectly fine to me. (Months later, when I wore it a second time, someone noted that both its purplish hue and narrow lapels of another fashion season gave away its age.) As I came out of the subway on Park Avenue, I realized how long it had been since I had been in Manhattan. The sleek, silver-skinned buildings loomed overhead, appearing to lean menacingly over the median dividing the busy street. Cabs came screaming out of the Grand Central underpass, hitting an uneven manhole with rattling regularity. People seemed to be running by me, jostling my slow-moving, tentative form, as I tried to remember which was the even side, which the odd, and had to cross Park three times before I reached my destination. I was in a city of ghosts; I walked like a man in a trance.

It's a wonder that the three men who were awaiting me (in decidedly more stylish suits)—the president of Westinghouse Broadcasting and two vice presidents—took me at all seriously. I imagined that they concluded, *Well, you know, these eccentric writers.* Win Baker, George Moynihan, and Don McGannon shook my hand, asked my preference in coffee, which was brought in elegant china on a tray by a secretary wearing a classic Dior suit. She sat the tray on a teak table, polished to shimmering perfection, between two copies of *Trying Out the Dream*, with tiny slips of paper peeking out between the pages.

"You've done something extraordinary here, Mr. Wilkes—may we call you Paul? . . ." the words trailed off, then came back in, a stronger signal, from a faraway radio station. ". . . a seminal work not only in journalism . . . an incisive portrait of American life never seen before." The words floated in the air. Didn't they know, hadn't I been clear that this was a life I had left behind? But then again, why was I here in the first place? Why did I dig out this suit? They were speaking, but the words weren't computing. "This is absolutely perfect for a major television series. . . ."

It was only when I got back to 80 Winthrop that the pieces started coming together. Donald was pacing the hallway, his footfalls like the drumbeat to which he very well may have been marching. Freddie's imaginary conversation was heating up; whomever he was talking with couldn't understand that the steam lines were out and the mess decks were closed. Only the mice were content, squealing in a feeding frenzy as they scampered over the Barcalounger. I closed the door to my room and sat on the Dorothy Day quilt. I had just been offered a prime-time television series based on my book. A contract was being drawn up for more money than I had ever made in my life. The fact that I had no television experience didn't seem to matter. I would be the on-air host and in charge of the entire production.

What was I doing?

∞

I never considered myself a journalist or writer "on the news." From the beginning, I had chosen magazine writing, not breaking news. Quite frankly, I never considered myself a quick or incisive thinker. I liked to tell a bigger story by telling a small story that was somehow representative, and that was exactly the thinking behind *Trying Out the Dream*. One family, average income (then about $12,000 a year), suburban, white, Protestant, two or three children, working father, stay-at-home mother, post–World War II migrants from an urban area. I had no idea I was writing about an institution about to undergo the most profound change it had experienced since the Industrial Revolution. I was writing about the kind of family that would in a generation be no more, reconfigured by the emerging role of women in the marketplace. Not only my marriage but half of all marriages would end in divorce. The classic family was about to become an endangered species.

Westinghouse's idea was not for me to film the Neumeyers, but to find representative families from across America, of different incomes, education levels, races, and occupations, and, using the technique of *Trying Out the Dream,* create a documentary portrait of the American family for the bicentennial year, 1976.

Looking back at how I was living in my life devoted to the poor, I am amazed that I just didn't say no. In trying to reach a decision, I employed the spiritual discipline of discernment, imploring God to show me the right path. I prayed, with head bowed at the kitchen table, with eyes upturned after Mass at Holy Cross Church. I read scripture, sifting the spiritual tea leaves. I tried to extract meaning from the parable of Christ being offered the world by a cunning devil. I thought of Peter and the cock crowing the third time. "The Lord is my shepherd; I shall not want." I picked up the phone to call Westinghouse to tell them no. I laid it back on the cradle so softly that not even God could hear. I looked for signs, even tiny and obscure ones. Something Freddie would say or a person who came to us with a special need, the way the Wandering Jew plant curled around the cord of a Venetian blind. Was it lovely or strangling? I tried to convince myself that I didn't have to choose. Yes, that could be the answer! I could do the series and continue to live at 80 Winthrop and work at CHIPS.

But my heart was telling me something else, something that made me profoundly sad.

As I looked at my life, I saw the supreme effort I was making. And I saw how deeply unhappy I really was. Try as I might, I did not see the face of Christ in my roommates or the people who came to CHIPS. When

I was honest about it, I realized that my prayer life was stifled, arid, forced. I was, in a certain way, "successful" in my work, but it was a hollow success. People looked at me as good and patient and caring. I imagine that those who didn't think I had gone completely mad admired me for having sacrificed everything to give my life to the poor.

One night, as Freddie was out in the kitchen preparing supper, I lay on my bed reading the *Catholic Worker*. Like a shaman, I continued to read the bones and twigs I kept tossing out before me, trying to discern what they were saying, what I should do. Maybe I would find the answer on these pages. Freddie had the radio on, something rare in our apartment. It was a familiar voice, but I mentally blocked my ears so that the voices of heroism and holiness could rise up from the *Worker* and bring my life back into focus. I wanted a line, a phrase to leap from those stark, unadorned pages, but that voice from the radio would not leave me alone. Was the song played more than once? The refrain crept into my consciousness, then pounded again and again, resounding down the long hallway, flinging open the door, assaulting me in my room as I lay there, defenseless.

Not Origen or Aquinas or Merton or Dorothy Day; not Matthew, Mark, Luke, or the lovely John. *Feed the hungry. Clothe the naked. Shelter the homeless.* The corporal works of mercy had been drowned out by Carole King. It's too late. It's too late. It's too late. It's too late. It's too late. The words echoed in my ears.

∞

I still try to pinpoint exactly what it was that caused me to leave the life I had sought so ardently and for which I had given up so much to live. Carole King? Freddie's mumblings? The smells? Grinding poverty, day in, day out? Angel's leg refusing to heal after all our good intentions and surgery? Or was it my visit a few weeks before to a second-floor apartment in a small house in Cobble Hill that underscored what a needy soul I was? A young college student, a CHIPS volunteer, had invited me over for coffee, and I went, knowing exactly what might happen. I never felt myself that attractive to women, and when she told me differently as we lay in a sun-drenched room on a blazingly white chenille bedspread, I didn't quite believe her. There before me was more woman than I had seen throughout my marriage, a marriage of nightgowns put on in closets, a marriage of quickly slipping our bodies between the sheets as if we should be embarrassed. I don't think J.C. and I ever saw each other, standing up, nude.

"Don't take this the wrong way," I sputtered. "This isn't a male chauvinist thing, okay? I'm not that kind of guy."

She said nothing.

"You have a beautiful body."

"Thank you."

I bit my lip, hoping it would pass. *Thank you.* I was done in by a simple "thank you" for an honest compliment on a subject off-limits for most of my life. I turned my head.

"It's all right, Paul. Believe me." Her voice was lost in the torrent of my tears that followed.

Should I have felt guilty for having sex outside the state of holy matrimony? Perhaps, but that subject was far from the contortions of my conscience. I had violated my calling, my self-imposed calling. I had disconnected my sexual urges, hadn't I, "offered them up" as we used to say, so that I could love all purely, without expecting anything in return? Without needing anything? Or so I tried to delude myself.

After that afternoon, I prayed, vowing to rededicate myself to the poor. But it was a hollow, forced prayer. Down deep, I knew it was already over. I spent less and less time at CHIPS. I avoided 80 Winthrop, sitting in Prospect Park and pretending I was reading. I drove my red, white, and blue Volkswagen van out to the Verrazano Narrows Bridge, crossed it, made a U-turn, and crossed it again. I lingered late over coffee at Snooky's on Seventh Avenue, a nocturnal creature in the window, right out of a Hopper painting. I walked through the Brooklyn Botanical Gardens, carefully reading each tiny sign in the midst of stubbles of brown deadness, killed by the winter, awaiting their spring. Something had died, and I couldn't fake it.

∞

On a blustery, cold, late spring day, Jacques helped me load my few possessions into the van and, as we stood at curbside on Winthrop Street, asked if I needed anything from the apartment to furnish my own. "Take whatever you need, Paaaul; we will find more," he said with that wonderful French lilt to his voice. "The bedspread; you must take eet with you," he said, turning to go back into the building. I took his arm.

"I think it needs to stay here, Jacques. I don't think . . . well, I don't think I'm the guy for it right now."

He looked up at me. He stood no more than five feet tall, so he looked up to most people. "Your face has ze look of a man who has failed. Someone who disappointed other people. Eet is not so. You will find ways to live with the Christ, new ways, fabulous ways that you cannot even imagine right now."

The world will never know of Jacques Travers. He will never be remembered in books of saints, his name never invoked in solemn tones in Masses on his feast day. But he will live in my heart forever, one of those anonymous saints who form the great "cloud of witnesses," without whom our world would not simply be poorer but would probably dissolve in sheer exhaustion at the venality of the rest of us. I have been blessed with many things in life, and to have known him was something that continues to shape my life. He knew how to be good in the simplest, happiest way. No choirs of angels, no drumroll. Just that impish grin. *Present.* Jacques Travers was present.

"I did disappoint you," I replied. "And the guys. I said I wanted to live this life. And I couldn't, Jacques. I just couldn't do it anymore." I had to look away; I was going to embarrass myself. I was ready to cry at all the wrong times, it seemed.

"You disappointed no one, *mon cher.* You served so well. Each day you were here, each smile you gave when you did not feel like smiling. You gave us so much. You must go where the heart leads. Not where a book tells you. Or someone wagging a finger to do theese or that. *Non.* God is a God of love. You cannot command love. It comes from here," he patted my chest. "Your heart ees good; listen to eet."

I held that little man in my arms for a long time until he gently pushed me away, giving me a little squeeze on the shoulder as he would often do to perk me up when I appeared down. "Au revoir for now. And come back to visit with us. Anytime. You are part of the family."

ABOVE: Margaret and Paul Wilkes on their wedding day, 1921. Aunt Rose is second from right.

RIGHT: This sweet little girl is me at about two years old, 1940. I didn't have a haircut until I was about three.

ABOVE: 11412 Forest Avenue, home to my father, mother, grandmother, and seven of us.

LEFT: In the backyard at Forest Avenue, 1942. Back row: my sisters, Frances, Pauline, Marion; Mom. Front row: Me (about four years old) and sister, Peg.

ABOVE: First Holy Communion, St. Benedict's, 1945. Father Leo at center. I am fourth from right, third row.

BELOW: My mother cuts the cake in honor of my Confirmation, 1950.

ABOVE: A noble man, my
father.

RIGHT: In the seventh grade,
wearing one of the few shirts
that wasn't a hand-me-down,
1951.

REPORT FOR SECOND QUARTER

PART I — SCHOLASTIC ACHIEVEMENT

PART II — CHRISTIAN CHARACTER DEVELOPMENT

ABOVE RIGHT: As is obvious, I wasn't the model Catholic school student.

ABOVE LEFT: Jergens lotion on my hair, ready for temptation at the CYO Canteen.

LEFT: Devotions were part of life at Cathedral Latin School, 1956.

LEFT: Marquette University graduation, 1960.

BELOW: Ltjg Wilkes, officer and gentleman, 1962.

ABOVE: *Boulder Daily Camera* reporter interviews Supreme Court Justice, Byron White, 1966.

BELOW: First book taking shape, 1970.

ABOVE: CHIPS, our storefront in Brooklyn, is born, 1973.

RIGHT: Jacques Travers, the saint I was privileged to know.

BELOW: The original Sag Harbor players, 1977. Wilfred Sheed, center, John Scanlon far right, standing. Me, the shirtless one, back row.

ABOVE: The "new man" in his Greenwich Village apartment, 1978.

RIGHT: In Jamaica, a few hours before I would be sobbing into the damp carpet.

ABOVE: The cruise to Bermuda with my brothers and sisters in 1978 should have been a reality check, but I went on with my alleged "new life."

RIGHT: Guests at one of my parties. Betty Friedan, right; Kurt Vonnegut; and Gene Young, my editor and the ex-wife of Gordon Parks, 1978.

BELOW: The famous suit for which I had a party.

ABOVE: My simple room at
Mount Saviour Monastery.

RIGHT: Tracy, the woman who
would save my life, and
Amanda Hanks, 1978.

ABOVE: An early date with Tracy; you can tell she is trying to figure out who is this guy looking off into the distance, 1978.

BELOW: Happy days with Tracy. We will break up later that week, 1980.

ABOVE: My hermit year, with friend, 1981.

RIGHT: With Father Mark Delary, Trappist monk and spiritual director, in the cornfield that will soon be overrun by raccoons.

RIGHT: Tracy, not exactly obeying the rules.

BELOW: Have I given this woman reason to worry? Our wedding day, 1982.

If the pope had only known what was in the book Father Greer brought him to bless, 1985.

ABOVE: Noah between us, Daniel, and the cuvacs, Hardwick, Massachusetts, 1989.

BELOW: The family today, Daniel on left, Noah on right.

PART FOUR

AS GOOD AS IT GETS?

19

ON THE PLAYING FIELDS OF THE HAMPTONS

WAS THIS A DREAM?

On a breezy, hot July day in the fashionable Hamptons, sixty miles and a thousand light years from 80 Winthrop Street in Brooklyn, here I am, incarnated as the New York Writer. The ball leaves the pitcher's hand. I crouch at home plate, a look of mock menace on my face, bat hovering over a bare shoulder. Curly hair, which looks devilishly unkempt but was in fact carefully sculpted for $75 in a chic Madison Avenue salon, spills onto my neck. Abercrombie and Fitch shorts cover the lower portion of my suntanned body, and underneath the well-tailored Egyptian cotton, the outline of a scant bathing suit breaks the flawless tone. My Brooks Brothers Golden Fleece Slim Fit Performance polo shirt rests on the arm of a very enthusiastic young woman on the sidelines. She is a *Time* researcher, graduate of a Seven Sisters school, with cascading blond hair, my date for the weekend.

On second base is someone new to the Hamptons scene this weekend. Fitted olive shorts and matching olive piping on the collar of her cream-colored pullover, very Talbot's of her. Excruciatingly long legs. She'll be at the beach at Amagansett this afternoon and maybe at the Scanlon's brunch tomorrow, or beachside near the Maidstone Club. There will be plenty of time to get to know her.

For this dreamworld I have traded in Peter Skelly's scab-crusted face, the homeless mother and her sniffling baby, the blind, the crippled, the deranged. I am now a charter and participating member of my generation's up-and-coming on the New York literary scene, just a short drive from Scotty Fitzgerald's fashionable, and just barely fictional, West Egg. My new companions are men and women in their twenties and thirties, now on a second or third media rung, but with eyes much further up the ladder. Walter Issacson, a barely adequate infielder, will go on to head Time, Inc., then write blockbusters on Franklin and Einstein. John Leo, once a leftie *Commonweal* Catholic, will continue his move to the right and become the intelligent darling of conservatives in his *U.S. News and World Report* column, eventually marrying the best of the women players, Jackie McCord, who will start up *Child* magazine and make them both millionaires many times over. Michael Fuchs, who always seems to be negotiating—and winning—even as he stands there at the plate, steely eyes demanding just the right pitch, will ride a tiny and then unknown startup called Home Box Office on to major media power. Ken Auletta, another writer, his friendliness tinged with just a hint of obsequiousness, cheers for whoever is at the plate. His wife, Amanda (aka Binky) Urban, the rising agent, stands on the sidelines, arms folded, her skin permanently tanned like a fine Coach handbag. Her eyes, like Fuchs's—for these two are an even more aggressive breed, with an even shorter attention span, within an already driven group of people—are always sizing up. In Binky's case, the few she selects will rise to the top of the heap, the 15 percent agent's commission she will extract but a small price to pay for what she will do for them. Then there's John Scanlon, the Friar Tuck of the game, whose counsel is sought by New York politicians and offered graciously to those who can pay handsomely. Nora and Delia Ephron, pale and thin and nervously laughing, will eventually leave the grimy East Coast for Hollywood. The game will draw Mort Zuckerman and Carl Bernstein and various other moguls and media stars of the moment. The Saturday morning softball game on a scraggly field behind Sag Harbor High School is considered the place to kick off a Hamptons weekend, where gossip is rich—and sometimes true—and word of the best parties is discreetly parceled out, but only to the wittiest, prettiest, and best connected.

I have arrived at a sort of fantastical summer camp for these toilers of word and image, who, for the other nine months in Manhattan, work the tips of their fingers to the bone. Here, no one has a past. Here, no one has an ex-wife. Here, no one has a worry that goes beyond what party to attend, no heartache greater than not being invited to the most desired of those events. A peaceable kingdom. A perfect world.

Back to home plate. The ball floats lazily through the hot morning air. Although I was hardly a great athlete in my younger years, here it is magically different. Everything is different; how could I be so blessed? Playing in the company of men and women who excel at other pursuits besides sports, I have emerged as somewhat of a star, a standout. On the field and off. Handsome, popular, and, despite my own insecurities, quite the lady's man. With a national television series in the works, a guest spot on *Good Morning America,* a lengthy interview with Terry Gross on NPR's

Fresh Air, dozens of stories nationwide, and a stylish Greenwich Village apartment, it seems only fitting. I swing, and what would be expected in this paradise found? The ball sails over the outfielders' heads. I clear the loaded bases at a leisurely jog and, as I come to home plate, jump upon it with a thump. Applause. Laughter. Another home run for the New York Writer—me.

Instead of fighting the traffic with the rest of the pedestrian weekenders, I leave my rented house in East Hampton just before noon on Monday morning. I stop for a drink at Bobby Van's in Bridgehampton. The usual crowd is there beneath the Tiffany lamps and old *Casablanca*-style fans. Truman Capote, the glory of *In Cold Blood* and the fabulous Black and White Ball now drowned in booze and relived in stories only the newest hangers-on haven't heard. So sweet and so lethal; how could one tiny body contain such balm and bile? His pale skin is stretched over cheekbones that threaten to poke through; he laughs uproariously, but his hollow eyes are sad. He extravagantly puffs away; one cigarette in his limp hand, two still burning in the ashtray. Next to him is James Jones, his tight little body withering under the assault of congestive heart failure, but still the soldier, standing there at the bar with a glass of warming seltzer, his gruff voice belying a gentle spirit within. Willie Morris, his tenure at *Harper's* magazine ended, his tiny bovine eyes sinking deeper into that florid face with each drink, his nature generous, his heart bitter at the New York that courted him so diligently and abandoned him so quickly.

I certainly am not yet worthy to sit in the pantheon with these writers, but there is a place for me on the temple steps. After all, Truman and I can trade stories of our writing. *Trying Out the Dream,* my foray into the little murders of suburbia, may not be the same in content as *In Cold Blood,* but the thrill of the reporter's hunt is similar. None of these men had any interest in the young women who came to Bobby Van's to sit among the famous, so there I prevailed. Moths drawn to the flame. Limitless, the possibilities.

∞

It did seem as though I were walking through a dream, so far from the musty sofa; from Freddie, Donald, and the Professor; from the acrid odor of cockroach droppings; from that rank, damp smell of poverty emanating from the people I lived with, slept alongside, and attempted to serve in Christlike love. So far from second-day bread and meat browned with age. So far from that red, white, and blue Volkswagen van, a life of voluntary poverty, a self-imposed vow of chastity.

So far from God.

In the Catholic tradition, there are many tales of dramatic conversion. St. Augustine turning away from the lush life of a decaying Roman society to become a towering theologian and apologist, his *Confessions* sounding the early rumble of Thomas Merton's life story sixteen centuries later. Saul of Tarsus, on the road to Damascus, ready to wreak havoc on the despicable Christians, blasted off his horse and into an awareness that the very God he hated was a God who loved and had great plans for him. Ignatius of Loyola, dissipated, affected and extravagant in hair and dress, consumed with the desire of winning glory on the battlefield, reconstituted into a soldier for God, whose followers, the Jesuits, would bring the face of Christ to millions and influence the very course of Western civilization. Charles de Foucauld, from champagne, foie gras, and the fleshpots of France to scurvy and isolation in the barren Sahara. Story after story of aimless, sinful lives transformed into lives of virtue.

My dramatic turnabout and latest persona were proving that conversion was a two-way street. I was traveling against the accepted traffic flow. I felt more like Peter, who ate elbow-to-elbow with Our Lord one night, professing his undying love, only to turn his back on him before the sun rose the next morning. Moral and spiritual whiplash. What was the Saint of Sixth Avenue doing, reincarnated as the Courtier of the Hamptons?

After leaving Jacques' community, I rented a modest fourth-floor walkup at 849 President Street, only a few blocks from CHIPS, still fooling myself that I would live parallel lives, working both on the television series and with the poor of Brooklyn. Frankly, I was a shell of a man, burned out physically, emotionally, spiritually. Only the adrenaline of the next crisis kept me going. I had lost something along the way. The picture in *Newsweek* was evidence of that. The missionary fervor and the sense of purpose and adventure that I felt so palpably when walking the streets of Brooklyn with Father Petroski had dissipated into lifeless and spiritless routine. The closeness to a God with whom I had felt such kinship had slowly faded, like taillights disappearing in a fog. I had tried so hard to maintain a spiritual life, praying and attending Mass daily, but my soul was not up to the hard work of confronting, day after day, the agonies and the needs of the poor, coupled with my own growing sense of loneliness. I did not have, as Tom Wolfe would later summarize what distinguished the astronauts, the "right stuff."

And then I was offered a New York I had only read about and imagined. I had an office at 90 Park Avenue, an unlimited expense account to travel the country, a clothes budget so I could have the "right look" on camera, a handsome, regular salary. Failing at shouldering the mantle of the "right stuff," I readily wrapped myself in the cheap garments comprised by the "right look." I emerged from three-and-a-half decades as a struggling, tepid, but acceptably good Christian, faithful husband, and street worker, where I abided by the rule of "if it feels good, you'd better *not* do it." I was catapulted into swinging, pre-AIDS New York in the mid-1970s, where that rule, in fact the whole rule book, had been tossed out the window. If it felt good, there was absolutely no reason *not* to do it. In fact, you should feel sort of bad if you didn't. The polarity of guilt had been reversed.

Such personal transformations don't happen overnight. Mine began innocently enough, in tears of both gratitude and remorse with that beautiful young woman on a chenille bedspread. Then there was the opera singer with exquisite taste suggested by Gerry Walker, my *Times* editor, to help me shop for the right wardrobe for my television series. First to Bonwit Teller for the beige tweed jacket, peach shirt, and beige silk tie and then home to her East Side apartment to try them on. And off. The public relations woman at Westinghouse Broadcasting suggested an after-work drink and then, after two Beefeater martinis, was ready for more than shop talk. Barry Jagoda's secretary was so taken with my kindness of bringing her a small bunch of daffodils that (as she would tell me later) she wanted to rip my clothes off as soon as I came to pick her up for our first date. We shopped Pottery Barn for dishes and flatware for my new life as a bachelor, then hurried back to her place for what I would, in the months ahead, delude myself into thinking was "instant intimacy."

> and you don't remember who you're talking to
> your concentration slips away . . .
>
> Don't sit cryin' for good times you had
> There's a girl right next to you
> and she's waiting for something to do
> Go ahead and love the one, love the one, love the one you're with
> love the one, love the one, love the one you're with
>
> Do it
> do it
> do it

I was a virtual teenager again. And this time—unlike during the 1950s and early 1960s in Cleveland—I was very much in the mainstream of 1970s America, with nothing to stop me from acting on every impulse. Love. Leave. Make up. Break up. All supposedly so I could be "true to myself." The new god had arrived. It was me.

The anthems of alienation and self-adoration spoke so logically and soothingly to my newly callow and hollow heart. Women would come, and they would go, I was assured by no less a prophetess than Stevie Nicks. And what of it? The rain, after all, would wash you clean. Stevie, thank you, thank you so much for these profound insights. They made no sense, of course, but I gustily blasted Fleetwood Mac songs from the tape deck of my sleek new car as I sped up FDR Drive, half tanked-up on the two or three vodkas or scotches I drank in preparation for still another ring on another apartment doorbell, another "Hey, [fill in the name], *great* to meet you!"

The Mommas and Papas; Crosby, Stills, Nash, and Young; the Jefferson Airplane—these troubadours of disaffection, self-absorption, and drugs were background echoes to my life. They provided my marching music. I was a little late for the revolution, but I was doing my best to make up for that sexually quiescent period, my sensual Dark Ages. Billie Joel comforted me that I was totally cool, totally right—after all, I was in a "New York state of mind." James Brown assured me, "I feel good!" Why? Because "I got you." And when things didn't go as well, the good den mother Linda Ronstadt was ready with consolation. Sure, I was cheated and mistreated, but when will I be loved? Poor me. Poor me.

The events occurring in those years that would shape America, the world, and the Catholic Church did not register as all that important. The hostages in Iran, Jim Jones and the Jonestown mass suicide, the execution of Gary Gilmore all passed before me like the illuminated, ephemeral news band on Times Square. Nothing touched me. Nothing affected me. And in the Catholic Church, with the declining years of Pope Paul VI, the march of Vatican II reform and openness that had so inflamed me and brought me back to the Church was losing momentum. With the election of a "smiling pope," the affable John Paul I, the promise of a return to the kind of Catholic Church that the beloved John XXIII had hoped for turned out to be short lived. He died thirty-three days after taking office. A new era would be ushered in with the charismatic but orthodox taskmaster, John Paul II.

Not that I would be thinking or writing about such things. My French-cut, nipped at the waist, Jean-Paul Germain blazer was far more important. Custom-made shirts became a necessity. I bought smooth calfskin boots and pelvis-hugging jeans so that I could disco with John Travolta–like agility and raw sexual power. Castoff clothes? *Moi?* One afternoon, walking with Barry Jagoda on Madison Avenue in search of a new suede jacket, I bridled at the fact that they were on sale at Abercrombie's, and promptly went down the street to Brooks Brothers, where I could pay full price. The more venal I was today, the more venal I could become tomorrow.

"In a dying culture, narcissism appears to embody—in the guise of personal 'growth' and 'awareness'—the highest attainment of spiritual enlightenment." How dare Christopher Lasch in *The Culture of Narcissism* write those words, dripping with irony? Marriage was out; "living together" was the only way, considered a noble and bold commitment in itself. Children? Really! We were all children, so how could we even think about bringing babies into our self-involved lives?

Names and phone numbers tumbled my way, as Catholic books once fell into Thomas Merton's hands, pressing him onward to conversion and eventually a monastic life. Just as inexorably, I raced in the opposite direction, not toward goodness, but away from it. It was as if the gears of the regulator that once controlled my conscience were stripped bare; nothing could stop or even slow my decent into hell. No instinct need be trammeled. For once in my life, I found myself one of the select on the supply side in the marketplace. I was an unattached, non-alimony-paying heterosexual with all his teeth and hair, pleasantly but not clinically neurotic, in his midthirties, and therefore eligible to date virtually any female between the age of high school graduation and that of the reception of her first Social Security check. I was considered a catch, as Merton had been in his early New York days, "a popular date."

At parties I would survey the women present and, like a sultan assessing his harem, select this one for tonight, that one for tomorrow, and place the rest on stand-by status, their phone numbers obtained. One afternoon, riding on a city bus, I spied an attractive woman, leaped off the bus, and told her we simply had to meet. There was something about her, I professed, so innocently, with such calculation. There was "something" about so many.

And before I knew what was happening to me, I was hooked. I had missed the dawning of the sexual revolution in Boulder. At Columbia, during that year when free love was in the air, I was the clueless guy with Vitalis on my slicked-down hair.

Born into a deep, unquestioning Catholic faith in Depression-era America, growing up in the sacrificing mentality of World War II, coming into adulthood in the conformist Silent Fifties, loveless and luckless as an undergraduate, then hermetically sealed in the smug cocoon of a stylized marriage as the fury of the sixties swept across the globe, I emerged to find that the world had completely changed. The Age of Aquarius had dawned. The seeds from the so-called Summer of Love in 1967 in San Francisco had wafted across America to find fertile soil in the cement and asphalt canyons of New York. Once I woke up, I found a sexual Disneyland, where fantasy became reality, where no one, if he so chose, ever had to grow up.

Something called Open Marriage was solemnly proclaimed "not a replacement, but an enhancement of marriage," thus canonizing marital infidelity. At Plato's Retreat, wrapped in a towel, a patron could stroll about the dimly lit basement of the Ansonia Hotel on the Upper West Side, choose a partner, have sex, and casually move on as if he or she had just inserted coins into a slot at the Horn and Hardart Automat for a serving of macaroni and cheese or a bologna sandwich. Two times, four? A dozen? Up to you if you had the stamina. The pill prevented, and penicillin cured. Sex was blame free, name free, attachment free. Plato's Retreat only routinized and commercialized what was happening in bedrooms, living rooms, kitchens, and hallways, on couches, beds and carpets, even cool tile, all over the city. Hannah Arendt talked of the "banality of evil" in Hitler's Germany. Seventies New York conspired to make the banality of casual sex a high calling. Singles bars were called meat markets—or meet markets, if you needed a sanitized spelling.

I had purchased a co-op apartment in the Peter Warren, a boxy, somewhat prosaic post–World War II building of red brick, at 45 West Tenth Street, between Fifth and Sixth avenues. It was a prime location, the heart of Greenwich Village. As I raised the blinds, I looked out over magnificent brownstones once occupied by Mark Twain, Edward Albee, Hart Crane, and Sinclair Lewis. I was certainly in the right company, at least; the spirits of the greats were here. And sunshine, that most precious of Manhattan commodities, flooded through a wall of windows into my apartment, 3-F, drenching the dining alcove with a soft yellow glow each morning as I sat there at a marble table, in a low-slung white leather chair, reading my *New York Times*. A Pavoni espresso machine produced excellent cappuccino, the Harmon Kardon stereo system provided perfect sound, the hardwood floors glistened. In the bedroom, a spacious queen-size bed was covered with a Marimekko print throw, the ultimate contemporary statement. And, along with sunshine above ground, below ground was a true Manhattan treasure. Accessible by elevator just outside the apartment's door—a crucial and strategic point—my new car awaited me in the parking garage. Like Batman, I was able to swoop in and out, with barely a notice. It was a single man's dream.

The Village was a wonderful place in those days, not yet overrun by people so rich that they hired out laundry, shopping, and dog walking, and even had their morning latte delivered. I loved to stroll those narrow, crowded streets, somehow convincing myself that the weary wanderer had finally found a true home. I strolled down to Puerto Rico Trading for my coffee beans, browsed at the legendary Eighth Avenue Bookshop, stopped at Zito's bakery for its luscious crusty bread and perhaps a chance encounter with Frank Sinatra, a good Italian boy and loyal customer. To Faicco's pork store for a ring of imported salsiccia; Murray's for St. André triple crème cheese. To the Jefferson Market or Balducci's for any vegetable or fruit I fancied, the season be damned. To the tiny shop off Bleecker for Roger Gallet sandalwood soap—I used no other. No more secondhand food, no more secondhand life. And all those wonderful smells.

On the corner of Waverly Place and Sixth Avenue, there was an odd building I often passed. Brilliant white Greek Revival columns rose up sublimely from the sidewalk to dissolve softly in the shadows of a portico. A shiny, black-painted wrought-iron fence was designed not to defy the clean lines of the building, yet was sturdy enough to keep it from defilement. It was several months and many passes-by—daytime and night, sober and not, alone or hand in hand with the lady of the moment—before I finally acknowledged that it was a Catholic church, St. Joseph's. And afterwards, in a conditioned reflex that even my headlong plunge into hedonism couldn't control, I would make the sign of the cross as I passed. It was never very obvious, more like swatting a pesky fly that buzzed to my forehead, chest, left shoulder and right. I'm sure no one knew. And I surely didn't want the ever-changing companion to know that en route to my apartment and that queen-size bed, this man had God on his mind.

My television series, a very occasional magazine article, and a feckless syndicated magazine series on singles life in New York kept me in a social world where the invitations, the possibilities multiplied exponentially. I even hosted my own television morning talk show for a summer in Baltimore, and usually chose to have the prettiest guest, preferably from New York, as my last on Friday morning, so we might travel back to New York together. With the aid of various mind-altering substances, unspeakable acts were staged during that five-hour drive.

I could have gone to a private party, book signing, art opening, or premiere every night, if I so chose. Sometimes there were two or three events an evening, allowing me to forage, as if at a sumptuous smorgasbord. On one night, you might find me in a Plaza Hotel suite with my friends Albert and David Maysles, the documentarians who shot an episode of my *Six American Families* television series, talking to tiny Mick Jagger, a flowered Chinese scarf trailing from his neck and toothy smile at the ready. I stood by knowingly at the PEN Center, as Jerzy Kosinski, his shock of hair piled atop his head, held court about the movie version of *Being There,* meanwhile doing his own foraging for new and kinky possibilities. I winked at Kurt Vonnegut in a sprawling penthouse apartment overlooking Central Park as he bemusedly peered over the top of his spectacles, nodding drunkenly, not hearing a word as a Berkeley literature exegete explained the symbolism in *Slaughterhouse-Five*. I sat across the table from Betty Friedan as she carried on a nonstop monologue on the role of women, and watched her face harden as she told how her husband's physical abuse rose right along with the ranking of *The Feminine Mystique* on the best-seller list.

But my favorite celebrity was a fellow Slovak, who loved this merry-go-round as much as I did. I saw him all the time, party after party. Andrew Warhola also had airbrushed his ethnicity, shortening his first name and dropping the *a* in the second. He would stand motionless, silent, with his corn-silk white hair and vague, completely undiscerning look. His Velvet Underground entourage—crimson-lipped, waiflike boys and girls, nipples startlingly peeking out of knit shirts, eyeliner neither reserved for nor rationed to either sex—giggled at just about everything, having come fortified with the best drugs the city had to offer. Like Kosinski, Warhol "loved to watch."

It was all going so swimmingly.

∞

I took a week off—a week *off* . . . from what?—and flew to Negril, a beach resort in Jamaica. I was four days and two women into my time there when it happened.

I had spent the day sunbathing and drinking at the pool, then was to go on to cocktails at the promontory overlooking the Caribbean. It was a perfect sunset, here on the westernmost tip of the island, a brilliant red ball ever so slowly falling into the blue water, a flash of light marking its nod to the day just past. I was to join a group of people for dinner, including both those women already obliged and those yet to be.

I came out of the shower and splashed on some Yves St. Laurent aftershave. I walked out into the sitting room, with its windows overlooking the beach, now bathed in the gentle light of a new moon. I turned to put on some clothes, but never made it to the closet. My knees suddenly buckled beneath me. I dropped to the ground. The next thing I knew, my face was pressed to the carpeting. No longer was my perfect world filled with the scent of blossoms that floated through the night air, or of my expensive aftershave, but the rank, putrid smell of damp, musty carpet. The rank, putrid smell of my life. How long I was there, I can't remember. I sobbed until the back of my throat ached. The utter hollowness of it all enveloped me, suffocating, searing, awful. I couldn't go anywhere. I didn't want even to be seen.

I crawled into bed, and left on the first plane the next morning.

20

THE PERFECT
GIRL FOR YOU

WAS THIS YET ANOTHER DREAM?

To the crowded room at a well-appointed reception at the Beverly Hills Wilshire Hotel, the booming, resonant voice of none other than Atticus Finch intones, "This impressive young man has changed the way we will look at the American family. What respect he has for those who have entrusted themselves to his care." I am seated nearby, my eyes are cast down, searching my folded hands. It is too great an honor, to be spoken of in words like these, from this iconic figure, in his deep, commanding voice. He goes on. "We owe him a great debt of gratitude for putting before us this mirror of who we are as an American people. It gives me great pleasure to introduce to you . . . Mr. Paul Wilkes." Applause. All rise to their feet. Wearing the excellent Bonwit Teller tweed jacket, the peach checked shirt and understated gold silk tie, I rise from my seat slowly, almost sheepishly, as if I hadn't expected this. My introducer smiles warmly as he shakes my hand and takes my elbow, gently encouraging me toward the microphone.

This evening, although Gregory Peck may look every bit like Atticus Finch, the righteous lawyer in *To Kill a Mockingbird*, the symbol of honesty and integrity, he and I share a secret. He is none of that. As the cold salmon and glasses of champagne on silvery trays are passed by white-gloved waiters, and fawning fans are pressing nearby to have their picture taken, he is simply earning his keep as the shill for an insurance company. Gregory Peck has also strayed from his high vocation and taken the easy path, praising shows he probably has not seen, mouthing words written by the PR department of my sponsor. *Six American Families,* my television series, was launched.

∞

Even after my Negril breakdown, I refused to take stock of what was happening to me, of the person I had become. As my social calendar was stuffed with events, openings, and parties to celebrate just about anything, I contributed in turn, hosting a few of my own gatherings in my very showable Greenwich Village apartment, doing my best to deepen the shallowness of my life. My thirty-eighth birthday party was at once the highest point of my "standing" in New York circles and one of those moments where an ominous gong should have sounded, or a bolt of lightning pierced that wall of glass overlooking magical Tenth Street and struck me dead. The guest list was impressive that night. Kurt Vonnegut and Jill Kremetz were there; Betty Friedan; my laconic but high-powered agent, Theron Raines, and his wife, Joan; Gordon Parks's ex-wife, Gene Young, who was my editor on *Trying Out the Dream,* the book that catapulted me to a degree of national prominence. Also in attendance were a few of my women friends. I opened my presents, the usual assortment of bottles of wine and popular books, none of which made anything close to a personal statement about giver or recipient. I offered a quick retort or dollop of repartee for each. I purposely mangled the pronunciation of a well-known French vineyard; I pulled a funny line from a recent *Times* review on the book cradled in my hand. How *en pointe* I could be. The last present awaited, this one carefully wrapped by an actual person, not a clerk. As if it were an Academy Award envelope, I ceremoniously removed the satin ribbon and peeled back the Degas-print paper. It was a baseball jersey, personalized. It was from Pamela, one of the ladies of the Hamptons summer past. How considerate of her. A huge 38 was emblazoned on the back. Above it, instead of my name, was another. "Scumbag." At first there was silence. Then an outburst of laughter. What a wonderful touch. Pam-e-la! Touché! How unique.

Scumbag, slang for a condom. A used condom.

I had left friends and family behind, all of life's connective and corrective tissue. There was no one who could confront me with who I was or remind me that I had been an entirely different person not that long before. I did sometimes go to Mass on Sundays, a habit engrained from my past that even this life couldn't break entirely, but I usually sat numbly in a back pew. Otherwise, my prayer life was nonexistent, except for fleeting, panicky incantations when I was drunk and afraid I was going to get in an accident, or when I woke up in a state of hungover dissipation and cried to heaven either to let me die immediately or to heal me quickly. In therapy, I occasionally noticed a furrow in Barbara Koltuv's brow, but the nature of psychoanalysis being what it is, the analysand, not the analyst, makes the value judgments. I careened through increasingly frightening intersections of God's grace and my wayward life, but nothing stopped me, or even slowed me down.

Things took on an even more ominous cast, strangely enough, at the very height of what would be fleeting prominence, when I went on a multicity tour for *Six American Families*. In Pittsburgh, I was promised a busy three days, with a round of newspaper interviews and talk show appearances. When I got there, picked up by a limousine at the airport, I was met by an obviously frightened junior production assistant from the local Westinghouse television station. I was presented with three heavy velum sheets of an itinerary that actually added up to nothing. Visits with the station's advertising department, lunch with some local writers' group, hastily arranged. A tour of the zoo. Desultory dinners with station interns. Some public relations "handler" had obviously not heard Gregory Peck's encomium and had dropped the ball.

I drank myself into oblivion each night I was there, and by the time I was limoed back to the airport at the end of the visit, I had completely lost my mental moorings. I remember trying to calm myself and focus on what people were saying. I couldn't even tell the agent at the counter where I was going. With ticket in hand—Baltimore—for some reason I left the terminal and started walking on the grass median out of the airport. Baltimore couldn't be that far away, and it was a pleasant day. Only an alarmed airport policeman saved me from getting killed. I lit a cigarette, took a few drags, put it out and lit another. The cavernous terminal was a hall of mirrors and echoes, like a carnival funhouse. People walking toward me grew to monstrous heights, then shrunk to pygmy size. Employees behind fast-food counters were watching my every move. The voice announcing flight arrivals and departures screeched at me in deafening waves. I ordered a double Rob Roy at the bar, then a second before I turned to straight scotch. I stumbled onto my plane only to be told it was the wrong one.

In the Navy aboard USS *Power*, we relied on the distant early warning (DEW) line to protect us from danger. DEW was a series of strategically positioned radar stations that scanned the arctic skies for signs of imminent danger coming from our nemesis at the time, the Russians. There was plenty of present danger with the way I was living, but my DEW system was obviously malfunctioning. I got off the plane in Baltimore, where I had once been a faithful married man and an idealistic young reporter for the *Sun*.

Dick Williams, my voluble classmate at Columbia journalism school, was the news director at one of the Baltimore television stations that had scheduled me for an appearance. Dick and I, both graduates of Catholic colleges, had been of one political mind during the early part of my time at Columbia, proving our righteousness and patriotism by throwing eggs at that ragtag group of protesting Vietnam veterans. Dick's politics had remained stably conservative since then, whereas mine had veered to the left; nonetheless we remained friends. A friend of his—Ron Kershaw, a junk-food-eating, alcoholic, TV news genius—happened to be in town. The last time I had seen Kershaw was at the Philadelphia apartment of his old girlfriend, Jessica Savitch, who would meteorically rise at NBC before she died some five years later when her Mercedes missed a turn leaving a restaurant and plunged into a ditch. That night I was with her and Kershaw, there was enough cocaine on her living room coffee table to get the entire City of Brotherly Love high. Ron and I howled about that evening, and he wolfed down a dozen Hostess Twinkies within five minutes to justify his reputation. As we traded stories before the show, trying to out-dissolute each other, we smoked a prodigious amount of marijuana. I remember little of that show, but before I went on, I went into the station manager's office and, for a joke, had them bring in the local weatherman. He was black and handsome, a rising star in this niche of programming. Gravely, I told him I was "from corporate," 90 Park in New York. "We" were profoundly disappointed in his on-air appearance and ratings. He was fired. His face went slack; he believed me. Kershaw and I howled again. "Gotcha!"

The videotape recording of the talk show is a harrowing visit with an insane man. There I am, eyes red and glassy, slouched in a chair wearing a Baltimore Orioles baseball jersey that I had somehow stolen from one of the offices. I mumble answers to questions, answers that make absolutely no sense. I laugh at my own answers. No one else does. All the signs were there that I was losing my mind. Still I marched on. The next morning I was on a plane for my last stop, Boston.

OO

If there were party nights, television appearances, dates, Hamptons weekends, hobnobbing with celebrities, and an address book filled with an ever-changing roster of women, there was another, hidden part of my life. I may leave the impression that I was always on my way to or from somewhere or something, with someone fabulous, but there were many more times that I felt overwhelmingly alone and lost. Had an anthropologist made even a cursory examination of the contents of my nightstand, he would have easily unearthed a truer picture of my life. On its polished mahogany top, next to a digital clock, whose face I stared at too many nights as one minute painfully hesitated before going on to the next, usually sat a glass or two. If there were two, one would have a lipstick imprint. There would be an ashtray, with a roach or two. But if the anthropologist dug deeper, he would unearth more: a dream notebook, with reoccurring themes of my appearing in public in rags or no clothes at all. Copies of *The Secret Strength of Depression* and Karen Horney's classic, *Neurosis and Human Growth,* the chapter on "The Tyranny of the Should" well underlined. And a small, plastic pharmacy bottle. "Librium. 10 mg. Take as needed." At the bottom of the drawer he would find a new copy of *The Asian Journal of Thomas Merton,* with the sales receipt at page 4, an indication of how far this wasted reader had been brave enough to travel.

I could usually stay ahead of that overpowering sense of loneliness during the day. There was work on the television series, the usual household chores, trips to Dr. Koltuv, and, of course, the complicated arrangements required by my social schedule. The sense of spiritual barrenness only got worse as the months wore on, even as I valiantly tried to schedule every night. After I had eaten supper—which I often did at home, alone—the demons, who had been cannily observing my frantic daytime efforts to convince myself that I was living a perfectly normal life, came to visit. There was no worse time than what I began to call the "hungry hours," from about seven to ten o'clock. I probably had had a few drinks by then, but I knew that if I went to bed I would wake up at two or three. I would try reading. I'd flick on the television set. Nothing held my attention. And then, in a burst, as if a fire alarm had sounded, I would splash on some cologne, grab a jacket, and bolt out the door.

Anything, it seemed, would do. Maybe it was some half-baked event I'd read about in the *Village Voice.* Or an art opening, store opening, a New School lecture like "Looking at Cinema in a New Way" or "The Principles of Biofeedback." Or, if it was the right night of the week, I would descend, like Batman, into the garage and then streak up to the Fourth Unitarian Universalist Church on Central Park West and West Seventy-sixth Street. This church knew exactly how to keep their doors open and budget balanced, through what was euphemistically called "adult education." The courses offered had ingenious titles that at first glance sounded interesting enough, but most of us who attended didn't base our choices on course content. We were the hunter-gatherers in the sexual jungle of New York, not intellectually curious night students. It was common knowledge that Fourth Unitarian provided a somewhat safe, somewhat respectable place to efficiently get laid. If the title sounded as if it would attract women, men signed up. "Love in the Age of Non-Commitment" and "Finding the Inner You" were sure bets.

As a last resort, I would stroll over to Benchley's, a bar on a corner of Hudson and Tenth, and drink away the evening, my standards for companionship going down as my alcohol level rose. If my barstool perch at Benchley's proved not the best vantage point, there were always the Village streets. It was only later in my life that I would come to appreciate the searing wisdom of the Psalms, but how accurately Psalm 88 applied to me on those nights:

> Friend and neighbor you have taken away
> My one companion is darkness

I walked about the Village in darkness, not so fast that I seemed in a hurry to get somewhere, nor so slowly that I looked like someone you wanted to avoid. On my rounds, women with children, older women, or very young girls could pass without my even registering them. My brain was disciplined, my eyes tightly focused. Yet if I were to say I was just looking for sex, I would be lying. That was the path sometimes taken, but this kind of sex was a dead end, and by now I knew it. If I could have seen more clearly then, I would have realized I was looking for so much more. Not for another diversion, another playmate in New York's sexual sandbox, but for that "other half" that Plato said every human being seeks. I was aching to meet someone with whom I shared true common ground, my old values, not these that I seemed not only to embrace but to embody. I wanted to sit over an espresso at Le Figaro, that wonderful café at MacDougal and Bleecker, and talk about Thomas Merton or Charles de Foucauld. I wanted to be with someone who might not have totally understood, but would have some inkling why I had started CHIPS and lived at 80 Winthrop. Someone who could talk about God without that sanctimonious, bloodless tone that J.C. was so good at. Someone who knew that life was an awful rowing toward God and that sometimes your boat simply got swamped. I wanted someone to see through this silly mask I was wearing, rip it off in fact, and reveal the person beneath: a person who still had at least the potential to be good and decent and kind. A person with whom she wanted to share not just a bed, but a life.

Out of the shadows of the side streets I would come, drawn to the main streets and traffic like a moth seeking the light of a flame. Along Bleecker or West Eighth Street or Sixth Avenue, lights from the businesses tantalizingly illuminated the faces of fast-walking Village women as I came toward them. In those precious few seconds, over and over again, I was looking for any sign—the arch of an eyebrow; a certain sway of the hip; thrown-back, confident shoulders; the gentle swell of breasts, large or small; creamy skin; just the right shade of lipstick; a well-cut coat or skirt—some admittedly surface attribute that would have deep metaphysical meaning and serve as a sign for me to do something, anything, to meet that person, right then. I fantasized that she and I would simultaneously stop at the same window, laugh at the coincidence, then start a conversation that would end up at that table at Le Figaro. I know I was half mad, but I was looking for divine intervention as I prowled the streets of New York. A miracle. Face after face, shape after shape approached me and swept by. With each, I felt first the flicker of yearning for what might be, then the terrible, sinking feeling of what was. I would be on these streets forever, condemned to be the single man's Sisyphus, pushing my hopes and desires up this mountain, only to be crushed time and again by the boulder of my own making.

Another man walking his own lonesome streets had a very different kind of experience. Thomas Merton, at the corner of Fourth and Walnut in Louisville, wrote in *Conjectures of a Guilty Bystander:*

> I was suddenly overwhelmed with the realization that I loved all these people, that they were mine and I was theirs, that we could not be alien to one another even though we were total strangers. I have the immense joy of being human, a member of the race in which God himself became incarnate. The sorrows and stupidities of the human condition can no longer overwhelm me, now that I realize what we all are. If only everybody could realize this! But it cannot be explained. There is no way of telling people that they are all walking around shining like the sun.

I had it all backward, didn't I? Love *me*. See *me*. Understand *me*. Me, me, and me. My interior monologue featured a man who said he wanted to share his life, but I was still a taker, not yet a partner. Such words and thoughts were only a thin veil over a gaping moral chasm.

One painfully lonely night, as I walked down Sixth Avenue, past Eighth Street, over the tops of the trees I saw a strange glow in the distance. For some reason I was drawn toward it, having nowhere in particular to go anyhow. It was higher than lights from a business, yet not as high as a streetlight, and not the more familiar yellowish light from an apartment window. There was a certain unnatural but diffused brilliance about it, a hazy but pure whiteness. Finally, as I peered into the distance, I could barely make out a stark, small cross barely visible against the night sky and the darkened, fluted pillars outlined against a vast expanse of white that was the portico of St. Joseph's Church. I crossed the street. A horn blared. I didn't hesitate. I was almost run over.

St. Joseph's was one of the mother churches of New York, built in 1833 in the midst of a bustling and very Protestant neighborhood, a symbol that Catholicism and immigrant Catholics might also have a place in the city. It was here in 1918 that another weary pilgrim came to exactly the spot where I was standing. Dorothy Day's life was also a mess. A tortured love affair was finally over, but she was pregnant. Almost without thinking, she had an abortion. She felt her life was meaningless, aimless. But beyond those tall, white, wooden doors that shone so brilliantly on this darkened stretch of Sixth Avenue, she found peace. I had been inside St. Joseph's a few times, for Mass. That night I felt the overpowering need to sit in one of those straight-backed pews and take in the clean, almost Puritan lines of the church. Yes, that was exactly what I had to do. Could I once again know the mysterious God whose presence I felt so palpably in such different ways in St. Benedict's in Cleveland, the dental school chapel in Milwaukee, the elegant St. Peter's in Rome, the prosaic auditorium of Brooklyn's St. Francis Xavier? I needed to know that the prodigal son could come home again, even after all he had done.

Step by tentative step, as if the roar of angry God—a God refusing to buy my facile arguments or petty rationalizations—could erupt at any moment, I came closer. Soon I was bathed in the glow of that light. Above the large doors was a forlorn statue of St. Joseph, his shoulders encrusted with the city's dirt and pigeon droppings, his eyes cast down. He looked so weary from watching over this busy street. He knew the secrets of all of us who passed by. The doors beneath this good and patient man were a brilliant white, beckoning, no more than a few yards away. I reached to open the wrought-iron gate. I didn't know how to pray anymore. I didn't know what to pray for. What would I do inside? I just needed a place to rest, a place to calm my mind so that I could get off the treadmill of my life. My hand closed around the cold metal, and I pulled.

The gate was locked.

My salvation was not going to come merely on the strength of an emotional, spur-of-the-moment midnight plea.

I shoved my hands into my pockets and headed back up Sixth Avenue toward the apartment. When I got to 45 West Tenth, I looked up at the lights of my own building. There he stood, like a statue in the second-floor window, bathed in his own soft glow. I never knew his name, but he was legendary in the building. Each night he took up his post, bare-chested and with a towel draped around his hips, waving to any man with whom he could make eye contact. To come up and see him. He waved to me, moving closer to the window. His bulging towel pressed against the windowpane.

I sensed it that night, but I know it for certain now. As disgusting as he was, we were not that much different. I was a man in exile from himself. In exile from God. Seeking whatever pleasure the moment could offer.

∞

It wasn't that my new life was the result of a conscious decision, the classic "I was a good Catholic boy, and now I want to be very bad and do everything I ever wanted to do." No. Rather, I conveniently put my conscience on hold. Or tried to. And, except for those awful times when I could no longer maintain the charade and broke down, I was successful. After all, I kept on rationalizing, I wasn't such a bad guy. I never forced myself on women. My various women friends could bring me home to meet the parents or introduce me to friends. I could talk about growing up in a family of seven with a $41 monthly house payment on the East Side of Cleveland or having lunch with a celebrity at La Grenouille. Really, you could take me anywhere, I said as I kept on trying to convince myself and Dr. Koltuv.

But, of course, something was very, very wrong. I did not kill in war or steal in everyday life, but now, given the opportunity, I discovered my capacity for sin. To be alienated from God. To place myself outside his care. Exiled, hidden from his loving gaze. We all have the capacity, and I was discovering how little it took to unleash it. It lays dormant in all of us—as does grace—awaiting its moment.

It might be offered in my defense that I was living in the 1970s, an adulterous, pleasure-seeking age. Bonhoeffer talked of "cheap grace"; mine was no more than a cheap excuse. So the pack of mad dogs was running; did I have to run along or, at times, even lead the pack? The adrenaline rush, the frenzy of a new adventure, a new conquest. And with each new excitement came the crushing disappointment that it not only had failed to bring anything close to true satisfaction but also had plunged me ever deeper into a kind of darkness I had never experienced before.

I remember one morning vividly. It was just after eight, and I was coming out of an apartment building near the Queen's Mid-Town Tunnel. I passed the doorman, who didn't even meet my eyes. He may not have known what apartment I was coming from, but my wrinkled shirt, unshaven face, uncombed hair, and vacant look marked me as a guest who had not planned to spend the night. He had seen my kind before. When I walked out onto the sidewalk, my unhurried step sluggishly falling behind people who actually had some purpose in their day, the smell of the city rose up to remind me of who I was.

A blast of choking, acrid car exhaust roiled out from a rotted, rattling muffler on a rusted and graffiti-covered truck that sped by. My eyes burned, and my nasal passages recoiled. The air was cool that morning, but heavy with humidity and with the odor of every Szechwan dish, dry cleaner load, pizza, and leftover beer of the night before. Leftover smells for a leftover man. For an instant, I held my breath as if I could escape. I ducked my face inside my new London Fog trench coat. The sweet and gentle aroma of my Guerlain Vetiver was so graciously and solicitously there to meet me, only to be enfolded in turn by the redolence of her Hermès. These almost supernatural smells could not have been wrung from mere buds or flowers. Once again, I had fended off the unpleasantness of the present moment.

But deeper, deeper within, there was still myself. Rising up like vengeance from hell to overwhelm these venal vapors, it came: the sourness of her own lower body and my own. I jerked my head out of the supposed sanctuary of my trench coat. I put my hand to my mouth as if someone were about to hit me. I walked faster now. The clotted slime of the gutter, held at bay in the cooler night air, was quickly warming, producing gagging fumes. I walked still faster, trying to outrun the decaying smell of my dying soul.

OO

While I was in Boston for my final stop on the *Six American Families* publicity tour, the Westinghouse station's publicity director, Linda Comstock, noting that I was single, said, "I've got someone you've absolutely got to meet back in New York. The perfect girl for you." I penciled in the name. The following week, I followed up to find that Cathy George was a gorgeous, neurotic, Japanese-Jewish woman who obviously was looking for a much bigger and richer catch than I (and which eventually would be hers). We went out a few times and then lost touch. I was surprised in October 1978 to get a call from her, inviting me to a Halloween party at her East Side apartment.

"I've got the perfect girl for you; do try to make it," she said.

"Didn't I hear this before? About you?"

"Hush. Just come; you'll see. This is the one for you."

I dutifully penciled in time and date—without a name. Cathy had failed to tell me who this perfect girl was.

21

TRACY

IT WASN'T REALLY LOVE AT FIRST SIGHT. IT WAS LUST. I joke about it to
this day, but it happens to be true.

At the epochal Halloween party, I was decked out in my nattily nipped-
at-waist, midnight blue blazer; tailor-made, monogrammed mauve shirt;
well-cut jeans; and a pair of custom-made, oh-so-supple, John Travolta
Saturday Night Fever shoes. And there she was, whirling about on the
smooth parquet floor of Cathy George's very uptown East Side apartment. The "perfect woman" had a great, alive face; radiant skin; lipstick
just the right crimson shade applied to luscious, very kissable lips. Try as
I might to make chitchat with other guests, I couldn't keep my eyes off
her form-fitting slacks as she twirled around and around to the thumping
beat of whatever was that moment's hottest disco hit.

Her name was Tracy Gochberg; she worked in advertising. I would find
out only later, but Cathy George had made the same "perfect girl" pitch
to two of us, so Barry Fox, whom I knew from the Hamptons summers,
was also interested. Tracy had come with a date, so she must have had her
hands full that night, juggling the attentions of three of us. I danced a few
times with her, probably making inane patter over the many decibels of
music and the voices of a couple dozen ever more imbibed, boisterous
partygoers.

When I got home early the next morning, I stopped just inside my
apartment door, closed it quietly behind me, and leaned my head back.
I peered past my darkened living room, past the glassy leaves of my schef-
flera plant, to the flood of streetlight that suffused my small dining area.
To the marble table, glistening and bare, to the leather chairs on either
side. They stood there so alertly, with their elegant, designer profile and
clean-cut chrome lines. So starkly alone. So empty. I went to the window
and looked out onto West Tenth Street. What was it about her? Why was
I standing here dumbly, staring out the window?

I didn't get Tracy's telephone number, but remembered she'd said she lived in the Village, and behold, there she was in the telephone book. At eight o'clock Sunday morning I rang her up, certainly not very New York of me. Little did I know that only a few feet from where she picked up the phone was her date from last night. I invited her over for coffee. She lived over on Jane Street, so we were only a few blocks apart. Tracy gave said sleeping date a lame excuse that she had to visit a sick friend (how ironic; I *was* kind of sick) and, with the Sunday *New York Times* tucked under her arm, appeared at my door an hour later.

I brewed a frothy cup of cappuccino on the Pavoni and topped it off with a sprinkle of cinnamon, a touch that got her thinking, I would later find out, that here was a guy with some domesticity. If New York women (they of the three containers of Dannon yogurt and a souring quart of skim milk in the refrigerator) were hardly Betty Crockers, New York men were not exactly known for well-provisioned kitchens or culinary prowess. As she perched cross-legged on my low-slung, pillowed couch, chatting on—and God Almighty, this woman could go on—my initial lust for Ms. Gochberg mutated to another emotion. In my life of passionate pursuits, it was a rather weak and strange emotion, more a gentle wave than the usual tsunami. I *liked* her. I really liked her. What was it? Her enthusiasm, energy, absolute lack of guile? Her streak of independence born of virtually raising herself?

Her father, Larry, was from an Orthodox Jewish shopkeeper family; Virginia, her mother, a proper Episcopalian whose father was a lawyer. Tracy was only two when the love match between two disparate religious worlds and cultures imploded. She was raised by her mother, loving and warm, but ineffectual and alcoholic, and a strong-willed grandmother who took her in after she had been kicked out of a very good and expensive boarding school ("for rebellious kids like me that neither parent wanted or could cope with"). She had been raised an Episcopalian, but when she wanted to find a church home in New York after many years away, she found the faux-British accents of the Episcopal pastors more than she could handle and had wandered into a small church on Sixth Avenue. Unbeknownst to this occasional and probably hungover visitor, she had been going to Mass at St. Joseph's. The first Sunday she went there, the priest encouraged the worshippers to sign a petition against nuclear proliferation. She liked the mix: mumbling homeless men and white-glove-wearing lace-curtain Irish ladies.

As we sipped on a second cappuccino and nibbled some biscotti, we quickly broke through the surface chatter of jobs and rent and parties, boring into the murkier strata beneath: where we each came from; our winding, rocky paths. I touched but lightly on the marriage to J.C., my exodus to CHIPS, the days at 80 Winthrop with Jacques. I didn't want to frighten her off. I found myself talking and even listening less, just watching her. She was only inches from me and smelled wonderful—Parfums Grès' intoxicating Cabochard, I would later find out. Behind her horn-rimmed glasses, she was beautiful in a girl-next-door yet very New York way, with fabulous eye makeup—a deep blue blush on her lids, dark and perfectly segmented lashes. (My eyes kept going to hers; I always did admire great makeup, well applied.)

It was nearing noon, and I knew exactly what I wanted.

I wanted Tracy to leave.

To write a crisp ending to a wonderful opening chapter. Nothing, no kiss, nothing at all that could possibly lead where I had been before and which too often ended in the same, unsatisfying way. Wednesday night for a movie? She said yes.

Was our first date the expression of a death wish? Or was I hanging out a warning sign? The opening scene of the movie we saw, François Truffaut's *The Man Who Loved Women,* is a slow pan, at the level of an open grave, of pair after pair of gorgeous legs, those of the women who have come to pay their last respects to the rogue being laid to rest. I squirmed in my seat. He simply *had* to have each and every one of them. Here I was, presenting Ms. Gochberg with an all-too-accurate portrait of the rogue sitting next to her. As we rode the Fifth Avenue bus back downtown, we laughed about the magnificent obsession of sad-eyed Bertrand Morane, but inside I was hoping that she wouldn't connect the dots. As she was talking, my eyes moved down over her tailored, black Calvin Klein coat, to the hem of a patterned Diane von Furstenberg silk dress, and on to a pair of very good midcalf leather boots. Yes, indeed, she could have been in the company of those women around the grave and would have shown quite nicely.

The trash can–stuffing incident came a week later.

It was after a party at Julian Bach's posh East Side townhouse, he the powerful New York agent (John Fowles, Theodore White, and Pat Conroy, to name a few clients) and the father of Pru Bach, one of Tracy's friends. I had had a few drinks and was making the rounds, blabbing on about paperback deals, movie options, and other such seminal events when, out of the corner of my eye, I spotted Tracy in a corner by Julian's impressive bookcase, talking to another man. Her hips were suggestively close to his, those luscious lips, as yet unkissed by me, inches away from his. It seemed that every time I saw her, she was in similar close quarters, *so* interested, so animated. I didn't say anything as we left the party, but my silence was short lived when she asked if anything was wrong. After all, she had had a great time; hadn't I? Wasn't this your crowd, writers and all, she asked?

"Look, you were all over him, all over everybody at the party, for God's sake. Putting your hand on his arm. Looking up with that coquettish little look. I'm not blind!" I was screaming.

"I just stand close to people when I talk. I'm animated; what do you want me to do? Go on a heavy dose of Valium?"

"I thought you came with me—"

"And I think I left with you. Is this pure jealousy or pure craziness?"

I was walking down Madison Avenue at a furious pace, with an incredulous "perfect woman" trailing in my wake. Jealous? Mr. No Commitment, the Urban Casanova? Mr. "I Have My Space and You Have Yours and Let's Keep It That Way?" Jealous?

"Well, what is it? We'd better settle this right now."

I turned. I don't know what possessed me. "I'll settle it. I'll settle it!" I picked up the perfect woman, slung her over my shoulder, and dumped her butt-first into the yawning maw of a huge metal mesh trash can on the corner of East Sixty-second Street.

Tracy was laughing uproariously. She thought it was perfectly hilarious that I could be jealous—not casually, a few angry words jealous—but so jealous that I would be driven to unceremoniously dump her into a fifty-five-gallon, three-cubic-foot Department of Sanitation waste receptacle. She had only known me for a matter of days, but, as I now realize, she knew me better than I knew myself. For who was I accusing of infidelity but myself? Of practicing the art of "instant intimacy," that up-close and personal way of talking that seductively focused so intently on the other? That physical closeness that promised more? She was innocent. I wasn't.

When I look back over the record of those years—the photos I took, the random scribbles on scraps of paper, diary notes, the two- and three-page reflections I wrote at the worst as well as the best times—it's a wonder that things turned out as they did. God's grace was surrounding me, the gracious and forgiving God whom I had run from and pushed to the margins of my life, the God who, I would only later *begin* to understand, was at work in his own quirky and mysterious ways.

The next few months were the happiest and most agonizing of my life since I had become a single man. Dinners over sake and teri maki at the Japanese Garden off Bleecker, long walks around Washington Square park, coffee and cannolis at Ferrara's in Little Italy, drives to Westchester County, snatching the tallest and most perfect cattails from the roadside of the New York Thruway as cars buzzed by. Watching that wonderful

smile spread from her bright eyes, like ripples on a still pond, to bring her
face alive, so fresh, so happy. A smile that knew me so completely and
took me in, just as I was. To see another smile, that certain smile, in the
surreal whitish-green mercury vapor streetlight spilling through the bedroom window, a light no longer shining on empty chairs and an empty
life. To awaken and just look at her, with a clear head and clear conscience, and start the day together.

It's not that we had these intense Heloise and Abelard, Francis and
Claire spiritual dialogues, but even as we were ostensibly outfitted in our
modern-day, New York uniforms provided by Jean-Paul Germain and
Diane von Furstenberg, there was more, much more, that neither of us
wanted to conceal. Beneath our very au courant life was something very
old-fashioned—the eternal verities, I would say. We both knew the emptiness Augustine described when he said that our human hearts are restless
until they rest in God. We felt the Sunday morning itch to be in church.
The need to help other people, to have our lives stand for something. But
as we individually sought God and meaning, we could, in the meantime,
match each other in inanity. I proffered my syndicated singles series, reading such ferverinos as "Be in the moment and make it yours; squeeze
every drop out of life." Tracy parried back with her work on the Wyler's
account, promising Americans true salvation through their choice of the
right lemonade. And if that wasn't enough, there was her sterling perfor-
mance on the Trojan condom account. After all was said and done, there
was always your trusty Trojan. I didn't mention my birthday present and
nickname. Scumbag.

Neither of us were conventional, by-the-book Christians; we were both
sinners. I was doing much better on this sinning account, but I had tried
with CHIPS and 80 Winthrop Street. Tracy visited Olga, an old, crotchety shut-in who abused her in inverse proportion to how kind Tracy was
to her that day. Tracy's aunt and uncle, Barbara and Rolf Kip, who helped
raise her, always had a patient or two from the mental ward of the local
VA hospital for holiday meals. Her grandmother, Jane Boyle, had decades
as a Gray Lady, volunteering at the hospital. I don't know if I was trying
to kill the relationship or give it the acid test, but I invited Tracy to come
with me for a community dinner at Jacques'. She gamely agreed, even
after I let her in on who some of her dinner companions might be.

With the help of my CHIPS cofounder, Ed Mohler, the pediatric orthopedic surgeon, Jacques had put a down payment on a rundown brownstone on Fourth Street, a few blocks from the storefront. This allowed
Jacques to take in even more homeless men and women. When Tracy and
I arrived, a series of uneven tables had been pushed together and set for

over twenty people. Jacques was his usual ebullient self: "O, my Tra-cee, *ma chère*, you are so beau-ti-ful! And Paaaul, the most famous writer, our good companion who means so much to us." Tracy gamely sat midtable and was having a heady discussion with a very distinguished man wearing an ascot—only slightly stained and tattered along the edges—about some item currently in the news, when he suddenly rejoined, "Well, before the march to Atlanta when I was on General Sherman's staff, he made it absolutely clear to us . . ." I tried to change the subject, or at least bring the conversation up a century. About this time we heard a strange, liquid sound, as if a pipe had sprung a leak. Tracy instinctively glanced toward the kitchen. Then, following the sound, she looked into the living room where the Professor was ensconced in his Barcalounger, and saw him unceremoniously peeing into a tall pineapple can, which beautifully amplified the sound. I leaped up from the table, but then stood there, hands at my side. What was I going to do: stop him?

She looked at me, I at her. Wordlessly she transmitted, *It's okay, buddy. I think I understand.*

We went on with our fancy parties, but that night at Jacques' marked one of those defining moments when all pretenses are wiped away, and either you walk away or grow closer.

With my life now so much in the open, Tracy, guileless by nature, had nothing to hide. She told me more about her early life, finding liquor bottles and making excuses when Mom "wasn't feeling well," wild adolescent years of drinking and drugs, a feeble suicide attempt, a nervous breakdown. One of the highlights of her youthful adventures was the night she ran away from home and showed up at the front gate of the forbidding compound of the Maryknoll fathers and sisters near the Kips' house in Ossining. She was desperately unhappy being bounced between her alcoholic mother and her father, who had remarried and was starting another family. She was ready to join, she assured the nun who answered the door. She might have been only ten years old and an Episcopalian, but she was sure God wanted her to be a Maryknoll nun. The kindly woman took her in and, instead of a habit, gave her a tuna fish sandwich and, with Tracy's permission, called her worried mother. It was such a wonderful story, I left my own remembrance of the gaunt Maryknoll priest for another day.

I know. I had found the perfect woman. So what did I do? I tried my best to screw it up. We would date for weeks, seeing each other daily, and then I would run away, with some phony excuse, just so I could go back out to the playground and act the petulant, testosterone-infused adolescent. Then, quickly realizing that the life I was once again living was killing my soul, I begged her to give us another chance. Us? Me. Tracy was totally there from the beginning.

There was one particularly horrific lunch at the Bean Sprout on lower Seventh Avenue that constituted grounds for justifiable homicide. My somber voice on the phone must have given it away, because Tracy arrived wearing a black sweater, already a widow. We were seated at a table within the glass-enclosed sidewalk café; pair after pair of impossibly happy lovers strolled by, hand in hand, arm in arm. I hated every last one of them. I wanted that for myself. Yet here, coming out of my mouth, was the latest flimsy excuse not to grow up—rather than, one hoped, grow old with this excellent woman. I muttered into the Thai salad that she wasn't "age appropriate." What the hell did that mean? She was then twenty-six going on twenty-seven, and I was forty going on nineteen. What it really meant was that I had met somebody else more accommo-dating, who didn't call me out of myself, who thought that such romantic flourishes as yellow roses for her mantel or violets for her fur really meant I cared.

A week later, I asked Tracy to move in with me.

Her father said she shouldn't. Her friends told her she was crazy. It wasn't just about the great leap into a serious commitment. It was far more than that. She had a spacious, one-bedroom apartment with a wood-burning fireplace. In New York, guys come and go; a good apartment nec-essarily needs to be more stable. But Tracy said yes, and Apartment 3-F now had two occupants. We even added a dog, appropriately rescued from the animal shelter. The perfect life was under way . . . until what we would always remember as the Brooklyn Bridge Massacre.

It was a gloomy Christmas Day afternoon, and we were headed across the bridge toward a friend's house. I can still hear the dull hum of the bridge grating beneath the tires. Then my voice saying, "It's just not working out."

"*What's* not working out?" came her disbelieving voice, as if I had just grown another head.

Tracy wanted to get married. To have children. To start a life together. She loved me. So here I was on Christmas Day—after she had made a wonderful mushroom omelet and helped me set the insecticide bombs that would de-roach our apartment—bailing out. In the rankings of lousy things men have visited on women, this one has to be near the top. She should have locked me inside to die with the other cockroaches.

So what was it, really? What was holding me back? I loved Tracy. We actually *were* Abelard and Heloise, or as close as you might come in Greenwich Village, circa 1980. Our paths to that spot on the Brooklyn

Bridge that day had certainly been quite different, she the WASP only child, I the Catholic from a large ethnic family, but, setting all the window dressing aside, we were alike in the things that really mattered.

If I am to be totally honest, it came down to this: married life seemed too *ordinary*.

I was not stupid enough to fail to realize that even though my playboy life might have a great present, there was no future. I wanted something else for my life. But to be a husband, Joe Husband? To have children, be a father? "Hey Dad, we're home." No drumroll in the background of that kind of life. I could just hear the dissonant anthem of the suburbs and a station wagon door slamming shut. No, no, not me.

I wanted more out of my life. I wanted to respond to a call, something impossible that demanded my every breath, my every waking hour. Something that would bring out the best in me. I wanted to be a hero—or, better put, to live heroically. The world did not have to take notice, but I wanted to know I had been measured to the highest standard. Even as we were breaking up, and even as I was about to descend even further into hell, I was thinking such idealistic thoughts. Churning deep within me was the yearning to feel once again that sensation I first knew kneeling on the grate on Forest Avenue. That presence which came to me in the dank dental school basement chapel at Marquette. The eyes of Dorothy Day searing the skin right off my face, vaporizing all the detritus that made up the external me, leaving behind a true human being. The art, the practice, the power of being *present*.

I didn't want much, just that perfect calling that would once and for all, like a gavel pounding down, settle everything.

Implicit in our relationship "not working out" was that Tracy would have to move out. I helped her find an apartment, over near Abington Square, more expensive and tiny in comparison to her place on Jane Street. Where she used to have a huge bedroom, she now would sleep on a day bed in the cramped living room. No fireplace. Her spacious kitchen was replaced by one ideal for the single woman, as only one person could safely fit in it. In New York, further grounds for murder. I moved her into 229 West Twelfth, got rid of the dog, and, quickly putting aside all those deep thoughts about the great calling, went back to my old ways.

If marijuana and alcohol were once enough to dull my mind and skew my judgment, they were no longer sufficient. Cocaine? Sure, why not? Pills? What's in it? Right, right, not to worry; let's go. One woman at a time? Why not two? Consider the possibilities. I was spiraling—plummeting—downward into my self-made hell. *Six American Families* had received outstanding reviews in newspapers and magazines across the country.

The series received a duPont-Columbia Award for documentary excellence, the equivalent of an Academy Award. On the night I was honored as an outstanding alumnus of Columbia University Graduate School of Journalism, I was surrounded with people whom I hadn't known a few months before and wouldn't know a few months after. It was the best I could do for "friends." When my name was called, I staggered to the podium, drunk, to accept the award. Marquette University proudly presented me, their distinguished graduate, with their highest journalism honor, the By-Line Award. My sisters and brothers, so proud of me, came to Milwaukee for the ceremony. I honored them by appearing at breakfast the next morning arm in arm with the enterprising senior journalism student with whom I had spent the night.

I soon was at the end of my rope financially as well and—by the kindness of the State of New York and the United States government—about to collect my last few unemployment checks. Put them away, plan for a rainy day? Please! How boringly practical. I traveled up to the best men's shop on Madison Avenue and selected a gorgeous three-piece Italian suit. My last three checks, $600, were invested in something that would surely make me a better person, would surely bring me closer to hearing and answering that call I was supposedly awaiting. I had it fitted, nipped, and tucked; it was a beautiful piece of work. No one caresses the body like those Italians. And, of course, one could not just bring it home and put it in a closet. *Sacre bleu!* What a wonderful occasion for a party. I mean, won't this be a different twist?

With the help of Nancy Anderson, a lady friend, we stuffed the sleeves and legs, arranged the silk hankie and tie just so, and when my playmates came through the door at West Tenth Street, there was the $600 suit draped over a piece of my Danish modern furniture. What a simply fabulous time we had that night and into the next morning, heaping praise on the suit, bowing to my ingenuity, admiring my sheer guts for spending my last paychecks on the most beautiful suit in New York City. Not only did this guy have taste, but the élan, the élan of it all!

The Romans had nothing on me. I could worship idols with the best of them.

OO

I traveled to Slovakia to work on a book that would never be published. When I returned, I called Tracy, and we started seeing each other again. One morning a few months later, sitting over a second cup of coffee, alone in the apartment, I finally realized what I had to do. I asked Tracy to lunch, avoiding the Bean Sprout and other scenes of other massacres, choosing a small bistro that had just opened on Eighth Street. I had shocked this woman with my snap decisions and masquerades so many times, but this would be, to say the least, unexpected. "Tracy, I'm subletting the apartment. I'm going to live as a hermit near a Trappist monastery up in Massachusetts. I . . . I think I have a monastic calling."

She looked at me carefully, as if to make sure voice, face, and content matched. "So you think you have a monastic vocation?" Her voice was drained of any emotion. "Are you nuts?"

"I didn't say I *did*. But I have to find out. If I don't, I'm going to go through my life always wondering. I've talked about this for twenty years, and, well, I have to see."

Her face hardened. "You keep your monasticism to yourself, Mr. Paul Wilkes. I was in this for another M word; they call it 'marriage,' strange and conventional as that might sound." She crumpled her napkin into a ball and threw it on the table, then stood up abruptly. "Marriage, get it? When you're serious about marriage, come back with a blood test and an engagement ring. Until then, buddy," and now she was bitter, "you're dead to me."

PART FIVE

GETTING BEARINGS

22

THE HERMIT

I HAD JUST RECEIVED HOLY COMMUNION. I slowly made my way past the rows of white-cowled monks who flanked me on either side, their heads bowed low at this profound moment. Here, in this magnificent architectural gem of towering splendor and Trappist reserve, I felt so small. With the harmony of scale and light perfected by their twelfth- and thirteenth-century brethren, the monks of St. Joseph Abbey in Spencer, Massachusetts, had built this paean to God, their own hands carefully, lovingly, prayerfully laying stone upon stone, brick upon brick. Soaring transepts thirty feet above me, stark arches majestically demarcating its sides, this was surely the home of the Most High God, a place of worship, awe, and comfort. So uncluttered, so austere, so minimal—how could such a church be so strangely lush? I was continually overwhelmed by the beauty of the place.

It was now Easter morning, 1981. I had shared the entire tridium of Holy Thursday, Good Friday, and Holy Saturday with these Trappist monks, suffering with Christ as he was mocked by his enemies and cavalierly rejected by those he loved so much, retracing each of his final, halting steps before dying with him on a rough-hewn cross. But then, with the power of God coursing through limp, lifeless flesh, casting off burial shrouds, I rose with him as the first of dawn's rays streamed through the magnificent rose window high overhead at the rear of the abbey church. Suddenly, just in front of me, as I neared my pew, a huge blue ball of light appeared, shimmering on the polished terrazzo floor.

It was one of those rare moments that monks and mystics describe when, in an unpredictable instant, they are swept into the presence of the elusive God. Breathless, I walked on, ever so slowly. I came closer, closer to that blaze of radiant light. The ball began to widen and stretch out, as if to form a path, beckoning me onward. I took one tentative step after another, sure that the next would bring me out of the darkness and into that place of brilliant light. I was trembling with anticipation, with terror. Finally, finally, I was one with him!

As I started to take the next, the ultimate step, the light flattened into a long, thin sliver. And disappeared.

∞

The idea is simple enough. It has made raving lunatics of some, saints of others. Leave the world, everything familiar, behind. Go to a place where silence speaks, where loneliness begets companionship. Discipline the body through prayer and fasting and never quite enough sleep. Seek only God, abandoning all else.

In the Catholic tradition, the godfather of such a spiritual path is good St. Benedict. He was but a boy of fourteen when he left the anarchic remains of a crumbling Roman empire in the sixth century to seek his God in the solitude of a cave near Subiaco, Italy. When he emerged three years later, his radiant face, his very presence spoke far more than his words could convey. Soon others were attracted to him; other men similarly saw their lives as shallow and meaningless. They too wanted to reach beyond the limitations of earthly bonds and needs to the Ineffable One.

Drawing on his own experiences as well as the wisdom of other seekers and desert dwellers of both Eastern and Western traditions, Benedict wrote what became known simply as the *Rule*—seventy-three rules, actually—that provided the structure for a new form of religious life. *Monos* they were called, men alone. Monks.

Benedictine monasteries proliferated throughout Europe during the Dark and then the early Middle Ages, their religious commitment, relative stability, and legions of scribes keeping civilization both intact and recorded. They also grew in great temporal power. Such divergence from Benedict's austere approach cried for renewal, and it became the province of a young French nobleman, Bernard, who joined a small group of disaffected Benedictines at a wretched outpost in a French backwater along the Cisteus River. These Cistercians—like Benedict in his time—touched a nerve within medieval man; monasteries soon dotted the French countryside. But even these eventually proved too grand and lax for Abbot Armand de Rance in the eighteenth century, whose abbey at La Trappe, also in France, harkened back to the Cistercian and Benedictine asceticism of silence, bodily mortification, and long hours of prayer and meditation. Thus the modern-day name of Trappists came to what is formally called the Order of Cistercians of the Strict Observance, OCSO. These proud letters followed the names of a handful of monks in three virtually unknown American monasteries when Thomas Merton entered one of them, Our Lady of Gethsemane in Kentucky, in 1941.

Merton, whose candor about his misspent youth, coupled with his innate hunger for meaning in life and his ability to look deeply into himself as he sought his God—and to write eloquently about it all—launched another monastic Golden Age. Who could resist such seduction as Merton offered in his classic *The Silent Life:* "These silent monasteries are now well known as the home of truly happy men. The life is difficult, no doubt, but the faith and self-sacrifice which make it possible also fill the heart of the monk with a peace the world cannot give."

All of which is a long preamble to the next chapter in my life. I was now in a small hermitage near St. Joseph's, living the life I had tasted at seventeen when I first encountered Merton, then had left behind during college, the Navy, a marriage, voluntary poverty with Jacques and CHIPS in Brooklyn, and, finally, the horrible excesses of my life in Greenwich Village. I was dead to Tracy. I was dead to the world. I no longer existed. On that Easter Sunday morning, everything changed. I was alive once more, raised from the dead. I felt the inexorable invitation of God. I would—I could—be a Trappist monk for the rest of my life. I knew this for certain. I wanted nothing less . . . or more.

Once a New York bon vivant, the life of the party who rubbed elbows with Capote and Vonnegut and Warhol, I was now a rural solitary, living in a simple, wood-shingled house set on a knoll that overlooked my freshly tilled garden and beyond. Tiny vegetable seedlings sprouted in the sunlight spilling through the glass doors leading out to my small porch. A Vermont Castings stove generated the only heat. Two young pigs rooted and snorted about in a pen I had built from scrap lumber cadged from a local mill. I was a bit of a mystery to the few neighbors, all farmers, along New Braintree Road in Oakham, a tiny town just a ten-minute drive to the monastery. I was somewhat of a mystery to myself. I had packed all the warm clothes I owned and left West Tenth Street the autumn before, telling no one but Tracy of my destination and intentions.

Six months later, on that Easter morning, there was finally some clarity to what for years had been a very confused and dissipated life. Those six months, though, were hardly so peaceful or pastoral. Actually, they were a living hell.

∞

I arrived in time for the onset of one of the bitterest Massachusetts winters in recent memory. I wore long johns, flannel shirts, even flannel-lined trousers, but the numbing cold penetrated any defense I could mount. Snow piled up against the side of my house, the drifts almost to the roof's gutters. One night, with the windchill factor at forty degrees below zero, my water pipes burst, flooding my basement, which quickly froze over. Cold was on my mind, all the time it seemed. During that Massachusetts winter, there were many times I was sure I was going mad. With the cold. With myself.

I didn't drink during the day, but come the arbitrary hour of five o'clock, I made up for lost time. Not every day, but on more days than I like to acknowledge. Jim Beam and Jack Daniels were my faithful companions, ready to provide good company, to warm me and dull the pain, at least temporarily. Although I was rising each morning at three to begin my life in tandem with the monks at Spencer, I often did it with heavy heart and head. During my morning meditation, when I sat yogi-style on a Zen bench Father Mark had given me, draped with a blanket or two, my tableau was a barren, snow-covered, windswept field behind the house. Certainly, it was an apt metaphor for my life.

On my knees, I pleaded in the words of the Psalm 108:

> I have become an object of scorn,
> All who see me toss their heads.
> Help me, Lord by God
> Save me because of your love
> Let them know this is your work,
> That this is your doing, O Lord

At my kitchen table, in addition to the Psalms, I read the New Testament as never before, my eyes burning as I waited for a phrase, a passage, one of the miracles to sear my brain. Loaves and fishes. The rich young man. Lazarus. The agony in the garden. The road to Emmaus. Haven't God's signs and wonders pointed the way for seekers throughout the ages? I wanted so badly to hear the call that, as one writer put it, "seemed to cost not less than everything." I wanted to live heroically for Christ, just as had the saints who formed my early impressions of what it was to be truly Catholic. I wanted to find a path to God, and if it led through frozen desolation, so be it.

I composed my own prayers:

> O, Lord, open my lips . . . that I might declare your praise.
> O, Lord, open my eyes . . . that they might see you in all things.

O, Lord, open my ears . . . that they might hear your voice.

O, Lord, awaken my body . . . that it might serve you this day.

O, Lord, awaken my mind . . . that I might understand your will
for me.

O, Lord, open my heart . . . that I might receive you.

Shivering, I prayed—on my knees, under the blankets, walking New
Braintree Road—emotions battling to surface, but I could not allow this,
because, once unleashed, they would be unstoppable.

In my pursuit to be a true man of God, I had failed at CHIPS, failed at
Jacques', and during this harsh winter I was failing again. I had been
given the grace to abruptly leave the city, but this was no more than a
first step, a gesture. I had finally gotten so sick of myself that I couldn't
go on. To be one with Dorothy Day or Jacques Travers or Antony or
Charles de Foucauld or Merton, I had to go deeper and deeper into this
desert of unknowing, with nothing familiar to grasp onto, no comforts,
no rest. It was terrifying and bewildering, just as the great spiritual masters had told, but was required by anyone who wishes to enter into the
mystery of being remade by God.

As if this haze of unknowing were not bad enough, the "midday
demon" often came to call. *Acedia* it is called, and solitaries know it
well. It is the opposite of desire, an abandonment of faith, the absence of
caring, a subtle but even worse agony. The fourth-century ascetic
Evagrius Ponticus explained, "it arouses in him an aversion for the place
where he is, even for his state in life . . . the demon makes him long for
other places, where he will find easily what he needs." The print in the
Bible before me, the texture of my table, the sound of the fluorescent
light over the sink, the lining of the trousers on my numb knees—all
unspeakable tortures. I wanted release. Anything. Anywhere. One night
I nearly catapulted myself out of a chair, threw on my parka, and drove
at breakneck speed into Spencer, to the Barn, a huge, shoddy, discount
store. I needed something, but when I got there, I didn't know what it
was. I hoped for a sign, but the only sign was in neon, flickering and half
lit. Acedia ruptures hope, courts despair.

I knew I must practice what some have called holy stubbornness. Concrete facts dictate what the will of God is for each person's life; Merton
had stressed this point over and over again in his insightful lectures to the
novices of Gethsemane. God's will was free, mine was free, Merton reas-
sured me. But this freedom seemed as vast and as barren as the surface of
the moon; I cried out for an answer, for the "facts" of my life to finally
take shape.

Throughout those dark months, before my Easter epiphany, while I incanted a mantra, "Lead me where you will, Lord," in my heart I already had the road and destination. It was so clear what I should be doing with my life. I wanted to be a Trappist monk. I was being tested. I just had to be patient, waiting for God to stamp my application "Approved."

23

ALMOST

"WELCOME TO THE WORLD OF SOUND."

I met with Father Mark Delary every week or so in a small reception room in the retreat house that was attached to, but kept very separate from, the cloistered inner sanctum of the monastery. With my hands folded—or clenched, given the state of my defenses—I would tell him of my spiritual reading, my aching soul, and my disciplined life. (I conveniently left out friends Jim and Jack and my extended cocktail hour.) He was maddeningly nonchalant about it all. He never once encouraged me to apply to the monastery. Instead he told me of recently written popular books he had read. John of the Cross, Ponticus, Aelred of Rievaulx, these were my choices. He nodded, without much interest.

To this day, I can close my eyes and recall the odor of this man and the claustrophobia of that room. Father Mark himself, like the nuns at St. Benedict's grade school, gave off only the odor of his clothes, but not of his body, as if such temporality had been blanched from him. Although the room was spacious enough, well appointed with a nineteenth-century antique refectory table and carved chairs donated by a wealthy benefactor, and a window crosshatched with medieval leading, I felt as though I were imprisoned in a KGB interrogation room.

But Father Mark was not the Grand Inquisitor. And who was bombarding me with questions impossible to easily answer but myself?

Some years later, I would take a little bit of Father Mark and add many fictional details to form the Father Columban of my one novel, *Temptations*. Father Columban also had an urban-exiled Catholic writer in spiritual direction. But he was hardly timid about laying out the options, as he saw them: the Trappist life or your old life, which will amount to nothing and bring you unhappiness. Father Columban was sure his directee had a vocation to monastic life. The real-life Father Mark was a far wiser spiritual guide, allowing me to wallow in my own purgatory. I looked to him for encouragement, to my reading and meditation for inspiration. I received none of the former, precious little of the latter.

But then came the brilliant blue light on Easter Sunday, and all the pieces suddenly seemed to fit. How can one explain such an experience? It is as if you are being electrocuted, yet there is no pain. As if you suddenly have no weight, yet you are walking. As if everything you heard about God, every thought, every effort you have mustered were returned to you, encapsulated in an instant of sublime sensation that actually has no feeling. As if you know everything you need to know, yet realize you "know" nothing at all. The unmistakable presence of God, that immutable "there" is with you, with such unbelievable comfort.

And, sadly—if the great spiritual writers are to be trusted—of little import.

Riding such a spiritual and emotional roller coaster, you find it difficult to know what is actually happening as you plummet down one incline, chug up another, and occasionally hit that point of stasis at the top where you can see forever. But one thing was settled, or at least I thought so. I had always feared that even with all my spiritual searching, my groaning for God, I could very well find myself, after all, insignificant and ordinary. I now triumphed in that thought.

Only when a person is able stand off to the side, at a distance of a few decades, does the truth become clear: that neither the tribulations nor the false hopes of those days were especially valid. Or lasting. I really had no idea of how even more "ordinary" I was to become.

∞

After the Easter experience, my spiritual life blossomed. Words of scripture spoke to me in new, fresh ways. St. Mark charted out my life in a few simple sentences: "Jesus looked at him and loved him. 'One thing you lack,' he said. 'Go, sell everything you have and give to the poor, and you will have treasure in heaven. Then come, follow me.'"

After all, I had done this once before, when I signed those separation papers and gave up everything I owned. But then I had abandoned the life of voluntary poverty, returning to grasp at the baubles of the world, all of which had made me increasingly more miserable. It was time to renounce everything, forever.

As I sat by the tiny creek across the road from my hermitage, Bible in hand, Psalm 1 came alive on a warm, late April morning: "He is like a tree planted by streams of water, which yields its fruit in due season and whose leaf does not wither. Whatever he does prospers."

My due season was at hand.

At my kitchen table, walking in the woods, sitting quietly in the side chapel at the monastery before daily Mass, I felt both a serenity and alertness I had never known. It seemed that every third or fourth line from the book I was reading urged me on. I was walking with Christ, in the shadow of Thomas Merton, Dorothy Day, Charles de Foucauld, my beloved Jacques Travers. All the effort I had expended now seemed like smoke drifting away. No longer was the path rocky and uncertain. The days flew by. As Merton exulted in his early days at Gethsemane, "Everything makes sense. Everything I wanted to do the most, I can now do all the time without interference. As soon as I got inside, I knew I was home where I never had been or would be a stranger."

To match the new freshness of my life, the hillside behind my home was now bedecked with a lush, brilliant blanket of green, the first growth of alfalfa. Soft spring winds nudged tufts of clouds across the sky. The air was so pure that I gulped it in each morning like a drowning man who couldn't believe his good fortune at being plucked from a raging sea and able to breathe again. I gave up drinking. I could now understand the sagacious regimen that Benedict had crafted—whereby community worship (Mass each morning and Compline ending the day at the monastery), individual reading, and contemplation are interspersed with periods of work—so that the weak would not be disheartened and the strong continually challenged. Each part of my day had its own place; no part hung heavy. There was no more of the emptiness I felt in the morning, the awful vacuum I used to feel after supper when I was living on West Tenth Street. I was in bed at eight, fast asleep before the "hungry hours" could take hold.

Merton was right: when one lacks spiritual pleasure in life, sensual pleasure rushes in to fill the gap. The recordings of his talks to novices reveal a voice completely confident that he had found true satisfaction in monastic life. Nothing he had ever experienced in the world could compare to his life as a self-professed "dead man."

I worked in the woods each morning with Brother Arthur, a cherubic, red-cheeked monk, clearing trees from swamps. I planted a huge garden. My uncut hair grew into curly tufts, my arms developed this strange lump between elbow and shoulder, my once soft hands grew so calloused that I gave up using gloves as I worked in my garden, chainsawed firewood, or helped my neighbor load bails of alfalfa into his barn. I had not been in such good shape physically since the Navy.

My past life receded further and further into memories that grew less and less tempting to revisit. The parade of women I had known seemed like something I had read about and not experienced. Tracy was different. She visited my dreams, and occasionally, when I'd be sitting at the table after Mass with my morning cappuccino (my one concession to venality: the Pavoni had made the trip north), thoughts of her, like a sudden cool breeze on an otherwise still, hot day, washed over me. I could see her in the morning light, sitting across from me at the marble table overlooking West Tenth Street. I could smell her perfume; feel the soft skin on her shoulder, visualize that wonderful smile she would have after we made love. I missed her, very much at times, but once this feeling was launched, I would quickly tamp it down with the rejoinder that sacrifice was part of the equation. In giving up the company and comfort of this wonderful woman, I soon would be more than compensated by the company of my Trappist brothers-to-be, not to mention an intimate relationship with God.

Most of the time, after the Easter experience, I convinced myself that mine was, finally, a perfect life, with perfect balance. But at the edges of my consciousness, patiently stalking me like a stealthy beast, something lurked. I discovered that I was not as strong as I kept telling myself I was.

Loneliness rushed into the vacuum of my perfect life, unsummoned, at full strength. When it struck, I felt my blood stop. I must be resolute, I told myself. I would meet loneliness head on. Thinking back, wasn't that loneliness I felt at the breakfast nook table in Cleveland, surrounded by brothers, sisters, mother, and father? Loneliness, in those waning years of my marriage to J.C. in the *House and Garden* townhouse? Lonely, even beneath the holy bedspread at 80 Winthrop Street? Lonely as I awoke next to women whose names I couldn't quite remember? This was the human condition, my human condition. It would always be there. As Merton himself explained in *The Seven Storey Mountain,* "I have always tended to resist any kind of a possessive affection on the part of any other human being—there has always been this profound instinct to keep clear, to keep free. And only with truly supernatural people have I ever felt really at my ease, really at peace."

There! Merton's own loneliness fueled his search for God, and look what became of him. I had no illusions about being another Merton; I did not have his gifts. But I did have the same gaping hole in my soul, the same emotional no-man's-land between me and other people. My years of analysis with Barbara Koltuv had helped me immeasurably. I had been presented with two basic tenets. The first: when presented with a fork in the road of life, even if one path is murky and unknown, choose it rather than the other, which—though it might be comfortable, predictable, and perhaps pleasurable—you have learned leads nowhere. My self-destructive, hedonistic New York days were exactly that. I chose the easy path again and again, and my unhappiness grew. If I were to return to that life, I would be guaranteeing my own misery. I wanted to take, as the popular book of the time so aptly named it, the road less traveled.

The second tenet, I realized, I still hadn't very successfully applied to my life. "Listen to your feelings, Paul." Every time Dr. Koltuv said anything close to those words, the alarm went off. Not only was this a hackneyed cliché, the bogus god of the 1970s, but "feelings" were the false beacon that the Catholicism of my upbringing had warned me to guard against. *Never* listen to your feelings! In contrast, Dr. Koltuv's psychoanalytic and Jungian training maintained that feelings were a window into the deepest part of me, piercing through the tough husk of my conscious self to the unconscious, the seat of the soul. I wasn't buying it—too risky, too out of control. After all, I had responded only too well to my feelings as I careened through my New York days. I had given in to every one of them! No, I had to pray more. God would answer my prayers.

∞

By late June, my backyard garden was the wonder of Oakham. Neighbors stopped by, incredulous that this city boy could have produced such a cornucopia. Six varieties of corn, kale and bok choy, yellow and green beans, carrots, potato plants, clusters of tomatoes, cauliflower, cantaloupe, watermelon. Cucumber vines burst the boundaries of the garden, spilling onto the grassy area so they might produce even more. If you had dropped by on that gorgeous, mild June day in 1981 that I will never forget, you would have seen a strapping, suntanned, shirtless man setting out feed for a few dozen white leghorn chickens, filling the trough with fresh-cut alfalfa in the sheep pen for two Dorsets, before striding out to the sun-dappled garden, a stack of cardboard boxes carefully balanced in his arms.

I piled huge heads of bok choy onto lithe zucchini, layered perfectly formed ears of corn beneath red and green leaf lettuce and splendid heads of romaine. Onions, carrots, leeks. I filled box after box and set them in a neat line at the edge of the garden. I looked down proudly at the fruits of my labor.

Then, without warning, I felt that awful throbbing in my throat. I was caught defenseless, blindsided. It came over me in an instant. I couldn't control myself. I started sobbing. Here, the hermit in Oakham, but it was the same overwhelming sense of emptiness I felt as the hedonist in Negril. Something—the same "thing" or merely its variation?—was so badly missing in my life.

∞

The soft footfall of one of the monks passing by the reception room in the St. Joseph Abbey guest house sounded like so many thunderclaps. Father Mark's hands lay one upon the other, his unblinking eyes—magnified by the thick lenses of his glasses—were fixed on me. I thought he was angry, very angry at what I was saying.

"I've done it all, Father," I said haltingly. "I've prayed, worked, meditated, given myself over completely. And here I am, instead of being ready to take the next steps to be admitted, I'm so confused, so damn confused." I swallowed. "After a year in the hermitage," I was now fighting to keep my voice steady, "I've come to a conclusion. I love this life, Benedict's way, away from the temptations of the world, alone with God. I'm in sync with it more than anything I've ever experienced. I've thought this over a million times: the Trappists are just about perfect, 99 percent right for me, but..."

His face remained impassive. I was sure he was boiling inside by now. After all, Mr. Ardent, Mr. Hermit, Mr. Seeker-of-the-Truth had just come up short, faded in the stretch, flunked out.

"Why?" His single word seemed to echo in the still room.

"I don't know why, Father. I just can't get there. It's as if I'm trying to put a left-hand glove on my right hand. It almost works; the right number of fingers, but it doesn't really fit."

"Then I think you should," Father Mark.

"You know how hard I tried, Father." I stumbled on, but his face softened just a bit, a sign that such excuses weren't needed. He understood. More completely than I did that morning. "I should do what?"

"I didn't become a Trappist because I figured it out. Because I prayed my way into it. Because I made up a list of pros and cons. Because I *tried,* for God's sake. Follow your heart, Paul." He was now rising out of his chair. "It's the only path to God."

"Father, please don't leave me hanging like this."

He smiled. "You don't look like you're hanging at all. I think you have the answer."

∞

A couple of weeks later, with cardboard boxes loaded with produce in my arms, I found myself upright and dry-eyed on the Fire Island ferry slip in Bay Shore, Long Island.

Tracy had rented a house with some friends for the week, and when I asked if I might visit, her voice was cold and distant. Who could blame her? Of course, all sorts of scenarios went through my mind—a new boyfriend would be there, topping the list. Jealousy, even though it involved a woman who looked upon me as dead and had not seen or heard from me for nearly a year, was still alive and well. Why did she allow me to come? It is a mystery to both of us to this day. Was a capricious God having a slow day in heaven and looking for a little diversion?

Fire Island is a spaghetti-thin, thirty-mile stretch of some of the most gorgeous beaches on the East Coast. Its communities vary from the staid Saltaire of moms, dads, and kids to the Pines and Cherry Grove, where gay men and women have vacationed for decades. No cars are allowed on the island; boardwalks are the only thoroughfares.

My garden extravaganza, as well as a couple of plump dressed chickens and a leg of lamb I'd brought packed in ice, dazzled Tracy and her housemates, but once the blanching of celery and the advantages of high-protein poultry feed were thoroughly discussed, it was time for us to walk. And walk we did, up one side of the island, across a boardwalk, down the other. In the morning, late at night.

I told her that I couldn't get her out of my mind. She countered that she did have a new boyfriend.

I said that as hard I was trying to be a Trappist monk, it wasn't working. I didn't know what to do. I still loved her. She changed the subject. She wasn't interested.

My words weren't coming out right. Even as I was speaking, I couldn't follow my own train of thought. Was it that I had been away from civilization for too long, or just that the war going on in me left me shell-shocked? Gradually, I said less and listened more. Her mother, a lifelong smoker and alcoholic, was about to have surgery for cancer of the esophagus, which would prolong her life, but not save it. They had never had the closest relationship, but Tracy was sad that Virginia, a wraith-like, witty woman whom I never saw completely sober, had never believed in herself enough to really live. Yet her daughter, who virtually raised herself, had become this indomitable spirit, a successful, independent New York career woman. But so unlike the many career women I had dated.

What was it about Tracy? Attractive, yes. Intelligent, sure. There was much more. She was completely without guile or pretension. She was honest, painfully honest. She never had an emotion she tried to hide. What you saw was what you got. I admired that so much because, when it suited my purposes, I was a master of artifice. Tracy had studied drama at Emerson College, but she was a terrible actress because she couldn't be anybody but herself.

And what else about Tracy? She loved me with a love that never wavered even as I did. For four years, she had seen something in me that I did not see in myself. She wanted to marry, to have children. If she kept choosing me, it meant she wanted me as a husband, a father. I knew all the facts, but I still refused to reach their logical conclusion. Three days later, with nothing resolved, I took the return ferry to Bay Shore and drove back to the hermitage.

When I pulled into the driveway on New Braintree Road, I noticed a strange indentation in my cornrows, as if some huge bird had lighted there. On closer inspection, I saw that the family of raccoons I had seen playfully scampering about on my late night and early morning walks had only been biding their time until my luscious midseason corn was mature. Scaling the stalks, they had broken every one before ruining the ears with no more than a greedy bite or two. I looked down the once erect and orderly rows, at the rows beside them with ears just forming, which could likely share a similar fate.

I desperately kept looking for *the* sign in those days, branching out from scripture readings to the shape of clouds during my morning meditation. To cornstalks. And so it was not at all odd that my mailbox that afternoon would open like the shaman's bag, but instead of stones and roots, bones and seeds, dried fungus and beads being cast before me, there, amid the letters and periodicals that I dumped onto my kitchen table, was the latest edition of the *Catholic Worker* and a new biography of Thomas Merton. The quiet of the hermitage enfolded me, and I did not leave for several days.

The *Catholic Worker* brought news of Jacques and our small community, which had grown to a dozen men and women. The rundown row house near CHIPS was now formally called the Arthur Sheehan House of Hospitality, after one of the Worker's earliest members. There was a gentle request by Jacques for additional help, as more and more deinstitutionalized mental patients and ever-growing ranks of the homeless came seeking shelter. Was this the message from God? Return to Brooklyn and the community?

Or was it in Merton's biography? When he was in his early forties— I was by now almost forty-two—he wondered if his life had been a monstrous mistake. If he had taken the wrong path. That what he had done amounted to nothing. That his future held nothing. He impetuously vowed to move to Russia so that he could be among the first victims if the Cold War erupted and a nuclear bomb were dropped. No, he was moving to Alaska. Nicaragua. He loved the monastery. He hated the monastery. Living within the community was a blessing. A curse. His hermit years were the best. He felt lonesome, exiled.

I scribbled down a line from the book and thrust it into my shirt pocket, close to my heart, an act like pushing tiny seeds into soil so that the magic and mystery of life might produce a fruitful plant. "Grace builds on nature." It seems I had come upon those words so many times in the past few weeks, and here they were again. In an inconsistent life, it was a constant theme for Merton: God provides grace for each of us to discover the true self and to escape the prison of the false self. But that grace is not generic; it works within the specific and unique nature of that individual. "Grace builds on nature." God's grace would be there for me; I wanted so to believe that. But what was the nature, my nature, that it would work with, build on?

I finished the Merton book during my morning reading, more confused than ever, deciding to break my self-imposed imprisonment and go to Mass at the monastery.

I swung into the monastery entrance on Massachusetts Route 31 and climbed the hill. The rising sun was in a perfect position to illuminate the golden cross atop the church, making it explode with light. It was hard to look at it directly. I slipped into my usual place, the last row, in the corner of the visitors' pews on the gospel side of the altar. I bowed my head in prayer, that I might shed all my false selves. That I might find the true self. That God would please show—in any way possible—the path I should take.

As the monks approached the altar to receive the Body and Blood of Christ at the magnificent slab of granite—so huge it had to be put in place first and the church built around it—I peered across the low wall that separated me from them. From my dream, my desire, my hope.

The oldest monks, most of whom I did not know well, were barely able to mount the stone steps. Abbot Thomas Keating, who would go on to become a famous spiritual writer, so tall and aristocratic, was that day a concelebrant at the Mass, humbly standing aside as Father Placid presided at the altar. Before them stood Arthur and his fellow brother monks, the workers who kept the monastery heated, the monks fed, the Trappist Preserves made. And the young monks, so holy, their hands precisely joined at this pregnant moment. I could be among them. If God would only listen to my fervent prayer that morning to wipe all doubt from my mind and take me to him. To grant me that 1 percent I was still lacking.

When I returned to the hermitage, I found a couple of envelopes with newly developed photos that had arrived by mail while I was away, and which I'd failed to open. This was my current life: pictures of my garden and livestock, Father Mark blessing my seedlings, my neighbor Prescott

Adams running his harrow over newly plowed soil. Piles of rocks I'd carried out by hand. The winter landscape of the now lush hillside, covered
with snow, so barren and gray. I opened a drawer where I kept my photographs. There was my past life: I standing arrogantly, a cigarette in one
hand, a manhattan in the other, surveying the stuffed suit at that last
party as bleary-eyed revelers surrounded me. The view from the windows
on West Tenth Street. A single picture of Jacques; it seems I was not taking many pictures then. And then a picture of Tracy. It was taken years
before, early in our dating days, when, on a whim, I had brought her up
to the monastery one weekend.

With a huge smile on her face, and her butt provocatively thrust
toward the camera, she pretends to climb over a fence on the monastery
grounds that demarcated the cloistered area. A sign warns, "Monastic
Enclosure. Women strictly forbidden."

What was the message here?

I softly kissed the picture.

24

A PLACE TO PARK

"HERE'S YOUR BLOOD TEST, MR. WILKES. Everything's fine. Just take it over to the town clerk's office over on Commercial Street for your license. When's the big day?"

"It's not exactly a question of 'when.'" I stared blankly at the nurse. "It's more a question of 'if.'"

She stared equally blankly back at me.

∞

Perhaps it had already happened, and I would be the last to know, but from all indications I was now certainly losing my mind. After returning from Fire Island, among other futilities, I repositioned my Zen bench for a different view and even took it out to the driveway on a warm summer's night and stared at the sky awash with stars. Could not the message be written here? I stayed after Mass each morning, fixed upon the huge crucifix on its blood-red frame hanging over the altar at St. Joseph's Abbey. Would God not answer this plea? My eyes traced the monastery's fieldstone walls. What did this granite Rorschach reveal? The sun's light reflected from a monk's window. Was this to be the sign? If so, what was it telling me—to come or to stay outside? I prayed at my bedside. I poured over the daily scripture readings with even more intensity. I tried to hold my soul still in silence so that I might know.

I realized I was simply worn out. I needed a place to think clearly, to stop this torture. I didn't know where to go or what to do. After all, I was already living a solitary, silent life. Strangely enough, I ended up in Provincetown, Massachusetts. Provincetown, one of America's most outrageously and openly gay towns, with afternoon tea parties, drag queen contests, Mates Leather and Meet Your Man weekends. Yes, Provincetown, not exactly considered the most religious or contemplative locale.

But then again, the Lord works in mysterious ways, and I guess that pat little adage was being put to the test.

I had friends in Provincetown—a woman I briefly dated and her boyfriend—and I knew they wouldn't ask too many questions. But that didn't stop me, even on the way there, from scribbling down the options:

1. Apply to join the Trappists.
2. Continue hermit life in Oakham.
3. Draw up a "rule" for a permanent, celibate consecrated state of prayer and bodily mortification and move to a more isolated place.
4. Go back to work at CHIPS.
5. Marry Tracy.
6. None of the above; return to my life on West Tenth Street.

Alone, I walked the beach at Race Point, among the beached fishing boats in Provincetown Harbor, between the towering dunes. Where the decision came from I still do not know. All of a sudden—which, of course, was not sudden at all, but something that had been germinating for a long time—I knew what I had to do. Or at least hoped I could do.

I had my blood drawn, walked into a jewelry store in Whaler's Wharf, and within minutes bought a gorgeous sapphire ring. I asked for a very specific kind of box—beautiful, narrow, and at least nine inches long. I jumped into my pickup truck, peeled away from the curb in Province-town, and made the three-hundred-mile trip from the tip of Cape Cod to Times Square in the heart of Manhattan in a terrifying four-and-a-half hours. Ricocheting from lane to lane on the Cross Bronx Expressway, I saw the sign for the George Washington Bridge. Paul Wilkes in another incarnation had approached that bridge with great expectations. Today he was bled of arrogance, amply endowed with self-doubt. I turned abruptly south onto the Henry Hudson Parkway and exited at the midtown exit, then careened across Forty-fourth Street, plunged into a parking garage, and was in the elevator on my way to the twenty-sixth floor before I somewhat came to my senses. I wasn't about to turn back now.

In gold letters, the stylized logo for Ashe-LeDonne, a theatrical advertising agency, adorned the richly grained mahogany door. I burst in. Alarmed, the receptionist looked up from her typewriter, "Can I help . . . you . . . sir . . . ," but I was already down the hallway. My heart was pounding. I paused outside the door of one "Tracy Gochberg, Account Executive," knocked on the door, and, without waiting, opened it.

Of course, Tracy could have been deep in a meeting or in the arms of a coworker (my twisted, jealous mind ever at work), but instead, there she was, punching away at the calculator on her desk, computing the advertising budget for Radio City Music Hall's Christmas show. I closed the door behind me. The Rockettes would have to wait. She looked shocked. For once she was speechless, as was I.

I put the plush-covered, elongated box on her desk.

She looked at it. Then up at me.

"Open it. Please."

She did, ever so slowly. She slipped the piece of paper that had been tightly rolled to fit inside the sapphire ring, the Commonwealth of Massachusetts informing her that the man standing before her was free of any sexually transmitted disease. She held the ring between thumb and index finger, but did not put it on.

"Remember what you said, that when I was serious about . . . about . . . ," I stuttered.

"I don't understand."

"I don't understand either."

I dropped to one knee. "Will you marry me?"

A quickly changing range of emotions flickered across her face. Danger. Incredulity. Doubt. Then a look came over her face that I had never seen before, as if all circuits had blown and the system had shut down.

"I don't know," she said, her voice flat.

I got to my feet and stood there dumbly, hands limp at my side.

"I've got to get these budgets done," she said. She handed me the keys to her apartment. "Let me think about this. I'll be working late."

The prospect of many hours of waiting was more than I could handle, so I ducked into the nearest Times Square theatre without even seeing what was playing. It happened to be *Raiders of the Lost Ark*. The sheer noise from the sound track was more than the ears of man who had spent much of the last year in silence could handle. I lasted a half hour and bolted from my seat. I went to Tracy's apartment—my smaller, more expensive legacy—on West Twelfth Street, knocked the decorative pillows onto the floor, and burrowed beneath the covers on the daybed. It was a hot summer's day. I was freezing.

The phone rang late in the afternoon. Another suitor calling? At first I was going to let it ring. Then I tentatively picked up the receiver.

"Ron Pine brought in some champagne," came Tracy's cheery voice. "We're celebrating."

"What?"

"I'm getting married."

"To me?"

"Yes, dummy, to you."

∞

I made any number of vows in the next six months, one of them being that if I didn't find a parking space near St. Joseph's Church around one o'clock on January 16, 1982, I would simply drive on. Always planning an exit strategy.

But there, surely by the grace of God it was, right on Sixth Avenue, no more than fifty yards from that iron gate. I inserted the quarters. With two hours on the meter for the business at hand, I took myself, wearing the legendary suit, in to be married.

So much had happened in the past six months. The cancer had finally prevailed over Tracy's mother's frail body. We had planned and almost unplanned our wedding as our emotions—mostly mine, I'm sure—ran wild. But there, waiting at the altar, was Father Robert Lott, tall, gaunt, unsmiling, who had calmly taken over the tiller and guided us through the troubled waters. This would be a thoroughly Catholic wedding, something that escaped me in the first marriage. Although there would be ample numbers of Christian believers and nonbelievers there in person, as well as a Jewish contingent—led by Tracy's father and grim-faced stepmother— others were there in spirit. There was Father Mark, who had told me to follow my heart, which I was finally attempting to do. Thomas Merton, who taught this reluctant novice that it is not in heraldic proclamations and visions but in real-life circumstances and concrete facts that God's will is revealed. My mother and father, the Notre Dame sisters, the Marianists from Cathedral Latin, the Jesuits from Marquette. And Barbara Koltuv, whose words about my not choosing "it," but "it" choosing me had once seemed like so much psychobabble, but had proved true.

I fought Tracy and her love because it had so much power over me.

It was a power I could not understand. And even while I stood there as Tracy, so lovely and glowing in an 1890s off-white Gibson Girl lace con-fection, processed slowly and so confidently toward our future, I felt the demons rising up. Demons of doubt. Demons of the fear of compromise. Demons of sheer, unabated terror as to what married life with this woman and the children she wanted to have would be like. The rings that we exchanged were of finely woven gold. In my first marriage, our rings were thick, solid, airless gold, as if to make a statement by sheer weight, creating a barricade against the outside world. These rings, with burnished beauty, allowed glimpses of flesh to show through, light and air to freely circulate among the strands. The first, impermeable. The second, with firm, but less vaunted, goals.

I climbed back into the pickup, my wife in full bridal gown in the other seat. I would later find that the common judgment of her friends was that the marriage would last about fifteen minutes. Just as Tracy was about to start down the aisle, her father had whispered to her, "You know you don't have to go through with this if you don't want to."

∞

Our first year of married life was as wonderful as it was tumultuous, as two strong spirits clashed and loved and generally tried to figure out what life at such close quarters was all about. There were the blissful moments, walking through the Brooklyn Botanical Gardens at cherry blossom time. Face to face, after making love, that smile on her face, not merely of sensual pleasure but of something so transcendent I had to look away. Or elbow to elbow at Mass, intoning those words that seemed to resonate with both of us: "O, Lord, I am not worthy to receive you, but only say the word and I shall be healed." Then, heads bowed, confident the word had been spoken, approaching the table to receive our sustenance before we went back to our lives.

We were in and out of marriage counseling, raging over such important issues as how much—and if—to spend on fresh-cut flowers, the wisdom of buying more than one roll of toilet paper at a time, and whether or not leaving dishes out to dry was more sanitary than drying them with a towel. But then we would stop and look at each other, finding it hard to remember exactly what had set us off—this time. We had a magic together that could bring us to laughter or tears, sometimes at the same time.

But what was really happening in our marriage was that I was dying. This time it was not the theoretical dying to which I had so dramatically consigned myself during the hermit year. This was death by marriage.

My wondrous ego was being impaled on the stake of ordinariness. I was now a married man, like so many others; nothing dramatic, nothing special. I was not the Saint of Sixth Avenue, I was not the monk-in-waiting. I was dying to that image of myself as "set apart," called, or different. I was also dying to a self whose universe for the past seven years had alternately revolved around his own navel, his libido, or his spiritual quest for a great summoning. We decided that 45 West Tenth just had too many ghosts in it, so it was sold, and we rented the upper two floors of a Brooklyn brownstone, just a few blocks from the brownstone I had bought, renovated, and given away. We were biding time, we knew that. New York would not be our home for long.

Then something propitious—and I use the word advisedly—happened in my working life, surely a blessing in more ways than I imagined at the time. An idea to do a documentary on Thomas Merton found some substantial funding, and soon I was on a plane for Thailand, on the first

leg of a journey that would take me around the world, filming key places
and people in Merton's life.

On that trip, I stood on the creaking oak floor and looked into the
dark corner of the bedroom where the newborn Thomas was laid in his
crib in Prades, a tiny town nestled in the foothills of the Pyrenees in the
south of France. I bowed my head in prayer exactly where Merton last
stood—on the drab, concrete floor in a bungalow on the grounds of a
Red Cross center outside Bangkok—when his wet hand touched a fan
with faulty wiring and 220 volts of electricity coursed through his body,
stopping his heart. I sat and talked with those who knew him best, his
Columbia buddy Bob Lax, editors James Laughlin and Robert Giroux,
his fellow monks at Gethsemane, the poet Lawrence Ferlinghetti, childhood friends, the Buddhist monk and peace activist Thich Nhat Hanh,
and, traveling to the far northern reaches of India, the Dalai Lama.

The man whose writing had quickened my own spiritual search, whose
telling portrayal of Trappist life had put this vocation in the forefront of
my mind at age seventeen and again at thirty-seven, Thomas Merton had
been my steadfast companion for much of my mature life. And, during
those months, I walked where he walked, prayed where he prayed, wept
where he wept. It was a great privilege, this pilgrimage. I felt close to
him, although I had never met the man. He had led me—circuitously
to be sure—not to the Trappists, but to Tracy.

Just four days before his accidental electrocution, Thomas Merton visited the statues at Gal Vihara within the ancient city of Polonnaruwa in
what was then known as Ceylon (and is now Sri Lanka). I stood where
he had stood, this time before the mammoth Buddhas, which, at the time he
was there, were considered little more than pagan idols by many in my
Catholic Church. The sandy apron before the statues undulated in the
withering heat of that day as the faces of the Buddhas, which at first
seemed impassive and lifeless, became strangely alive and alert. It was
almost as if they were ready to speak, yet to speak would have been so
superfluous and unnecessary. Merton's words haunted me then as they do
today: "I know and have seen what I was obscurely looking for."

The spiritual life is a journey into the unknown. Married life is a journey into the unknown. Like Abraham, we are called to leave the
recognizable and go to a place uncharted. The familiar landscape is abandoned; the unfamiliar appears on the hazy horizon. We are called to trust
in God that we will know how to navigate this new terrain, that we will
find food and shelter—and what we are really looking for.

Merton's own enlightenment came in this exotic place on the other
side of the world from the monastery in which he had spent twenty-seven
years, half his life. Would I be so fortunate to have such an experience in

this lifetime, and if so, where? I, too, in one way or another, sought "the face of God," throughout my life, and so deliberately in my days as a hermit, only to have God conceal himself even further from my view and dance beyond my paltry grasp. "The face of God." Even to use this term is a pious conceit. I simply wanted to know that my life had meaning, that I had lived for something worthwhile and—as the good nuns at St. Benedict's first sowed the seeds—somehow made the world a better place. That I, even though I would probably never fully know it, had done God's will. I was embarking on another phase of my life, with more reservations than convictions. But I did not exactly think of marriage as a "vocation." It was more a state in life than a true calling.

I was still a product of that part of my grade-school education which taught that the highest state (on earth, that is) for men or women was the religious life. Next was "single blessedness," a sort of limbo where the person never married and supposedly lived a holy, virginal life. At the lowest rung of this hierarchy of life choices was marriage, with lust and concupiscence given into. I had taken the easy way, it appeared.

∞

Soon after my return from the round-the-world trip for the Merton documentary, Tracy lost her job at the advertising agency. Her exit would have been either laughable or lamentable, if advertising were a serious business in the first place. The color of the envelopes sent out for some Radio City Music Hall extravaganza hadn't exactly matched the invitation within, and that was that. In her final days, she called me at the Merton editing room.

"Congratulations, Daddy!"

I can date exactly when that child was conceived. I was going in for back surgery in late August, and the night before I would be put out of commission for some weeks, unable to flex the body in that direction, we made love.

We couldn't afford to live in New York on a freelance writer's precarious income, so we moved into the tiny hermitage in Oakham. Neither our New York friends (still wondering when this marriage was going to implode) nor the taciturn neighbors on New Braintree Road could quite figure out what we were doing there. But Tracy, now beginning to swell with the baby, proved the model country wife. With style, of course. She planted a lovely garden, presenting me with an artfully designed scroll detailing every cucumber plant and cantaloupe mound. I still have it. She made a hermitage into a home with wildflowers gathered, curtains in place of Venetian blinds, and carpets vacuumed on a regular basis.

She never failed to wear makeup, looking gorgeous even before venturing out to feed the chickens each morning.

The Oakham house was certainly going to be too small, so with the money from the sale of the Greenwich Village apartment, we bought what was a bit ostentatiously called Goat Hill Farm, a lovely 1860s clapboard home with attached barn, set on a hill with three acres of rolling pasture. We, the urban creatures who could barely see the sky from our respective New York apartments, were now so remote that we could see plenty of sky, but not another house. We had a spectacular vista from our upstairs bedroom, overlooking the sweep of a cornfield on the Hanson Farm in the valley below. We had moved a few miles from Oakham to Hardwick, Massachusetts, where the cow population was greater than the human.

As the months passed, we took to the rhythm of country life, making this venerable house our own, going to bed early, rising with the sun. But, as I look back, I realize I was only partially there. I was playing the part of the expectant father without fully acknowledging that Tracy's ever-expanding midsection would actually yield a child. It seems my personality had been retooled so often and so radically, from the staid, childless brownstoner to CHIPS street worker to urban Lothario to Antony of the Desert, that my system was resisting still another transmutation.

OO

I had experienced feelings of disconnectedness and vertigo before, where everything was slightly out of focus. But here in the JCPenney store in Eastfield Mall, Springfield, Massachusetts, I experienced it once again. On my right, row after row of baby bottles, nipples, pacifiers towered over me. Different sizes, shapes, colors; dizzying, looming displays. On my left, through the vertiginous haze, mounds of blankets, diapers, pins, plastic pants. Before me, a miasma of pinks and blues, tiny sleepers no bigger than a large sock, booties no bigger than my thumb. What alien creatures could these be for?

"Paul, what about . . ."

That voice; who was speaking to me?

This woman waddling alongside me was the vivid reminder that I was call-less at the moment. This beautiful woman, on whose flat stomach I once could lay my head, was now ripe and full. She had been virtually carrying twigs around in her mouth as we prepared for this birth. That night in Springfield, I finally gave in to her nagging. If we didn't get the "baby stuff" *tonight*, she emphasized, we'd be stopping on the way back from the hospital. With "it" in the car seat. Oh, yes, car seat, one aisle over. With plastic tray? Washable? Would it conform to the seatbelts in

the Toyota—oh my God!—station wagon? Yes, a station wagon. Where
had I gone wrong?

Tracy might have been wondering the same thing. Used to shopping at
Lord & Taylor and Bloomingdale's, she had had a similar experience a few
months back when she made her first JCPenney purchase, a maternity
dress. She actually liked it, she had to admit, but then again she was always
more adaptable than I, no matter my deluded visions of myself.

OO

The birth of Paul Noah Wilkes, as my photographs in the delivery room
document so graphically, was a bloody mess. The floor was covered with
blood; Dr. Karen Green's surgical gown was soaked with blood; Tracy's
thighs, which I had so lovingly stroked, were caked and streaked with
blood. And by the time my firstborn son's purplish, banana-shaped head
finally poked its way into the world, Tracy had lost so much blood that
her skin had turned a sickly olive color.

Noah would never do things the normal way, and his birth, face up and
pounding into Tracy's pelvic bones, was a preview of coming events. But
there he was at 4:47 PM on April 8, 1982, seven pounds and twenty-one
inches of life-changing reality. As in the scripture, they wrapped him in
swaddling clothes and then laid him in his mother's arms. Tracy smiled
weakly, her blood pressure continuing to drop, until an alert nurse grabbed
the baby, and Tracy was given a bracing injection of Naloxone to counter-
act an overdose of anesthetic.

Two months later, Tracy and I stood before my beaming spiritual director, Father Mark, in the tiny retreat house chapel at St. Joseph's Abbey.
We were just a few yards from the KGB interrogation room in which
I had spent so many tortured hours of discernment. But my path had ultimately led here, just down the hallway, with a baby, my baby, sleeping
peacefully in my arms. Infants are usually not baptized at monasteries,
but Father Mark made an exception for us, pronouncing the words and
pouring holy water onto Paul Noah's round, now perfectly shaped head,
welcoming him into the Catholic faith and Church.

There I was, repeating vows, not as the monk I hoped I'd be, but as a
father I never imagined I wanted to be. There wasn't another Catholic
among the godparents we had chosen—two Episcopalians, a Methodist,
and a Jew—so Brother Aidan Logan, the acolyte for the baptism, had to
step in as Noah's godfather.

What would Thomas Merton have thought of the irony—and
strangeness—of it all? As best I could tell, he would have thrown back his
head and roared with laughter at the sense of humor of this God of ours.

25

FATHER GREER

THE STROLLER BUMPED ALONG THE UNEVEN ASPHALT ROADBED, victim of
the heaving and thawing of Massachusetts winters, as the rising sun sent
blazing shafts of light through the tall maples lining Upper Church Street.
I had a feeling—deep beneath thermal underwear, flannel shirt, wool
sweater, and Hollofil II–insulated L.L.Bean parka—that my chest was
about to explode. There, looking back from the recesses of an Aprica
stroller, bundled against the minus-ten-degree morning, was the grinning,
red-cheeked face of my son, Noah.

Life at Goat Hill Farm, life as a husband and father—much to my
amazement—was producing, on a daily basis, some of the happiest
moments of my life. We planted an enormous garden and raised a few
sheep and a flock of chickens, which provided us with all the vegetables
and meat we needed. One of the rooms of the barn was now a coop for
laying chickens, and fresh brown eggs awaited us each morning. A wood-
burning stove in the kitchen warmed most of the house. Tracy had turned
complete Earth Mother, freezing vegetables, rounding up runaway sheep,
hauling firewood from the barn, cooing to Noah in a rocking chair as he
fell asleep in her loving arms.

The otherworldly quality of the "blue light" experience at the monastery now regularly burst into my life. On that morning, I was
exhausted from a fitful night's sleep, yet looking into that angelic,
trusting face in the stroller, I was tingling with energy, more alive than
I had ever—yes, *ever*—felt before in my life. Such crystalline moments
could happen while I was putting on my high-topped barn boots to go
out to gather eggs. Or taking diapers out of the washer to put them in
the dryer. Reading a line from a favorite storybook. Seeing hoarfrost
glisten in the morning sun as it began to yield to that pale, warming,
first light.

As unpredictable as they were breathtaking, these moments of serenity seemed to signal that the stars and planets had finally aligned and that I was exactly where I was supposed to be, doing exactly what I was supposed to be doing. As I was wont to do, I tried to write a headline for this story, and the best I could was come up with was a corny "peace with a purpose." I never felt peace at CHIPS, although I had a great purpose. What passed for peace in my New York days was manufactured and hollow and fleeting, and was certainly with no purpose. Even as a hermit, there was so much *effort* expended, there was nothing left over to ever feel at ease in that moment, in this activity—which is another way of describing being at peace.

Charles de Foucauld living in his tiny hut with the Tuareg in the bleak Algerian desert. Dorothy Day ladling soup on the bowery. St. Sebastian, eyes cast heavenward, with arrows sticking out from every inch of his body. Those were once my role models. Were they no more than idols I worshipped? Thomas Merton certainly knew of false gods, because he too once paid them homage. Only one who has experienced this profound an alienation of affection could write, as he did in *New Seeds of Contemplation*, words that I had read so many times, vainly trying to understand what in fact was so apparent: "Every one of us is shadowed by an illusory person: a false self. This is the man I want myself to be but who cannot exist, because God does not know anything about him. And to be unknown to God is altogether too much privacy."

And, then, if that were so, "For me to be a saint means to be myself. Therefore, the problem of sanctity and salvation is in fact the problem of finding out who I am and of discovering my true self."

Getting up in the middle of the night to comfort a screaming baby with a painful ear infection? Changing a diaper? Going on early morning walks so Mom could get some needed rest? Was this the "it" I had been chasing all these years? All I knew was that I loved being a father and a husband. It felt completely natural. In statistics and psychology, they call it "goodness of fit," where the circumstances or data mesh with the givens, both seemingly unpredictable, but in fact totally predictable. I know little about psychology and nothing about statistics, but this symphonic interaction was working beautifully. I hadn't figured my way here. My heart—not my head—was learning how to steer my life.

Strangely enough, with all this paternal bliss, what I once called my spiritual life had withered away. We bought Goat Hill Farm to keep me within a short drive of the monastery, so I could continue to go to daily Mass there. Noah, married life, and the work of our tiny farm had not been let in on such a grand plan. My prayer life had devolved into an

exhausted minute or two on my knees each night. We began to attend
Sunday Mass at the tiny parish in nearby Wheelwright. There, a priest
who organized wrestling nights and trading card afternoons for the local
children and sent everyone birthday greetings, but whose sermons
wouldn't have earned him a passing grade in the basic seminary homilet-
ics course, had us hungering for something at least minimally stimulating
or inspiring. We went down to Gilbertville, where the pastor, obviously
an intelligent man, verbally crucified us each Sunday. He made it clear we
were indeed the sinners that most of us, in our hearts, had the sneaking
suspicion we just might be. "And now let us listen *attentively* to God's
holy word," he would punitively intone before the reading of the scripture. Polish himself, he spoke to his largely Polish congregation as if they
were little more than illiterate peasants, dumb oxen. It reminded me of
St. Benedict's in Cleveland, and Father Leo looking down from the pulpit
at us Slovaks, other stupid beasts among the Slavic herd. But Vatican II had
come along. Hadn't our Gilbertville priest gotten the word about the
"priesthood of all believers" being charged with sanctifying the world?
This was a difficult assignment to carry out while mumbling a litany of
mea culpas.

   If my spiritual life was in intensive care, my writing life was on life
support. My outlook was of such tragic dimensions that, just after ten
each morning as I sat before my mute, black Royal upright typewriter,
I came to dread the approach of our rural postman's sputtering old
Plymouth. The clunking sound of his shifting into a lower gear as the car
eased down the hill was ominous, foreboding. The squeal of brakes as he
coasted to a stop in front of our house started the palpitations. Then the
ethereal screech, like a long-buried coffin being pried open, reduced me to
a limp rag. I peeked from behind the curtains, hoping I wouldn't be seen,
awaiting another fatal verdict.

   What would that oblong sarcophagus of a mailbox hold this morning?
Among the junk mail and bills, another rejection letter—or two—another
"no thanks" to what I had foolishly thought was a reasonably good idea
or acceptable piece of writing. I tried to keep a positive attitude—I had
gone through similar dry periods before—but I was slowly eroding inside.
Then there was one rejection that just about finished me off.

   I had gotten an assignment from *Yankee* magazine to profile four monasteries in the Northeast. *Yankee* was then a self-consciously back-to-the-
land magazine at a time when "spirituality" had supplanted mere religious
conviction, and compost and organic arugula were rising stocks among
people who were turning their backs on convention, careers, and city life.
When I did preliminary research on the magazine before submitting the

monastery idea, I cringed. As I scanned the front of the magazine, it appeared that all the editors had beards, smoked pipes, and wore Wellington boots. I was desperate, so I agreed to do the piece for said Wellington-wearing editors, all for the munificent sum of $700.

After six weeks of work, when *Yankee* rejected that piece and so graciously sent along a "kill fee" of $200, I wanted to travel up to their offices in Dublin, New Hampshire, and fulfill the contract by personally stomping the twerps to death with those Wellingtons.

It had reached a point where I didn't think the local free shopper would have accepted one of my pieces. I had even written an essay, "The Dark Night of the Writer's Soul," about my agonies. Like everything else I was writing, it was rejected. Even an essay about rejection, rejected. I mean, how pitiful could it be?

Only a part-time job teaching writing at Clark University kept the chickens, sheep, and Wilkes family one step ahead of public assistance. I began to wonder if the newfound happiness of fatherhood was an Agent Orange–like defoliant, wafting over my life, destroying both my spiritual and my writing lives. It seemed that way, but this purgatory of rejection and spiritual malnourishment was only preparing me for the most significant—and long-lasting—religious awakening of my life.

∞

"Mr. Wilkes, this is Bob Gottlieb from the *New Yorker* magazine. Mr. Wilkes?"

"B-b-b—"

"Mr. Wilkes, do you have a moment to talk?"

"B-b-b-Bob Gottlieb?"

By moments like these are lives completely changed.

It was about seven o'clock on a Friday evening, and some friends had come up from New York. We were well into a much-extended cocktail hour when the phone rang. Tracy airily answered, "Wilkes place!" She was asked if there were a "Mr. Wilkes" there. I took the phone, expecting to be solicited for a new chimney, siding, or paint job. Instead, Robert Gottlieb, editor of the *New Yorker*, was about to resuscitate my writing life and launch my relationship with one Joseph Terrence Greer Jr., priest of the Archdiocese of Boston.

I had quite a few ideas for articles or books floating around in my brain—the typical freelance writer's bounty and fate—most of which never got much further than a few scribbled lines on the back of an envelope or supermarket receipt. But one idea that kept coming back to me was to do a modern-day version of Georges Bernanos's classic, *The Diary of a Country Priest*. In that book, a priest in a small French village struggles with his faith, his seeming ineffectiveness, and his downright failures as he becomes sicker and sicker with what will be a fatal disease. My idea was to follow an American priest, one who had a limited time to live. I wanted to see how a man of faith lived his final days, if he was buttressed by his beliefs or crushed by the weight of his imminent death. If he sensed God with him. Or felt abandoned by him. Father Greer was recommended to me by another Boston priest, Father Ernest Serino, who had had a heart attack but was not in imminent danger of dying. "Joe Greer has a diagnosis of a fatal cancer," Father Serino told me. "He's always been a good priest, a little cocky, but solid, though not particularly distinguished. The cancer's had a profound effect on him. If he'll do it, he would be perfect."

I had sent letters to the personnel directors in the Worcester and Springfield dioceses and the Archdiocese of Boston with this strange request: I wished to talk with priests about to die. Father Greer was the twenty-sixth priest I had interviewed, and for a variety of reasons, some visceral and some more practical, none of the first twenty-five seemed quite right. As a writer, you need to have a certain connection with a subject, especially when you will spend months with him or her. Out of frustration or panic, you may be tempted to feel that the connection is there when it is not, but a sixth sense keeps you looking until it is. When Father Greer first walked into the dark-paneled reception room within the St. Patrick's rectory, I immediately fell in love with the man.

As I would eventually describe him, first in the *New Yorker* and then, bowing to Bernanos in the title of my book, *In Mysterious Ways: The Death and Life of a Parish Priest*: "Father Greer is fifty-six years old and has black hair that ascends to a small wave before being slicked back from his face. The face itself is handsome, strong, and ruddy, relatively wrinkle-free, and traced with a fine pattern of broken blood vessels, the result—he is not shy to admit—of too many hours of work, a bit too much drinking (especially during the hectic days of school integration in Boston), and the overall wear of thirty years as a priest." He had a very 1950s look about him, but I would eventually discover that Father Greer was very much a priest of his time, a protean and magnificent man in his triumphs as well as his failures.

The *New Yorker* assignment was surely an act of divine intervention; there is no reason it should have happened. After that initial visit with Father Greer, I had switched gears, for the moment setting aside the book idea. Instead, I felt that he would make a perfect *New Yorker* profile, and through him, I could look at the larger Church, declining Mass attendance, the accelerating shortage of priests, and the loss of their once inalienable authority. I sent Gottlieb what writers call a query letter, which outlines the story idea briskly and enticingly, explaining why it is appropriate for that publication. Borne to the sarcophagus of my mailbox by the hearse of an old Plymouth with squealing brakes, Gottlieb's prompt and curt initial reply informed me that the magazine did not commission articles by writers unknown to them. I was used to rejections, but for some reason, I was not going to let this be the final note. Hmm . . . unknown writer.

At the time, I had a few books behind me, as well as the *Six American Families* series, but those were years before. There had been the extended dry spell, divided between hedonism and eremitism. The most recent piece I had was a somewhat dated and rather perfunctory one for the *New York Times Magazine* on the election of the Episcopal Church's presiding bishop. I retrieved a nonyellowed copy of that article, but I knew that would not be enough. How could I convince Gottlieb that this could be a great article and that I was the writer to bring it off? First, what did a *New Yorker* profile actually sound like? I had admired the magazine from a distance, but had never actually read it much. I went to the Ware Public Library and paged through a few back issues. Returning home, making the sign of the cross, and, possessed in a sort of fugue state, I sat before the Royal upright and rattled off a page and a half, saying to Gottlieb, "This is the way the piece might begin . . ."

> The Roman Catholic parish of St. Patrick—Father Joseph Greer's parish—covers almost four square miles of the town of Natick, and, with eighty-five hundred parishioners, is one of the larger Catholic communities in suburban Boston. Its church, which consists of a main sanctuary and a smaller church below ground level, seats eleven hundred. In addition, there is a sixteen-acre cemetery, a huge elementary-school building and adjoining hall, an eighteen-bedroom convent, and twenty-seven room rectory, converted from a Civil War–era roadhouse. St. Patrick's, which was itself founded in 1860, is the mother Catholic church of Natick, and was at one time considered a dream assignment. For decades, the pastor of St. Patrick's . . .

I went on to say that that dream was no more. Since Vatican II, these have been rocky years in the Catholic Church, this parish, and this man's life. I quietly slipped those typewritten pages into a large brown envelope and made the sign of the cross over the sealed edge.

∞

At the end of Gottlieb's Friday evening call, blessedly giving me the assignment even after my stuttering response, he instructed me to call the "money person" on Monday. When I did, she asked how much I wanted for an advance, something I had never gotten before for a magazine article. "Oh, I think a thousand—"

"Would five thousand do?" she interrupted.

"Yes, that's fine," I gulped.

"And expenses? Two thousand to begin with?"

"Sure. Perfect." My lips were quivering on the mouthpiece. If I could have transmitted a kiss over AT&T's long lines, I would have happily done so. The Wilkes family was eating again.

∞

For the first few weeks, I didn't ask Father Greer a single question, just tagged along as he went about being a parish priest in Natick . . . and a cancer patient at the New England Medical Center in Boston. I sat with him as he consoled a sad widow at her kitchen table in her tiny apartment; as he haggled with a Boston College classmate over the price of a new, environmentally sound oil tank to replace the rusting hulk deep beneath the rectory's front lawn; as he held the hand of a teenage accident victim in the hospital; as he joked with fellow priests about the blizzard of mail they received from the chancery office, the bulk of which Father Greer deposited in a wastebasket, unopened.

There were many trips—sadly too many—to the cancer ward of the medical center to see the physicians who were guiding his care. The year before, he had been diagnosed with multiple myeloma. Malignant plasma cells were dividing unchecked in his body, damaging healthy tissue and collecting in his bone marrow, causing severe pain in his back while compromising his immune system. This cancer had no "cure." Father Greer's only hope was a regime of radiation and chemotherapy, and eventually, if his body could withstand it, to have a bone marrow transplant, which would extend, but not save, his life.

At the end of a normal workday in the parish, we would go up to his second-floor suite of rooms, brightly decorated in shades of blue—so different from the unremitting beiges and browns of most rectories I had visited—and Father Greer would mix a healthy batch of manhattans that we would leisurely sip as we watched the evening news, alert for the tinkle of a bell downstairs, summoning us to dinner. He was not a man to quickly open up beyond surface chitchat and basic facts, but gradually we began to talk more deeply about his early life, his call to the priesthood—which occurred while he was engaged to be married— his views on the Church, his cancer. And, late one evening, we talked of his violation of the sacred vow of celibacy. I grew to treasure those hours, both of us inevitably a little lightheaded from alcohol, when the tough, fast-quipping bravado was set aside and a mortal man, with a death sentence, was laid bare. Then he spoke plainly and simply about his faith as well as his doubts.

Although clouds of rage occasionally darkened the landscape of his mind ("God, I've tried to do my best; why me?"), Father Greer was not a man to allow himself extended bouts of self-pity. Life wasn't about fairness or bargaining or rewards for good intentions. He was a Celtic existentialist. What was, was. One made the best of it. God's graces flowed in adversity, ebbed when all seemed to go well. A dark pessimism danced with a deep, no-nonsense faith, so typically Irish.

If I were to invite you to visit, ever so briefly, with Father Greer, that you might get some measure of the man, I would ask you to be present on two occasions, to show his marvelous range.

A breezy couple, both with substantial jobs in Boston's booming high-tech sector (Father Greer would later refer to them as "the hundred-thousand-dollar couple" for their combined income, quite a sum at the time), came to make wedding arrangements. It soon became evident that they were more awed by the beauty and majesty of St. Patrick's as a tableau for the exchange of their vows than interested in the sacrament of marriage that would take place therein. It was apparent that they were living together and were not practicing Catholics.

After listening to the details of flowers, gowns, caterer, and guest list, Father Greer interposed, "About that guest list. I think you forgot someone." The young woman reached into her Gucci bag for a pen. "Jesus. I don't think he made the list," Father Greer said dryly. "Look, I'm barely batting .500 on the marriages I've performed. I'm not looking for another divorce. Let's do this the best way we can, with the circumstances at hand." More the Hound of Heaven than the Badger of the Boston Archdiocese, he prescribed weekly attendance at Mass, which he would gently monitor at the church's door. Acknowledging that Boston rents precluded a more radical solution, he asked them to live apart for at least a week or two before the wedding. "You want this to be a special day, don't you?" Although at the time he was not overly optimistic for their continuing Catholic practice, Father Greer would be pleasantly surprised in the months following the wedding, when the couple became regular attendees.

There were a number of funerals I attended with him, but one stands out. A call had come from a young couple whose baby had died shortly after birth. As they weren't churchgoing Catholics, their pleas to several parishes, the house of a religious order, and the archdiocesan offices had proved fruitless. "Somebody's got to do it," Father Greer said, without hesitation. He had never met them before the day that he stood in front of a raw gash in the ground at the parish cemetery, the tiny white coffin flanked by a sobbing mother, her abdomen still swollen, and an ashen-faced father rubbing his calloused hands together. He looked at them. "Most of us have to wait sixty, seventy, eighty years to be with Christ in heaven. Your baby, only a day. She is with him right now. That much we know. We know it for sure."

It was his unerring sense of place, his ability to size up a situation quickly and to speak practically about God, about the balm that was Catholicism, that continually endeared him to me. He was imperfect. After Vatican II, when many priests were leaving and the strict rules that kept priests bound to their rectories and clerical life were loosening, Father Greer hung his trademark black suit in the closet one evening, put on a tweed sports jacket and a pair of slacks, and ventured out into the world. He frequented cocktail lounges—certainly none within his parish—and did far more than chat with the young women he met.

He admitted he was a racist. When the Boston public schools were being integrated and the call went out for priests to ride with black schoolchildren into the white bastion of Charlestown, his priest friends scoffed at the idea. Father Greer volunteered, only to have former parishioners throw rotten fruit and spit on him, screaming that he was a "nigger lover." He put it this way one night as we talked: "Do I love them as much as I love my Irish people? No, I don't. But, God didn't make any garbage. These people aren't garbage."

He was certainly charismatic, but not the Ron Petroski type, who, though I didn't know it, was about to resign his priesthood. Father Petroski had been accused of molesting one or perhaps more of the teenage boys at my Brooklyn parish, boys that I knew, boys who also were inspired by him. Years later, he would die of AIDS. No, Father Greer was a tattered but more whole piece of cloth. He was a man whose deep spirituality, once you spent time with him and began to notice, glowed through his actions. He never called attention to himself; he brushed aside thanks and kudos. He found an enormous pleasure in helping people, in making connections so that a marginal student could get into his beloved Boston College, poor kids could get free Red Sox tickets, or his parking lot would be the first plowed by Natick Public Works on snowy Sunday mornings.

∞

The profile of Father Greer appeared in the June 13, 1988, issue of the *New Yorker*. It generated more mail than I received on anything I'd written before or since. The *New Yorker* itself was flooded with letters. Father Greer's story had touched a nerve in Catholic America. Priests wrote to say that, finally, someone had captured their life and presented an honest and appealing portrait of a priest who was as human as he was holy. Lay Catholics said he was the kind of priest they wanted as their pastor. I was overwhelmed with the response, and when I took a sheaf of letters to show Father Greer, he typically changed the subject. He had not even read the entire article.

Who could not love a man like that?

I received seven book offers and so was able to continue spending time with him. *In Mysterious Ways: The Death and Life of a Parish Priest* went on to chronicle the horrific trial of his bone marrow transplant, whereby he was basically killed—irradiated with x-rays and poisonous chemicals—such that only the infusion of his own previously harvested peripheral stem cells would bring him back to life. Balding, his mouth and esophagus scalded with painful canker sores, he precariously hung on to life, then slowly grew stronger. He eventually returned to St. Patrick's. Inevitably, the disease came back. I was with Father Greer until the end—even after the book was published—reading the Psalms from his well-worn breviary at his bedside in the intensive care unit of New England Medical Center as he gasped for life and the cancer relentlessly wore him down. From diagnosis to death, he had lived seven years, remarkable in itself, testimony to his will to live and his love for his work as a parish priest.

∞

After his funeral, I sat alone with the bronze casket perched atop a green catafalque at the cemetery. It was a raw February day, a perfectly appropriate day for a Son of the Sod to be buried, with a bone-chilling wind whispering through the bare trees, rattling the few dry leaves left to cling tentatively to the spindly branches.

I had lost not just a perfect subject to write about, but a man who I genuinely enjoyed being with, a man who, just for who he was, constantly made me want to be a better person. In a journalist's life, there are thousands of interviews, hours upon hours of observation, but it is rare—at least it was for me, being a man with such a short attention span—to hunger for still more time together. But I knew as I stood there that Father Greer had implanted something in me that would be unaffected by the mere fact that he was no more.

Father Greer had laid a cornerstone. A new kind of faith was beginning to take shape within me. At a time in the larger Catholic Church when Pope John Paul II was continuing on a path toward obedience and orthodoxy and away from the liberating power of Vatican II, many Catholics were simply giving up on the Church in frustration over its imperiousness and insensitivity. Bishops faithfully carried out Vatican edicts, seeing it as both their calling and as a step to higher office to condemn the wayward, meanwhile asserting an authority that had been conferred by Rome, but that—to me, at least—had not been earned in the eyes of the local faithful. That was not the kind of Catholicism I wanted to live. There was another way, not that it was so dramatic or rebellious. It just seemed to make more sense. In Father Greer, I saw the New Testament come alive as he strolled the streets of Natick, as he healed with a word or a look, as he forgave, as he took people where they were and infused their ordinary actions with a measure of transcending grace.

The various jagged pieces, collected so randomly and for the most part unconsciously during the first fifty years of my life, were coming together. I now saw a way to live my life. It was a strange and mystical mixture of my father's basic integrity, my mother's selfless love, and what the sisters, brothers, and priests had imparted through my seventeen years of Catholic education. The objective, they taught, was to make the world a better place, with whatever time or talent one had. Your thanks would rise up from the good you have done, a soft mist of knowing that in some small way you mattered, you made a difference. The world would not acclaim you. Only your soul would know, occasionally. Those days with Jacques Travers had helped bring this life into focus. Jacques, a man who could smile at the bruise on his forehead after he was mugged and who would spend his last $10 for a good bottle of Pouilly Fuisse.

This was not theology or philosophy or psychology learned in a classroom, but wisdom revealed during my months in the company of my unlikely guru, one Joseph Terrence Greer Jr. Father Greer, who so casually dumped praise and rejection into the same pot. Be ready, he so profoundly and simply said, "to take the pokes with the strokes. You're gonna get both, and don't make much of either." If every priest should have a plaque with those words emblazoned on it, so should every writer. Father Greer drolly took aim at my hand wringing and doubting if I was doing enough with my life or was being a good enough father: "Life is lacing up your sneakers every morning and getting out on the court to play as best as you can. Let God take care of the rest."

He knew the limitations of his own humanity. This once by-the-book, rigid priest had, before the upheavals of the post Vatican II Church, unflinchingly upheld every jot and tiddle of Catholic doctrine. Now he joined the ranks of sinners and the diseased, and grew closer to God. His life as a priest, as a man in prayer, blossomed. When I asked him what he told couples who were having difficulties with the Church's unflinching stand on artificial birth control as confirmed in the 1979 papal encyclical, *Humanae Vitae*, he smiled, "In the old days, I gave no quarter. But after facing my own shortcomings, I looked for extenuating circumstances. And I always found them."

It was a Christlike mercy he demonstrated, not a high-priest's perfection.

Just as my own father never told me what it was to be Catholic, but showed me, Father Greer demonstrated the richness of a life with Christ, a life not predicated on personal accomplishments and glib ecclesial assurances, but tempered and tested by the doubt we all experience, the halting steps we take. I saw in Father Greer the example of a human nature transformed by God into something beautiful and good. Grace *did* build on nature. It built on his nature; it would build on mine. I had no grand plan or road map for my life, but I had the growing confidence that God would provide the light and insight for the next step. And the next.

I dropped to my knees on the frozen ground beside the casket. I remained there in silence for a long time, not wanting to leave him. The wind diminished to a soft murmur, a final good-bye. A faint light broke through the low, fast-moving clouds, then disappeared. I got to my feet to walk back out into the world of the living and into the days that lay ahead.

PART SIX

LIFE, LIVED

26

THE WRITING LIFE

IT WAS A PECULIAR, MUFFLED SOUND, like a huge log striking a giant rug, echoing from the mist-shrouded foothills of the Velez Mountains to the east. It sounded a second, then a third time, followed by an eerie silence. But then it gradually rose up, first as no more than a gentle whistle, like that of a shepherd minding his flocks on one of the lush upland pastures surrounding the city. Louder. Louder still, until the whistle became a deafening screech, a high-pitched wail from hell.

I pressed the small of my back into the roughhewn stone of the building on Matije Gupca Street. It was fall 1992, and I was on assignment, covering the Bosnian War. I had stopped to watch workmen laying cinder block to repair the building's face, surgically peeled off by a bomb. The workmen, cigarettes dangling from their mouths, seemed hardly concerned as they straightened up from their work and lay down their trowels. A deafening thud sounded; the earth beneath me trembled. I jerked around to see a column of smoke spiral into the air behind some low buildings to the north, no more than a half mile away. There was a second and then a third impact; three neat plumes rose over the otherwise quiet city of Mostar. I turned back to the worksite. The laborers were gone. I was alone. What I had hastily written in my reporter's notebook was an illegible scrawl. I was sweating profusely, my Kevlar bulletproof vest not allowing even the vapor of my perspiration to venture into the world outside its secure perimeter. Shoving my notebook into my pants pocket, I ran as fast I could back down the street, Leica pounding at my chest.

I hustled past the shell of the once beautiful church of SS. Peter and Paul—its bare, ruined arches standing starkly in the early morning light, no longer with anything to support—and to the gates of the adjoining Franciscan monastery. This was my refuge, itself a most tempting target for the Serb gun emplacements in the mountains. In the enemy's eyes, so went the local wisdom, any symbol that God was present in Mostar had to be pounded into inconsequential dust.

∞

When I married and faced the prospect of having children, I experienced a fear that may not have been on a par with what I was feeling on Matije Gupca Street, but it was a substantial fear nonetheless. A fear that my writing life would be snuffed out, eclipsed by the demands of fatherhood and providing for a family, that my creative juices would dry up. That my few functioning brain cells would atrophy. That I would have to agree to that most dreaded of sentences for the freelance writer: getting a real job.

Strangely, just the opposite had happened. My sons, Noah and Daniel, were now in grade school; Tracy had earned, with honors, a master of social work degree from Boston College and was working in a family services agency. Whatever periods of time there were between household and farm chores, helping teach Daniel his letters and Noah his addition tables, shopping at the local Big Y supermarket, carpooling to T-ball and soccer practice, seemed *dyanu*, a fine Jewish word I learned while spending time with a Conservative rabbi and writing a book about a year in his life. *Dyanu*. Enough. In their Passover Seder, Jews express thanks to a God of deliverance, a God at work beyond their limitations. He always proved to be on time and sufficient. *Dyanu*.

This was the God I was coming to experience, although my understanding was typically lagging behind what was actually happening.

Now here I was in Mostar, ducking artillery rounds, quoting Hebrew words from a rabbi whom I would accompany to pray at the Wailing Wall in Jerusalem, having just returned from a trip to El Salvador where I stood amid red rosebushes on the hallowed ground where six Jesuits, their housekeeper, and her daughter were slaughtered by government soldiers. I would soon walk the halls of the papal palace in the Vatican, sit with cardinals and speculate—quite prematurely—on who the next pope might be when John Paul II was called home. The self-involved New York years, when I had an infinite amount of time to travel anywhere and stay as long as I wanted, had produced nothing. I had gone nowhere, in more ways than not writing anything more meaningful than the pitiful series on the vicissitudes of being single. My finite number of hours as a married man and father seemed like the five barley loaves and two fishes—woefully inadequate in the face of the great need at hand, yet miraculously sufficient. *Dyanu*.

A different kind of spiritual and religious life was slowly taking shape, intermingled with a writing life I could have only dreamed about. The constraints of a family, blessed stability, and a sense of purpose conspired to focus me as never before in my life. I was discovering a new voice as a writer, a clarity about what to write about, and a way to write about it.

What was this voice? I honestly do not know. After all, one does not wake up one morning and begin to write in "the voice." .

Where did it come from? For that I can at least venture a guess. It may have seen its birth at the breakfast nook table in Cleveland when my father, mellowed by a few shots and beers, would offhandedly tell his stories. Like the one about the day in the coal mines when a frightened, first-day miner forgot his lunch and my father said gruffly, "I can't eat this damn ham and cheese sandwich; ya want it, kid?" It was nurtured by the hagiographic wonderment of Butler's *Lives of the Saints* and flavored by the clean smell of the Notre Dame nun as she whisked by, lining us up for lunch. It was reinforced by Father McEvoy holding a host above the simple wooden altar in the basement of Marquette's dental school chapel. It was confirmed by the gentle look on Jacques Travers' face as he rearranged the coverlet over the Professor's bony knees.

The sights, the sounds, the smells of Catholicism captured my imagination and pierced my heart far more deeply than the Church's dogmas, doctrines, laws, and prohibitions. It is the difference between *wanting* to believe in something I found attractive rather than *having* to believe in something I was told I must. After all, from an early age I was not the best rule follower. And as a journalist, I had the inclinations of a magazine writer, not a reporter of the news and facts. The facts were often some of the least important elements of a story, and often misleading, no more than a Potemkin village hiding the reality. I wanted the story behind those facts. What made people do the things they did? Why did they act this way? Who and what had influenced and formed them? Who were they on the surface and deep inside? What mattered most to them? Least?

In my first twenty years as a writer, I had written about New York City's garbage, the election of Elks officers, why detectives don't solve more crimes, a wild dog in Central Park, teenage outcasts in Baltimore's Monument Park, brownstones in Brooklyn, and a soldier coming home, sealed in a casket. I had interviewed a sitting U.S. Supreme Court justice and a future vice president of the United States. I had lunched with movie starlets in five-star restaurants, sat in locker rooms with sports legends, and looked out from the glass-sheathed corner offices of business moguls. If Joseph had a coat of many colors, my clipping file was a

patchwork of disparate people and subjects. But I had now come to the
realization that yes, garbage men and celebrities needed to have their
say, but someone else would have to write about them. There was nothing wrong with those kinds of stories, but I had lost my interest in them.
To receive an assignment from a major national magazine on an idea
cooked up during its editorial board meeting just wasn't enough anymore. I wanted to write about what belief and faith in God really meant.
How did it motivate people to do what they did? Where was it healthy
and beneficial? Where was it corrupted?

It's hardly a secret that many writers choose subjects because, down
deep, they are trying to sort out their own lives in the process. They
might write about sports because, Walter Mitty–like, they are on the field.
Politics, because they want to influence. Power, because they are
seduced—or repelled—by it. It was certainly that way with me. I often
felt that I was merely *playing* at being a Catholic. I was struggling with
my own faith, what believing in God really meant, how it steered a life.
I was not a man on some holy mission, not at all. It was hardly that conscious. It was more a combination of happenstance and animal instinct
than design.

God's grace and guidance were building on the natural instincts, likes,
and dislikes that I possessed, the ancient mariner steering me away from
shoal waters, leading me toward open sea. The creative hand of God,
Aquinas would say, was at work in the being that was uniquely mine, in
the specific events of my life. For nothing in our human nature is defiled;
everything has the potential for holiness. God is in it all. Few of us see
this in the moment, and only after God has passed by do we know that
he had been present. I look back now and realize that he was there palpably during this crucial hinge in my life.

It is a bit strange that I would begin to write almost exclusively on
subjects, issues, and people where religion and religious belief had a bearing. I was hardly the model Christian. By certain measures, I was not
even a very good Catholic.

I had major problems with the so-called institutional Church, with the
sometimes barely adequate men who served as pastors in parishes
I attended, with the Medici-like pomposity of the hierarchy, parading
about in medieval gowns, cascading lace, soaring miters atop their heads.
The unspeakable burden heaped on the backs of the divorced, who were
denied the Eucharist; the disdain with which "objectively disordered"
homosexuals were looked on; the threat of excommunication for those
contemplating an abortion or supporting those who made this choice—
none of this squared with the expansiveness and forgiveness of the

Christ of the New Testament. A Christ I was beginning to know as, each morning, I read dispatches from the portrayal of his life as reported by Matthew, Mark, Luke, and John.

So what does one do about such a conflicted relationship? For me, the only answer was to write about it.

My theology, my ecclesiology, had become simpler and simpler. Along with the brutality and stupidity of everyday life, there was grace abounding, erupting in the most unlikely places. Every so often, the curtain was pulled back for an instant, and there the face of God was revealed. Although I could not say it in those words, that is what I wanted to write about. I wanted to write about common goodness found in uncommon places. I wanted to be inspired by lives of quiet virtue and in turn provide the conduit—as I had done with Father Greer—so that others would know that their humanity, too, was the good soil onto which God randomly and recklessly scattered many rich seeds of opportunity. I wanted to write about living a truly Christ-centered life, in hopes that I myself might do it more successfully. And I saw no other way to do it than through the only prism I had, a Catholic prism. I would write about other religious traditions, but more and more, Catholic subjects found their way to me. I wanted to find and write about what was good about the Church and Catholics, but I would not look for excuses or allow the Church to hide behind convoluted defenses when I saw the institution or us Catholics forfeiting the magnificent mandate we had been given. For certain, I would not be an apologist for the Church, right or wrong. I was a writer who was Catholic. I was not a Catholic writer. I loved the Catholic Church enough to engage it, in my own small and insignificant way. I respected my profession enough to approach subjects and issues with a reporter's open mind.

Father Petroski had introduced me to the power and potential of a Vatican II way of living a Catholic life. Father Greer had shown so poignantly how an otherwise ordinary, fallible man could influence lives through a certain commonsense application of the virtues as well as the shortcomings he had been apportioned. There was a kind of Catholic DNA, a way of regarding the world I had taken from him. I wanted to speak to and for the people occupying Catholicism's Middle Earth, people like myself, questioning, confused, hopeful, realizing we were neither angry enough to be on one end of the spectrum—and perhaps out of the Church altogether—nor sure enough for the other extreme and willing to unthinkingly vow, "My Church, right or wrong."

As a reporter looking for documentation of how and why I came to this understanding of my role in life, I am embarrassed with the paucity of information I have to back it up. Whereas I have notebooks of reflections and agonized diary entries for my troubled days in New York, I have embarrassingly little documentation for this period. At the same time, I have boxes upon boxes of photographs of my wife and children, their drawings, and various mementos. All I have about my own life (as I was the picture taker, I am in precious few of the photos) are the books and the magazine articles I wrote, mostly for the *New Yorker*. Better than my explanations, revisiting three of them here will illustrate what God had set in my path and what I would write about. I would find a Church conflicted, a Church redeemed, and a Church disgraced.

BOSNIA: A CHURCH CONFLICTED. I thought I was allaying at least some of Tracy's fears when I went down to the Hanson farm and asked Gus Hanson to spray-paint the helmet I had bought a bright shade of sky blue. The helmet, which had arrived by overnight delivery, was in military khaki; I thought the color would mark me as a combatant. Tracy was not terribly enthusiastic about this hastily arranged reporting trip for the *New Yorker*, but she at least approved of the blue helmet as we talked over breakfast on the day I was to leave. Perhaps this would keep me alive. I had read about a monastery in the city of Mostar that was helping refugees, and I wanted to see how faith was lived out in this terrible conflict. Little did I know that this exact shade of blue was used by the United Nations troops in Bosnia and that the UN troops were hated by *all* sides as the slaughter went on. Little did I know that Mostar would be in the news every night I was there and that Tracy would begin to wonder how my body would be shipped home.

My research had shown that the besieged city of Mostar was once one of the jewels in Communism's tawdry crown. Josef Tito had masterfully laid before its people a life of abundance with good jobs, good income, ample food, and plenty of drink, a bounty their ancestors had never known. Despite his authoritarian rule, there still was a modicum of freedom of speech and travel. In the bargain, there was one thing Yugoslavs did have to agree to sacrifice—their faith in God. Tito made the mockery of religion a fine art: who needed God when you, comrades, had all this!

With Tito's death and the collapse of the Soviet Union, the synthetic entity called Yugoslavia began to dissolve, as long-standing hatred between Serb and Croat, Christian and Muslim bubbled to the surface. Sarajevo was much in the news in the early 1990s as troops led by a hard-line nationalist Communist thug named Slobodan Milošević indiscriminately killed, raped, and ravaged throughout the country, fueled by the dream of a "greater Serbia." But I was heading for Mostar, which had suffered even greater loss of life and had witnessed appalling damage. And the Mostar story had hardly been told.

The horrors and indignities of war were readily apparent when I finally made it from the seaport city of Split through friendly and enemy lines to the city, in the company of Galal Abbas, an intrepid Sudanese student. God had provided a coal-black guardian angel who spoke fluent Croatian. The city's main park was now a cemetery. Galal and I walked among fresh mounds of dirt that almost touched each other to conserve space, marking the continuing and most recent sacrifice. In the distance, row after row of other mounds were slowly subsiding and growing stubs of grass. There was virtually no food for sale in Mostar, so all its people had become beggars, their only sustenance what relief agencies could bring in. Well-dressed women, their dyed hair now combed into convoluted styles to hide the roots they could neither bend nor blend to their wishes, stood in line with the women who used to clean their well-appointed houses. A once opulent shopping mall had been incinerated, its aluminum facade melted like so much wax.

"I would not say what has happened here deepens faith. It makes faith a question." Father Thomaslav Pervan's measured response to my question about the effects of this horrible and lengthy siege of Mostar was neither righteous nor vindictive. He and the community of ten Franciscan monks, scorned for decades, were now the only semblance of order, the only place to turn for life's basic needs. Beneath his cracked window, lines of people waited for their humble daily ration of a few cans of food, a small bag of beans, a potato or two.

Father Pervan, a husky man with a disconcertingly fixed, vague smile on his face, spoke in a voice cauterized of emotion. There was a Slavic melancholy about him; so many oppressors had come this way— Ottomans, Hapsburgs, Nazis, and, within memory, the Communist partisans who slaughtered dozens of his brother monks. Dealing with this latest onslaught, Father Pervan had not shown himself to be the saint I had come here to find and canonize in print. Even as he fed Muslims and gave them the medicines they needed, it was apparent that he distrusted, disliked, and perhaps even hated them. Although I was in search of a story that would show that the Catholic Church had risen above ethnicity and religion during this horrible time, I didn't find it. I drove over roads pockmarked from artillery barrages with Father Jakob Renic, past the graveyard at Voyno where he buried—mostly at night because of sniper fire—dozens of soldiers and civilians slaughtered in an orgy of hate. I stood with soldiers in camouflage fatigues at the front line in a mountain outpost high above Voyno, as Father Renic placed a host on their tongues, their breath heavy with cigarettes and *lozovaca,* the local plum brandy that numbed their minds and increased their courage. These good Catholic boys and Father Renic happily posed for a picture afterwards, and several of the soldiers thrust their arms high in a Nazi-style salute, an uncomfortable throwback to their role in World War II, when they, not the Serbs, had the upper hand. Again, my hoped-for story, ruined.

EL SALVADOR: A CHURCH REDEEMED. I was the journalist traveling to dangerous places, but it was Tracy whose bravery and audacity made the local news column of the *Ware River News.* Our sheep had once again breeched the pitiful fencing, and Tracy, still in her nightgown, but otherwise fully made up and about to begin her day as the farm wife, part-time social worker, and mother of two young sons, grabbed a bucket of feed and ran out onto Upper Church. In a lilting voice, she hollered, "Sheep, sheep, sheep," but it was perhaps the rattling of the feed in the bucket that lured them back into the pasture. I applauded her—and thought this was as good a time as any to mention that the story idea I'd suggested to Bob Gottlieb had been approved at the *New Yorker.* I would be traveling to El Salvador. I tried to soft-sell the trip: "You had more of a chance to get hurt than I will."

She was not to be convinced. I showed the boys where El Salvador was on the map. "Isn't that where they're fighting, Dad?" asked Noah. "A little bit, but remember, I'm a bigger chicken than the ones out in the coop. Don't worry; I'll be careful." The boys were excited that their father was going someplace they had seen on television news. Tracy was still not convinced. I promised I'd call home as often as I could.

One night, calling from a roadside stand in San Salvador, I mentioned the name of an otherwise quiet provincial capital I'd passed through earlier in the day. "It's on the news right now," Tracy said. "Oh, God, the rebels just shelled it!" There was static on the line. "Couldn't you just come home right now?"

When I got to El Salvador, it was not hard to see that the One, Holy, Catholic and Apostolic Church was, in reality, two Catholic Churches. There was the Church that sided with the landed oligarchy and a right-wing military that promised stability. Then there was the Church that sided with the landless peasants and the left-wing insurgents who promised revolution. Oscar Romero was part of both; he had seen the Church both ways. His early days as the archbishop of San Salvador garnered invitations to the finest houses and the halls of power, and the tacit approval of his superiors in Rome. His conversion to the second Church earned him scorn and dire warnings from Rome and, finally, a single .22

caliber bullet, fired from the door of the nun's chapel at the Convent of the Good Shepherd, which pierced his heart.

El Salvador presented a complex, confusing situation, as left-wing politics and basic gospel values faced off against a more predictable but oppressive government and—predominantly Catholic—ruling class, where Washington and Rome saw their best interests and future hopes preserved by the status quo. The U.S. government would eventually send $10 billion in guns, equipment, and helicopters, meanwhile helping train Salvadoran military in the arts of counterterrorism, combating guerilla warfare, and torture masked as "interrogation." Pope John Paul II, fearing that the theology of liberation that was sweeping Central America was less religious belief than political ideology—just another incarnation of the Communist thought he so hated in his native Poland—also opted to speak out forcefully against the revolutionaries and for the government.

Caught in the middle was Romero, once a conveniently quiet and pious prelate. It was only after the assassination of his friend and fellow student Father Rutilio Grande, whose clerical path had led him to the poor villages where death squads routinely killed anyone who opposed the government, that Romero became an ardent advocate for the *pobrecitos* of his country. The war dragged on; U.S. aid continued. And then, in 1989, six Jesuits were killed, execution-style, along with their housekeeper and her daughter. The one-year anniversary of their deaths provided me with a perfect opportunity to visit this troubled country.

In the Catholic tradition, the Via Dolorosa commonly refers to the Way of the Cross that pilgrims trace through the streets of Jerusalem's Old City, in a sense walking with Christ from condemnation at the hands of Pilate to his tomb in the sepulcher. I had symbolically taken that journey hundreds of times in St. Benedict's Church as we recited the stations of the cross. As a boy, saying the rote prayers that recalled those fourteen events, I would constantly let my mind wander. I was already not a budding news reporter with a string of facts but a magazine writer filling in the details. I could hear the jeering crowds, the whip upon his back, the cross bumping over the cobblestone street. I could visualize his face, contorted in agony, caked with blood, dust, sweat, spittle. The Good Shepherd, the Healer, the Promised One. How could his life have ended this way?

How fortunate I was to be steeped in the rich folklore of Catholicism, to have my brain etched in those impressionable days with an indelible image of Christ. It had prepared me to travel another Via Dolorosa, this one recalling not a figure in a rough wool tunic but rather men and women in El Salvador in cotton slacks and short-sleeved shirts or blouses, who confronted not ancient imperial powers but those of this day and our own making.

A cool evening breeze rustled the tall eucalyptus trees overlooking a grassy knoll at the heart of the campus of the Universidad Centroamericana (UCA) in the capital of San Salvador, bringing slight relief to the thousands of people assembled. It was time for the Offertory of the Mass. Eight apothecary jars were brought in a solemn procession to the makeshift elevated altar near where I was standing. Carried high in the air, each was borne by a campesino who had known them in life. *Elba Ramos. Celina Ramos. Amando López Quintana. Ignacio Ellacuria. Juan Ramón Moreno Pardo. Ignacio Martín Baro. Segundo Montes Mozo. José Joaquin López y López.* Each jar had a simple white label with black lettering. No honorifics, no separation of clergy and lay, all equal in death. Within the jars were soil, dried grass, and twigs, all bathed in blood, reverentially collected after the bodies were removed. Relics now.

These, the latest Catholic martyrs of El Salvador, were unlikely revolutionaries, not all of them brave and forceful like Father Ellacuria, who was their outspoken leader. The six Jesuits; the three Catholic nuns and the lay missioner, Jean Donovan; Romero; and so many other Catholics had found that the mere "practicing" of their faith was no longer enough. They read the scriptures, not as abstract history, but as light shining upon their decisions. In villages, they formed small base communities to study and pray together. In different ways, they all came to a similar conclusion: they could not obediently bow to the authority of a government or a Church that did not square with the image of justice in their hearts. With all its ambiguities, with all the confusing mixing of contemporary politics and venerable religion, theirs was both an anguished cry and a sweet song of the soul, a strong and forceful Catholicism, at once bound to Mother Church, yet free to be obedient to conscience and the *Cristo*.

In grade school, reading the lives of the saints, I felt the call to live a fearless Catholic life. I never felt that more strongly than that night on the UCA campus. I felt it rise up in my chest as I stood beside the graves of the two Maryknoll sisters in a San Salvador cemetery. I was covered with gooseflesh when I looked into the closet in Oscar Romero's tiny room on the grounds of Divine Providence Hospital to see the blood-soaked alb he wore as he said his last Mass. His blood was spilled on the altar; some say drops fell into the chalice. I felt both rage and determination as I stood in the simple adobe hut in El Mozote, before the painting on the wall depicting that horrific night when the helicopter gunship hovered overhead and blew women and children to bits with round after round of U.S.-supplied ammunition. As I walked the rutted, dusty streets of the villages of Chalatenago with Father Jon Sobrino, where he and the Jesuits who had been killed had devoted so much of their time, I could see what they meant to these campesinos. When all else seemed hopeless, Christ was there among them in the presence of these unlikely martyrs.

I was not a proselytizer for the Catholic faith. I was the dispassionate reporter. But the facts from these stories were so compelling, I knew as I formed them into an article that I was writing about a kind of religious belief that profoundly influences lives, not one that simply obeys the rules. My grasp of scripture, like that of most Catholics, was pitiful. But Christ didn't say to adore him, but to *follow* him. Along whatever straight or crooked path or Via Dolorosa that is each of our lives.

WHEELWRIGHT, MASSACHUSETTS: A CHURCH DISGRACED. I reentered the rhythm of country life back in Massachusetts, happy to be home and out of danger. The boys and I tended the garden and helped our great white dog, Gemma, a Slovak Cuvac, give birth to twelve puppies that looked like slimy rats. I attended PTA meetings and ran successfully for the town council. I wondered where the next story would take me. That a *New Yorker* profile would be set only a few miles from our little farm was both a surprise and a tragedy. It would be of a priest, my pastor.

Father Ronald Provost, the pastor of St. Augustine, our tiny parish in Wheelwright, Massachusetts, was a peculiar man. He was always smiling, yet distant and almost childlike in certain ways. Preoccupied, he never seemed at ease with adults, never making eye contact, and abruptly cutting conversations short. In contrast, he was tremendously popular with the children of the parish for the outings to amusement parks, the baseball card trading or wrestling events organized. His sermons were banal, disjointed, and always off the cuff, with no notes to guide him. There was not enough content to either offend or inspire. But as that time was the beginning of a difficult period for the Catholic Church in the United States, we felt lucky even to have any priest at all in our parish.

With the demands of my work and family, I was finding it impossible to go to the monastery on any regular basis. I wanted to do something that would bring me back into the gentle rhythms of prayer that mark the monastic day, and considered buying the Liturgy of the Hours, the breviary that priests use, which contains prayers for various times of the day. I don't know why, but I happened to mention this to Father Provost one Sunday after still another of his deadening liturgies. He quickly volunteered to give me his set. "I never use them," he said cheerily, as if it were a relief to be rid of them, as though he were disposing of an ill-fitting shirt he'd found at the back of closet. "I never really learned how to use them in the seminary." I felt a flicker of sadness for a man whose own prayer life was that anemic, but thought no more about it.

One Sunday morning, our tiny congregation looked up to the altar, expecting to see Father Provost, but he was inexplicably gone, to be replaced each ensuing week by one of a string of visiting priests who said nothing about his hasty departure. It was as if we didn't need to know and had no right to ask. Seven months later, I heard that Father Provost was back in Worcester. I still hadn't gotten the breviary set, so I contacted him, and we agreed to meet for lunch. He told me that he had badly needed a rest and was eager to resume his duties. He handed me a brown paper grocery bag with the four leather-bound volumes within, his name on the first page of each.

Two days later, I opened the *Worcester Telegram and Gazette* to find Father Provost the subject of the lead story. He had been indicted on a child pornography charge. According to the indictment, on one of the outings with parish children for which he was so beloved, he had "posed a child in a state of nudity." When I eventually saw the pictures he had taken of that young boy, which would be entered as evidence, my blood ran cold. My own sons were then seven and nine. The boy in the photograph was ten. Had someone not accidentally caught Father Provost taking those pictures, the face staring back at me from those photos could have been that of Noah or Daniel.

I knew I had to write this story, and not only about the charge and the eventual outcome of the case. What had shaped this man? More important, were there any warning signs that something was amiss? Had my Church been culpable? There was a small but growing number of stories hinting that Church officials in some dioceses may have shuffled priests from parish to parish, even after accusations of inappropriate behavior with minors and blatant child molestation had been brought to their attention. It was almost too horrible to consider: Were there even more priests—men who occupied such a position of trust in Catholicism—violating our children?

At his trial a year later, Father Provost was defended by James Gavin Reardon Jr., an aggressive, bellicose lawyer retained by the diocese, who unashamedly tried to discredit the boy by saying he had willingly posed for the priest, meanwhile mounting a razor-thin argument that the photos did not precisely meet the Commonwealth's standard for pornography. Reardon succeeded at having dismissed as possible evidence Father Provost's prior treatment at a now-disgraced center for sex addicts as well as the extensive collection of nude and seminude photographs of young boys that were found by a housekeeper in a parish he had previously served. Nevertheless, Provost was convicted of child pornography and placed on probation, but received no jail time with the understanding that he would be removed and permanently barred from the priesthood.

The story I wrote for the *New Yorker* in 1993 appeared at a time when allegations about priestly abuse were continuing to surface with alarming regularity, but the most powerful cardinals in America—Law in Boston, Bevilacqua in Philadelphia, and O'Connor in New York—steadfastly resisted any intervention by civil authorities, countering that these were "isolated cases." And, after all, the priests had dedicated their lives to God's service. The media were bitterly criticized for scandal monger-ing, the lawyers representing the alleged victims for trying to bilk the Church. The Vatican maintained that ecclesial, not secular, courts would sit in judgment and that, in any case, a priest's ordination marked a man for life, and such men should be treated with deference. It would be almost another ten years before the *Boston Globe*'s sweeping investiga-tion revealed not only the sickening depth of abuse by priests in the Archdiocese of Boston and beyond but also how the Church had covered up the repeated offenses of known abusers and moved them on to other, unsuspecting parishes.

Not that my article was the line drawn demarcating the age of inno-cence about clergy sexual abuse from the age of realization, but after "Unholy Acts" was published, no one who had read the article could say that he or she did not know the gravity of the situation.

I exhaustively detailed that pedophilia was so ingrained an obsession that it could not be cured by reassignment or treatment. It was like hav-ing brown eyes or blue. When a child was abused, it was not—except in rare cases—a single episode. Provost's life story was riddled with markers that should have alerted his superiors. He had been caught with child pornographic material years before. Other priests had complained of his obsession with children. He had been moved from parish to parish more than any other priest of the diocese of Worcester because he could not live in an environment with other adults. He was a shadowy figure on the margins; no priest I talked to really knew anything about him; he was called a ghost. His superiors knew that he was a damaged man, yet they inflicted him on parish after parish, eventually giving him his own parish in remote Wheelwright where "he couldn't do much harm," as one dioc-esan official told me. Of course, just the opposite was true. He had free rein and no oversight. In his room at the rectory, detectives found a huge envelope crammed with pictures of little boys in various states and poses of undress and total nudity. Although prevented from being introduced in court, it was mute evidence that Father Provost's sick gallery was the diligent product of many years, in my parish and others he served.

Years later, the playwright John Patrick Shanley would write about the genesis of *Doubt,* his Broadway play about a priest accused of molesting a child. "We had, like many animals, flocked together for warmth and safety. And as a result we were terribly vulnerable to anyone who chose to hunt us. When trust is the order of the day, predators are free to plunder. And plunder they did. As the ever widening Church scandals reveal, the hunters had a field day. And the shepherds, so invested in the surface, sacrificed actual good for perceived virtue."

My research revealed the draconian measures the Church had used, intimidating parents who came forward to complain of sexual abuse, and demanding that children confront the priest-abuser with evidence. Dioceses steadfastly held to a policy that only when the abuser admitted his abuse—a point impossible for the pathological minds of these men to reach—would anything be done. The children—some as young as three, four, and five years old—were painted as the seducers, the priest the innocent victim of their wiles. My Catholic Church had protected the abuser and prosecuted the abused. My Church had followed the rules, bowing to the false God of ordination as if the ontological sign were impermeable, its bearer not only forgiven these most horrible of sins but then allowed to abuse again.

A sordid tale like this could harden one's heart. Religious belief and trust had been carefully and diabolically manipulated, not as pathways to God or holiness, but as the crude instruments of perversion. Priests would actually tell children they were honoring God as they were being fondled, raped, sodomized. As tiny trousers were being pulled down and a priest's zipper opened, a Hail Mary or Our Father might be intoned. Scores of Catholics would leave the Church in disgust over the continuing clergy abuse scandal. Just as Jews asked where their God was during the Holocaust and, finding no good answer, vowed they would worship him no more, Catholics felt betrayed, their faith in God, the Church, the priesthood shattered.

Writing about what effect his play might have, Shanley continued: "The beginning of change is the moment of Doubt. It is that crucial moment when I renew my humanity or become a lie."

I had begun to use Father Provost's breviary, hoping in some way to pray for him, but after a while I couldn't pick it up without becoming overwhelmed with nausea and anger. So I turned back to scripture each morning, hoping to find guidance. As I was working on his story, one passage kept playing in my mind with haunting regularity: "Where can

I go, Lord; you have the words of eternal life." So this is what it was to be a follower of Christ when everything seemed to point away from him.

I admire the deep faith of Methodists, Lutherans, Presbyterians, Episcopalians, and the millions in evangelical churches. There were many aspects of non-Christian traditions, from Buddhism to Judaism, that were enormously attractive to me—Buddhist mindfulness, Judaism's rich rituals, for example. I could readily embrace so many parts of these various faiths, but my heart was not with them. As imperfect as it was, I was not about to leave the Catholic Church. I couldn't. I wouldn't know where to go. I was ashamed of what priests had done and bishops had covered up. This devastating trauma that thousands of children had experienced would mentally scar them for life.

Even at that dark time, when Catholics lay low and priests stopped wearing the Roman collars in public, I was still proud to be called a Catholic. Our sacramental life, our tradition of spiritual masters, the social encyclicals, the charitable work done around the world—what religion so tenderly brought a person into a more intimate relationship with God or persistently forced that person back out into the world? Conflicted as I was, I loved the Catholic Church, and I wanted to continue to write about how Catholicism was lived out—not merely as a myriad of dogma and doctrine, rights and wrongs—but as a life force. If that meant holding up the best example or exposing the worst, I would tell that story.

My Catholic education had taught me well: I could name the spiritual and corporal works of mercy; I could recite the three things that needed to be present to commit a mortal sin. But there was something more, far more, to Catholic experience. I was coming to know—as did a young Thomas Merton gazing upon the frescoes in the Roman church of SS. Cosmas and Damian—"Something of who this person was that men called Christ." This was not a Christ of numbing rules and pomposity of office. I wanted to write about the Christ in Catholicism. How, as Catholics, our souls wend their way through the rocky soil of life—like hair-thin, thirsty roots—to find refreshment and sustenance in him.

I write these words today, but I didn't have that clear an idea in those days. But something was further taking form within me. I was not the zealous streetworker at CHIPS, the ascetic hermit and ersatz monk, but a father sitting at a MacDonald's table eating hamburgers and French fries with my family, a reporter filling note pads with my sometimes-illegible scrawl and then trying to make some sense of those words. I was called arrogant and a heretic, condemned for being too critical and not obedient enough to my Church. All I could do when I doubted myself was go back to the clear mandate of Vatican II that one's fully formed conscience is the final arbiter in one's life. And, as I approached the altar to receive the Eucharist, to say those words over and over, "Lord, I am not worthy to believe you, but only say the word and I shall be healed." The muddled cry often rose up from within me: "Lord, I believe. Help my unbelief."

After Father Provost, there would be many other stories through which I had the opportunity to talk about the magnificence and reach of my Church, about the power of Jesus Christ in the world. I would spend time at a poor Trappist monastery in India, where Indian monks in saffron robes lived out the Rule of St. Benedict, sang Gregorian chant and the Bagavad Gita, and provided a good bull for their neighbor's cows or a dowry for a poor village girl. At a table in a trattoria in Rome, I would sit across from Belgium's prophetic Cardinal Godfried Daneels, dressed in simple clerical garb, as he told of a vision of what the Catholic Church could really be.

I continued to believe. And to pray for my unbelief.

27

A MONK, AT LAST

IT WAS THE MIDDLE OF THE NIGHT. I suddenly sat bolt upright in bed. A lightning strike? I sniffed. No smell of flesh burning. A heart attack? I was a perfect 120 over 70, with low cholesterol, my weight in proportion to my height. I put forefinger and middle finger to my wrist. Steady pulse. The last of three descending chimes sounded dully in my room. Then again. Three, two, one. Like distant echoes, the chimes sounded in rooms down a long hallway. Was I dying? Was this what it was like? My head was slowly clearing. I realized where I was. It was 3 AM. It was time for Vigils. It was not the last minutes of my life but the first hour of the monastic day.

I threw my legs over the side of the bed and groggily rose to my feet. In other cells, only the occasional sound of the soft rush of water in toilet or sink disturbed the quiet. No voices, of course, as this was still the monastic period called the Great Silence, which began at the conclusion of Compline the night before and would not be over until after Mass this morning. All of us were rising. All of us knowing where we would be when the next bell was rung. And the next. The next. Blessed uniformity. We were all the same here, all awakening in the same ten-foot-by-twelve-foot cell, all of us with no more furniture than a single bed, a small desk, and a straight-backed, unpadded chair. A few wooden pegs were sufficient to hold what few clothes each of us used.

I splashed water on my face and quickly dressed. The soft, late spring air of the South Carolina low country, stirred by the gentle wind along the Cooper River, enfolded me in its moist, sensual embrace. So conflicted and so rich this sultry air, earthy and dank with the smell from decaying fish and logs washed up on the banks of the slow-moving river, yet fragrant from the huge magnolia blossoms bursting from the tips of branches on towering trees overhead. The old rotting away, the new coming to life. Never all one or the other. The never-ending, maddening yin and yang of it all. Life, death. The stale, the fresh. The river flows on, silently, surely. Another day was beginning here at Mepkin Abbey as I joined the line of Trappist monks, heads buried within their hooded cowls, approaching the chapel. Another day for brother monks and myself to attempt to draw closer to God, to do his will, to find him in the ordinariness of whatever these next hours would bring. Another day of dying to self so that he might come alive within our earthly shells.

I took my place in the stall assigned, alongside Brother Joseph, one of the most senior monks. I had a special place in my heart for Joseph. Just last month he had given me a piece of the belt that had girded him throughout his first fifty-eight years of Trappist life, beginning at Gethsemane (it did not escape me that that belt had once been in the presence of Thomas Merton), then here at Mepkin, where he was one of the founders. The thick leather had eventually worn out, but Brother Joseph had not. I kept that curled, cracked length of leather on my desk, next to the pictures of the seven Trappist monks of the Algerian monastery of Tibhirine in the Atlas Mountains who were slaughtered a few years before by some of the very people they came to serve. Belt and pictures, each was an icon to me, a symbol of what was best about the Trappists, a life built upon the abiding faith in God that he would direct each of us on the right path to the right place. Secure in the trust that he would never leave our side, whether desolation set in or consolation was at hand. These were qualities I so badly wanted for my life. That was the very reason I was here.

I had only a few moments to say a silent prayer, my eyes closed, before the bells sounded high in the tower outside the abbey church. Moments later, a single, harsh rap of the abbot's knuckles on the arm of his wooden stall resounded through the still church. We bowed in unison. *O God, open my lips, that my mouth shall declare your praise.* Across the centuries, the words have not changed. We chanted in English, joining with Trappists around the world in a chorus of dozens of languages, all greeting our God with the words of Psalm 51. After Vigils, I sat for a half hour in silent meditation and then returned to my cell to continue the fourth chapter of St. Luke's Gospel, my *lectio divina,* or holy reading. A light breakfast of cereal and toast, Holy Mass, and then the morning work period, repairing screens on the doors of the guest houses. Lunch, a short nap, more screen repair, some reading and prayer, in bed after Compline at 8:15. At no point in the day would I have to think about what next to do. I basked in the gentle rhythm, the symmetry and balance so wisely crafted by St. Benedict. The weak will not be disheartened; the strong would always find they could still strive for more. The perfect life. I was living it.

Three days a month.

∞

The spiritual guide whose unwitting wisdom had set me on the path to
Mepkin and—even if a bit truncated—a monastic life, was a brash, irreli-
gious Englishwoman. The unlikely setting for this footnote in the annals
of spiritual direction was her elegant office on the seventeenth floor of the
gleaming skyscraper just off Times Square at 20 West Forty-third Street.
Tina Brown, the moment's reigning doyenne of publishing, had replaced
Bob Gottlieb as the editor of the *New Yorker* magazine; she greeted me
with a firm handshake and a steely smile. (Strange that two worldly *New
Yorker* editors would have so much to do with my interior life.) "Faaabu-
lous, Pwwaul," she cooed disarmingly in her British accent. "We just
need you to do more and more for the magazine. We simply love your
work on religion. Love it. You bring a unique voice to the magazine."
Well, it wasn't Gregory Peck. Tina Brown had a reputation for chewing
up a few writers each day before her morning tea was served, on bone
china, at her desk.

Running through my mind was a mantra, not quite spiritual in tone:
"Take me, Tina; I'm yours." What more could a writer want than to have
the premier magazine in the country want "more and more"? Unlimited
expense-account lunches. Travel to wherever to write about whatever.
Prestige. Book editors clamoring. After all the years of struggle, I was
finally home. I offered a hint of a smile, but inside I was beaming, a
Cheshire Cat's grin.

"Let's see, what shall we have you do next?" Her eyes mystically
searched the ceiling. "Bruce Ritter! Yes, Bruce Ritter. Where is he now?
Fabulous. You're perfect for it. Per-fect." Father Bruce Ritter had founded
Covenant House in New York, which had gained a national reputation
for its work with runaways. Father Ritter went on to be indicted for
molesting some of the boys he had taken in to help.

At first, I said nothing. Then it came out of my mouth in a burst, even
before I had a chance to realize what I was saying—and its probable
affect: "Tina-if-there-are-ten-people-on-the-face-of-the-earth . . ." The
words stumbled on, even as "Take me; I'm yours," was still playing softly
in the background. ". . . I don't want to meet—or do a story about—one
of them is Bruce Ritter."

"Oh."

With that "oh," my life at Tina Brown's *New Yorker* was over. I was
homeless once more, a wandering pilgrim.

I had written about Father Provost because what had happened in my
tiny rural town was so chillingly close to home, I couldn't do otherwise.

My stories about the role of religion and individuals' religious beliefs usually excited me; I couldn't wait to do the interviews, the research. The story on Father Provost sickened me each day I worked on it. Conflict, differing ways of living out the gospel, the vacuum in leadership among our bishops, Vatican muscle-flexing—yes, these I could write about. I didn't want to make a career out of writing about what was sick and aberrant in the Catholic Church. There was only the dank smell and none of the fragrance in her story idea.

Mostly at my urging, our family had moved from Goat Hill Farm in Massachusetts to Wilmington, North Carolina, a move precipitated by an extraordinarily snowy Massachusetts winter and the feeling that although our years in the country had been idyllic, it was time for a change and to get back to a more peopled part of the planet. And a warmer part of the United States. As I had always had a Trappist monastery in my life— Gethsemane first, then Spencer—I found that the closest monastery to Wilmington was Mepkin Abbey, just three-and-a-half hours south.

On my first visit there, when I turned off Dr. Evans Road and passed under the massive, gnarled live oaks that line the main road into the monastery, I let out a sigh. I knew I had found a resting place for my soul, a place I could go to reflect on God and my life. Mepkin had a rich history. Native Americans lived and hunted here for centuries. It then became a rice plantation for Revolutionary War hero Henry Laurens, the first president of the Continental Congress. It eventually was a hunting refuge for Henry and Claire Boothe Luce, he the founder of Time, Inc., and she the playwright, U.S. ambassador, and Bishop Fulton Sheen's celebrated Catholic convert. When both Hank and Claire lost children who were in their early twenties, Mepkin no longer had its appeal as a getaway, and they donated some four thousand acres to the Trappists for a foundation. It was at a time, after World War II and Merton's *The Seven Storey Mountain,* when men were joining the order in droves; in fact, some were living in tents at Gethsemane. Twenty-nine Gethsemane monks, including a then young Brother Joseph, were sent to be the founders.

I visited this beautiful oasis a few more times and tried to hold on to and put into practice what I learned. My life was not the tempest it was during the Spencer years; I expected more of myself. I wanted to become a deeper man of prayer, more centered, calmer, less wedded to the vagaries of acclaim and recognition that—when I was honest with myself— I silently sought. Tina Brown proved that again, brilliantly, as the Brits are wont to say. I yearned to live in the freedom and excitement of the gospel, to be Christlike, compassionate, and open to the opportunities each day presented. I knew enough about monks and monasticism to understand that their life held no pat answers, but as I looked back over my life, starting with Thomas Merton's writings, I had always found in them ways to navigate my life.

On those first Mepkin visits, I experienced that heady cocktail of a profound sense of serenity and the spiritual high that people often have with a few days of retreat, which is quickly trampled by life in the real world. The first car cutting you off or a child with a smart answer can grind all the best of intentions and blazing insights into dust. After such seeming bliss, you wake up to a bad hangover, laced with guilt and self-hate. But my utter failure at taking monastic principles and wisdom into the rest of my life actually turned out to be a very good thing, excavating a hole that something inside me wanted to fill. Finally it came to me: I would visit the monastery every month for a year and write about what I experienced and how it worked—or didn't—in my life. And so for a part of a week each month I was living as a monk. Strange, wasn't it, that I had written about single life as if *it* were a calling. Strange, wasn't it, that aspiring monk and aspiring writer at last were introduced to each other. Thus the divine mystery of God was at work once more.

The table of contents for what eventually became *Beyond the Walls: Monastic Wisdom for Everyday Life* might give the wrong impression. The book developed in a far less orderly manner than that. My first visits held more anxiety than insight, the usual hand wringing and wailing of an impatient man. I gradually found that as my expectations decreased and I stopped trying so bloody hard to see God peeking at me from behind every magnolia tree or leaping out of every line of scripture, he graciously calmed my spirit and opened me to himself. As St. Augustine said, "God is not what you imagine or think you understand. If you understand him, you have failed." My experiences began to fall into some reasonably discrete, classic categories.

Indirection: finding the true path

Faith: the core of our lives

Conversatio: incremental heroism

Stability: a sense of where you are

Detachment: freedom of the heart

Discernment: charting life's path

Mysticism: eternity now

Chastity: true freedom

Prayer: mutual desire

Vocation . . . within vocation, within vocation . . .

Community: many churches

The simple path: monastic wisdom for everyday life

As I read, thought, prayed, and eventually wrote about what went into the twelve concepts that served as the book's orderly chapter headings in a very disorderly life, I found the static lessening and a clearer and simpler message coming through. When monks make their solemn profession, they promise obedience and stability, but it is *conversatio*, or "conversion of manners," that is the sturdy backbone of monastic life. Conversatio called on me not to have a one-time, apocalyptic, Road to Emmaus experience, but to continually assess my life and actions in the light of grace and experience and to act accordingly. To enact small, sometimes imperceptible daily conversions. I knew I had to continually cut myself loose from those seductive, stubborn habits—the lust for acknowledgment; the bullheaded need, on the home front, to have the final word on just about everything; the impatience that I had canonized as a certain kind of intellectual acuity. I had to come out of the shadows into the light.

In the shadows, I was a person who still drank too much. I loved to cook, but I also loved the fact that, alone in the kitchen, with refrigerator and liquor cabinet at hand, I could drink as much as I wanted, with no one the wiser. Hey, just having a taste! And another. I could lock myself in the bathroom and have my way with the scantily clad models in the Victoria's Secret catalog I conveniently had sent to the house, claiming it was only so I could buy Tracy a frilly piece of lingerie every so often. Hey, who am I hurting in here? In prayer, I could go even further into the shadows, hiding my messy self from God, piously mouthing what I thought he wanted to hear. "Hey, God, doing my best, doing my best. Lacing up the sneakers, just like Father Greer said. See?"

During Lent of that year, 1995, I gave up drinking, as I usually did, and discovered that I was waking up each morning feeling more alert, more alive. On Easter Sunday, when I would have poured myself a good tumbler of Stolichnaya as a well-deserved reward, I hesitated. Conversatio. I went through that day and the next and next. I didn't have to hide in that shadow anymore; my drinking days were over. I canceled the catalogs and focused on the beautiful, voluptuous, sensuous woman who was my wife. I stopped talking to God as if God didn't know much about human nature, instead of being the loving, present father and good friend I now knew him to be.

Something happened. As I stopped looking for God, I began to see him. I stopped listening for special messages, yet I heard the soft whisper of God's urging. I stopped waiting for signs and wonders, and little miracles kept occurring.

It was grace. God's grace. It was what Karl Rahner, the great theologian and architect of some of Vatican II's most powerful documents, called the "mysticism of everyday life." That year in my life marked the true Vatican II liberation of my soul. It was a year of tears and laughter. Tears at my stumbling, laughter at the presence of God in the ordinariness of my life. It was a year of flying dust, as I swept the attic of stale, musty ideas of God, and opened the windows to his fresh, clean air.

It was tough to kill that false self, and death came slowly. But perhaps I was finally growing up, to see that the saints I so admired and sought to emulate had their particular places in the cosmic dance and I had mine. Each of us is called to our own kind of sainthood, each within the circumstances of our lives, each placed in exactly that place by a somewhat capricious but always loving God. I was not in the desert with de Foucauld or in a monastery with Merton or in the Bowery with Dorothy Day. I was a fifty-something American male, whose calling was to be a father to two sons, then at the onset of their teenage years; a husband to a social worker wife; and a tradesman who worked with words. We lived in a middle-class section of Wilmington called Forest Hills and drove Volvos—old ones, but still Volvos. During my CHIPS and hermit days, if I had ever fast-forwarded my life to see such a resume, I would have shuddered.

OO

I am a reporter, given to trying to find the "significant detail," that telling moment which unmistakably illustrates the point I'm trying to make, hoping to etch that image so vividly that the reader is not reading words but is actually there. During that year, first scrawled on the back of an envelope or in the slim margin of a dollar bill, and even occasionally in a notebook, tiny, fleeting flashes of God's presence appeared in my life. There were many such moments during that year, but three stand out.

The first occurred during my early days at Mepkin. I was sleepy after a restless night, so after Vigils I needed to remain on my feet if I were to stay awake. It was a dark, moonless night, and as I walked away from the church, I could see that the tiny lights embedded alongside the roadway would soon end. A black void lay beyond. I reached the last light and found my heart pounding with anxiety. How would I see where to go?

I would surely go off the road into a ditch. I stepped into that void, only to find that it was not total blackness at all. The moon might have been hidden from my sight, but its soft glow gave just enough light for one step, then another, then another. I couldn't see far ahead, but enough for the moment. The glow was with me.

Was this not the way God was guiding me, one step at a time? After all, how many steps can one take at one time?

The second was on a busy day in New York when I had appointments to see various publishers about my work, past, present, and, I hoped, future. I thought back to the young man on the George Washington Bridge howling to the New York skyline like some demented animal. I decided to walk more modestly—and prayerfully—and to punctuate this day as the monks punctuated theirs, with prayer. After all, we were each going about our vocation, weren't we? Between breakfast, lunch, and dinner meetings, visits to various editors and television executives, I slipped into St. Vincent Ferrar on Lexington, a tiny midtown chapel, and St. Paul the Apostle on the corner of West Fifty-ninth and Columbus. I didn't pray for a lucrative contract or an exciting overseas assignment. I prayed that I wouldn't be another Willie Loman hawking my goods. I prayed that I would find worthwhile, honorable work, pleasing to God. I can't even recall if all that blur of meetings produced anything, but when I slipped into a cab at the end of the day, I looked at the empty seat next to me. He was there, as he had been all day long. What a feeling, a transcendent feeling in the back of a Yellow cab hurtling up Broadway.

The third was in the Grand Canyon. Noah was far ahead on our assent from the canyon floor, followed by Daniel, then Tracy. We approached an especially sharp cutback, a steep section of the trail, and I lost sight of them. I was both a little miffed that my boys hadn't heeded my words not to go too far ahead and terrified that someone would get hurt. Tiny rocks skittered over the edge of the narrow pathway ahead of me. I looked up to what appeared to be a solid face of sandstone to see one head, then a second and third, as if emerging from the very rock itself. Noah's blond hair blazed in the morning sun, Daniel's dark brown hair dazzled with red highlights, and Tracy's lighter auburn was aglow. God had parted the veil for just an instant to let me know that he was there. Everything was all right. The river was flowing on, silently, surely, carrying me gently along.

28

WHY? WHY NOT?

THE UNASSUMING, UNMARKED BUILDING AT 2801 North Meridian Street in Indianapolis could easily pass for the headquarters of a midsize Midwestern insurance company. Or a huge mausoleum. Certainly not the repository—in spirit, if not in reality—of fifteen billion Eli Lilly family dollars. Although not well known to most of us, the Lilly Endowment was, at the time, the world's second-largest philanthropic foundation; only the Bill and Melinda Gates Foundation has more resources. The Lillys, good Methodists that they were, while making their fortune in pharmaceuticals—from the first injectable insulin, to the miracles of penicillin, erythromycin, and the Ceclor that cured my Daniel's many ear infections, to the modern-day balm of Prozac—did not forget their religious roots. One of the endowment's stated goals is to assist in the furtherance of religious belief and practice. Approaching the endowment's humble portals daily, proposals in hand and hope in their hearts, many supplicants hope (and pray) for some small share in this bounty. As I was hoping and praying on that crisp, sunny spring morning in 1997.

After a short wait in the lobby, I was directed to the second-floor office of a Lilly grants officer. My fate was foretold by the prelude of a practiced "As worthy as your idea is, [insert supplicant's first name], I'm very sorry that our answer must be . . ." Condolences aside, it was an unequivocal rejection of an idea so viable, extraordinary, and prescient that I can't even remember what it was. But I do remember what Fred Hofheinz, the grants officer, and I had for lunch. Over creamed chicken on a bed of flavored rice, and green beans almandine seasoned with a liberal sprinkling of desolation in one of the more modest corporate cafeterias in Indianapolis, something actually viable, extraordinary, and prescient was about to be born. As I was discovering in my life, the "oh's" and "no's" were exactly what was needed for God to shunt me onto another uncharted—and unchosen—path.

∞

I had just returned from giving what is called a mission, three nights of talks, at the Church of the Presentation, a Catholic parish in Upper Saddle River, New Jersey. One of my books or articles seemingly had sparked the interest of the pastor and staff, and they took a chance that I might be a reasonable choice for this yearly event, which took place during Lent. I thought of many inspiring titles for my talks, but finally, grasping about for what could be a theme, the best I could do was "The Good Enough Catholic: A Guide for the Perplexed." It was certainly a commentary on my life, but it also had another source, the prominent British psychologist D. W. Winnicott. Winnicott, a wise observer of family dynamics, found that the healthiest children grew up in families with what he called "good enough" parents, parents who certainly asked for excellence and demanded sacrifice, but who understood that along with successes and good behavior would come many failures and awful behavior. Children of such parents would know that they were loved and accepted even when they were just "good enough" and would thrive and go on to live happier, fuller lives. It struck me as a perfect way to talk about our relationship with a God who asks for our very best, but accepts whoever we are at the moment. A perfect way to talk about living a healthy, holy Catholic life.

And so I mounted the impressive pulpit at the Church of the Presentation and found myself facing five hundred people, there to be instructed, guided, and, I hoped inspired. I talked about what I saw as a Church turning inward and away from the vision and power of Vatican II and how we couldn't let that happen. I assured them that they had good reason to be perplexed. I certainly was. I told a few stories about my own faith journey, leaving out the more grisly details. I tried to make the point that faith in God and an honest attempt at religious practice—in our case, Catholicism (but not that Catholics exclusively had the ear of God)—were elastic enough to accommodate different approaches and durable enough to see us through the various seasons in our lives. Although I had never publicly talked about my own struggles with faith and belief, I found myself speaking of God in personal terms, both of his tremendous love and a rich sense of humor as he gazed upon the calamities we continued to visit upon ourselves.

I had carefully prepared notes, and the talks seemed to be going smoothly enough, but then strange things began to happen. Now and then—and it would last only an instant, come and gone so quickly that

I wondered at first if it had happened at all—another channel would flicker alive. In the wash of faces before me, one would suddenly come into focus. It might happen as I looked up from my notes or when I paused to emphasize a point. In those moments, in those faces, I imagined I saw something of who these people were. I could visualize their night of desolation at the wrought-iron gates of their St. Joseph's Church, their chance meetings with a Jacques Travers or Father Greer, their disgust at the smell of their sins, their unabated hunger for God, their time in a self-imposed hermitage, their finding the right life partner. I could see old men as young once again, overseas and away from home; older women as they processed down the aisle so many years before, their waists narrow and hopes high. I could see the young men growing old and bent, the young women hearing the awful words of the diagnosis they most feared. I could see couples praying together, growing old in a love that deepened each year. Those faces before me at times were transformed into so many tiny points of light. At other times, a single face's glow grew in intensity, so powerful and blinding that I had to look away. It was my imagination. But it was more than that.

I was in each one of them. Each one of them was in me. We had all been on so many stages in our lives, so many acts, playing so many characters. We were of the tribe called Catholic, sinner and saint, trudging along together, some of us of wavering faith and others rock solid. I couldn't quite understand what was happening. I found myself breathless, light-headed at the end of my talks, not from the exertion of speaking, but from seeing in their glowing faces who they were now, were once, and some day would be. As I spent my days at Presentation and looked further into what was going on here, it became clear that this was a parish unlike any I had ever witnessed or been part of. This was a quantum leap from my experience with Father Petroski and the small group of kids that had gathered around him. This was an entire parish on to something that brought them alive. Through a blizzard of over a hundred lay-run ministries, Presentation saw to the needs of young at-home mothers as well as a sizeable retired contingent. Women who had had an abortion found a supportive place to talk; the divorced sailed the Hudson River at sundown to feel a fresh breeze in their lives. After a funeral, the mourners were provided a lovingly prepared meal, free of charge. Presentation fed the hungry, clothed the naked, and provided shelter to the homeless, meanwhile enflaming young singles who flocked to the 6 PM Sunday Mass in Talbot's dresses, Brooks Brothers jackets, and BMWs, their PDAs and cell phones silenced. I had never witnessed such energy, determination, sheer goodness, and deep holiness in a parish. It was as if the spirit of God—actually God in person—had been allowed to come down from the altar, shed his ecclesiastical robes, blow out the vigil lamps, and run wild through the well-maintained streets of this affluent suburb.

On the plane home, the words I had written about Thomas Merton's first visit to the Abbey of Gethsemane vividly surfaced in my mind. "What he saw and what he felt during that week would change him forever."

I had just witnessed the difference between *being* Catholic and *living* Catholic. And it *would* change me forever. The difference between being Catholic and living Catholic might seem like a fine distinction, but at the Church of the Presentation, I felt the exhilarating power the first disciples must have felt in the presence of Jesus Christ when nothing was too much of a challenge, there was nothing to fear, and everything was possible.

The people at Presentation were not the uber-Catholics, daily communicants, their rosaries spilling nonstop through pious fingers. These were not the vigilant ones who reported every liturgical infraction to the bishop, every seeming deviance from dogma, every person who might have a view contrary to the magisterium. No, these were ordinary people given a vision that they could do great and holy things in each other's presence, in God's presence. Who knew what sins they had committed, where they had diverged from the "fullness of the faith," that narrow gate through which, according to the righteous, anyone daring to call themselves Catholic must pass. Their sheer goodness radiated. This parish was their monastery, to which God had called them. This was the crucible in which they would be purified, the community they could depend on for support, a holy home enriched by their presence. This was Catholicism at its best. The true, wounded, triumphant Body of Christ. Where had I been? Why had I never seen this before?

Were these people before me that different than the saints we know by name? Were their trials, their temptations, their bouts of fatigue any less intense than that of those we formally canonize? Their groaning so different? Did God—knowing exactly the makeup of their every cell—not smile lovingly upon them and every so often gently pull back the curtain to reveal himself? Did he not call them by name as they lived in the unique circumstances of this day?

In a documentary about his life, Bob Dylan said his inspiration in the 1950s came from folk singers like Woody Guthrie, Odetta, and Pete Seeger at a time when "How Much Is That Doggie in the Window" and other safe, banal songs of a safe, banal age were topping the charts. "Their music taught you how to live," Dylan said. That was exactly what Presentation was doing, offering the gospel as a liberating force to its people, with a power to transform them. To use a military image, it was as if by attending Presentation they were accepting a commission to be the Special Forces of Christianity. Every one of them had a heroic vocation.

Upper Saddle River, New Jersey, the Elysian Fields of two-car garages, three bedrooms, two-and-a-half baths, and grass-obsessed homeowners? The epitome of shopping mall America? The stereotypes didn't escape me as I tried to sort out what I had witnessed. At first I tried to shrug it off. After all, I was the outrider, the dissenter, the skeptic of "institutional Church." But God chose this suburban rendezvous in New Jersey in a place, at a time, when I least expected to encounter him, unleashing something I couldn't deny, meanwhile wondering why I had never seen it before.

I was a cradle Catholic. I had been educated in Catholic schools from kindergarten through college. I had written extensively about the Catholic Church, priests, bishops, issues. But I had never really looked at the very building blocks of Catholicism: its parishes. They were a given, so much cement and wood pews, just *there*. Yet, in Upper Saddle River, it was as if I had come upon an entirely new religion. I felt an excitement about my faith I had not felt since the days at CHIPS. But here was the big difference—or, at least it seemed to me—this was available to every Catholic. You didn't have to open a Brooklyn storefront or live in the slums of Calcutta or spend your life in the cloister. This spiritually rich life could be available in that most common outpost of the universal Church—the parish.

OO

After my talks at Presentation, I headed back to Wilmington, wondering: Could my own parish become like Presentation? I excitedly told Tracy and the boys what I had seen and felt. Tracy narrowed her eyes; this was not a Catholic church she had yet seen during our first fifteen years of married life. The boys seemed unimpressed; their parochial schooling had asked them to memorize catechetical answers, but had hardly ignited a flame within them. I was eager to tell my own pastor, but I knew I had to do it carefully. Our parish was certainly better than those I had experienced in Massachusetts, yet it was hardly happy or dynamic. It was a place where parishioners were wary of the pastor's moods, brought on, he would say, by his diabetes. But blood sugar levels were only a small part of it. Ours was a parish, like many others, where it was tacitly understood that the priest was in charge, that lay people were supposed to be helpful but not assertive, and that if an idea surfaced, it would have the best chance of succeeding if it actually or apparently originated in the rectory.

I briskly walked into the parish office. The parish secretary greeted my enthusiastic hello with a silent nod.

"Is Father in?"

"No." Ah, that word again. Her voice was as expressionless as her face. Keep going, I told myself. My enthusiasm may not be her enthusiasm.

"When will he be back?"

"I don't know."

"I'd like to talk to him about—"

"Father is very busy."

"I was wondering if—"

"I'm going to lunch now; I have to lock the door."

I sat in my car, feeling like a punctured balloon slowly losing its air. Deflation is not a natural state for me. Gradually another emotion rose up within me, filling the vacuum. It was not merely disappointment. It wasn't even anger. I surprised myself. It was boiling-hot rage. Why did our parish have to be a spiritless, inhospitable, afraid to bother or even approach the pastor kind of place? I had just seen the gospel come alive, a place where people were excited about being Catholic and *were* lacing up their sneakers, where fresh approaches and new ways of helping or reaching people were encouraged and acted on. The seven deadly words of church life— "We've never done it that way before"—were not to be heard. Instead of "Why?" the response at Presentation to new ideas was "Why not?"

It was now the late 1990s, and church attendance in all but evangelical churches was precipitously dropping as more and more people walked away from traditional religion, some of them opting for New Age approaches, others simply choosing nothing. The Catholic Church was regularly in the news, and the news, for the most part, was not good. Cases of clergy sexual abuse surfaced almost weekly; vocations to the priesthood continued their downward trend; smaller parishes were beginning to be closed for lack of a pastor. Where the ratio of Catholics to parish priests had been less than one thousand to one when I was growing up, it was now over three thousand to one. Religious sisters who once were the backbone of parish schools and activities were becoming an endangered species. Their number had also shrunk by two-thirds. There were now only two hundred thousand sisters. Once they numbered six hundred thousand. Their average age was around seventy. Church attendance, which not many years before had been well over 50 percent of American Catholics, was no more than half that.

Reflecting what was happening in the country at large, the rise of a Religious Right in the Church—such groups as Opus Dei and Legionnaires of

Christ—signaled a move to blunt the openness and pluralistic thought of
Vatican II. Catholic men who were attracted to a structured environment
and sure answers found the priesthood appealing. The pastoral bishops
appointed when John XXIII was pope were aging and being replaced by
more loyal sons of the Church, who could be counted on for unquestioning
allegiance. Innovative parishes—like Presentation, I would later find out—
were often in trouble with diocesan officials. An almost guaranteed way
to ensure that a priest would never be elevated to bishop was for him to
diverge from standard practices. I was not alone in concluding that there
were forces in my Church that wanted to turn back the clock. Tens of millions of American Catholics—something unimaginable just a generation
before—had dropped out.

Yet there was Presentation, with packed masses each weekend, where
Catholics traveled as much as an hour to attend, driving by many other
parishes. They came from an astounding sixty-two ZIP codes. Presentation was doing something very right, resonating with a range of late-
twentieth-century Americans. It was the best example of Vatican II in
action I had ever seen, a complement of priestly and lay talents, different
in role, equal in discipleship, each with a vocation to live out.

∞

So, back at the Lilly Endowment, crestfallen and running out of fresh
ways to recast my rejected proposal, I touched on the New Jersey experience over custard pie and coffee, expecting to be eventually shown the
way out onto Meridian Street, well fed but empty handed. Surprisingly,
Fred Hofheinz's expressionless face slowly warmed. "Interesting. Why
don't you write something about *that*?"

Arrogant as I was, writing about parish life was not exactly what I had
in mind when I came to Lilly that morning. But then, there were those
faces. I couldn't get them out of my mind. Presentation had given
those people a new vision of their worth, their place before God.
Although these parishioners had tried alternatives, the restlessness for
God that Augustine wrote about couldn't be satisfied with yoga, tran-
scendental meditation, or sunrise walks on the beach. They found they
couldn't go it alone. Had I inadvertently discovered something? Were
there were other parishes like Presentation? As a Catholic, I was inspired
by what I had experienced. As a journalist, I realized that if this was happening elsewhere, there was a great story waiting to be told.

Messages from God come in different ways and kinds of packaging.
This one was via first-class mail. A few months later, I was not a little

surprised (honestly: shocked) to find a large brown envelope in my mailbox. Whatever I had said in my Lilly Endowment grant proposal had made sense. The next two years of my life would take me on a most amazing odyssey through Catholic America. As much as I loved my Catholic Church, I had often written about what was wrong with it. And there was plenty. I now had the opportunity to tell what was right. I would find there was even more to report on.

From St. Peter Claver in the most crime-ridden neighborhood in New Orleans, its churchyard ringed with barbed wire, to five tiny, clustered parishes in heartland Minnesota, surrounded by corn and soy bean fields, God was alive, well, and thriving in Catholic parishes. The elegant St. James Cathedral in Seattle and shabby St. Francis of Assisi in Portland, Oregon—each was bringing the Mass alive for its people. St. Pius X in El Paso, Texas, built upon deep Hispanic reverence to recast faith with a Vatican II hue. At St. Mark's in Boise, Idaho, teenagers crafted their own Sunday night liturgy, drawing the young into a life of worship and service to the poor.

My research would eventually result in a book about some three hundred excellent parishes I found. They were rural, urban, suburban, Hispanic, African American, white, small, large; they were led by charismatic pastors and by men and women of more modest talents; they had budgets of every size and were located in every part of the country. As I was finishing the book, assessing what these excellent parishes had in common, I found it could be summarized by the words of Tip O'Neill, the consummate politician: "All politics are local." These parishes' focus was local, but not parochial. They reminded me of religious groups that met immigrants landing at Ellis Island. How can we help you right now? What are your needs? These parishes viewed themselves not as diocesan franchises—a sort of religious Wendy's or McDonald's, offering predictable, standardized fare—but as scrappy missionary outposts. The idea was not simply to dispense sacraments and ensure good order, but to bring Jesus down off that cross in the sanctuary and into people's lives.

∞.

With my book on excellent Catholic parishes—and another on excellent Protestant churches—published, more calls came in, asking me to give talks. What was happening? I was a writer, not a speaker. And who was I to be standing in front of a group of Catholics, I the public sinner whose ragged life made St. Augustine look like no more than a naughty schoolboy? What right did I have to talk about the state of the Church, about what *I* thought made for excellent parishes—I, whose only training in theology was a couple of courses at Marquette, where I squeaked by with a C?

I found the answer one morning, the house quiet, as I sat on the back steps with my morning reading of scripture. I memorized this sentence and would recite it many times in the years ahead just before giving a talk: "Do not worry about how you are to speak or what you are to say; for what you are to say will be given to you at that time; for it is not you who speak, but the Spirit of your Father speaking through you."

I would like to say that I immediately took those words literally, but I didn't. I took them incrementally. Slowly, over the months ahead, these simple and searing words pierced layers of doubt, tentativeness, and wavering faith.

PART SEVEN

RETURNING

29

KOLINOVCE

IT IS THE SIMPLEST OF CHURCHES. Three narrow windows are humbly spaced along its roughly plastered side walls, almost apologetically, so as not to covet too much outside light. Its exterior walls are burnt beige, an earth tone meant not to intrude. A half-moon pane of glass rests astride a single wooden door, itself no bigger or grander than those in the village houses clustered at the foot of the small hill. The roof is an indigenous red tile. The steeple, in keeping with the scale, modest, does not soar but gently raises its head, as if after prayer. Within the church, it is dark and cold on this overcast April day. Heat was a luxury then as it is now.

As I slowly approach the wooden altar, I run my hand over the worn edges of the pews. There are only three rows of pews on either side of a threadbare rug, not entirely successful in hiding, protecting, or enhancing a narrow path of worn, wide-plank flooring that serves as the main and only aisle. Over the altar is a mournful portrait, darkened by the years, of St. Francis of Assisi, his hands tenderly enfolding the base of a crucifix, his eyes raised, fixed on the face of the Crucified One above. To look at it once is to immediately understand the artist's intention. To linger on the image is to be drawn into the suffering itself, sharing all the agony of the cross and little of the ecstasy of beholding the One hung there. For this is the church of St. František Seraf, so named for the moment Francis received the wounds of the crucified Christ—the stigmata—from one of the seraphim, angels burning with love for God, and those considered closest to him. How apt a saint for this tiny village in Slovakia, which had seen so many crucifixions of its own.

It was 1998, and I was now nearing my sixtieth year; my boys were teenagers. I had traveled the world and across the United States to write about God and faith and religious belief. It was time I came here, for this place—far more than St. Benedict's or the basement of the Marquette

dental school or the Brooklyn church or the Church of the Presentation—was the true wellspring of my faith. For here in Kolinovce, people
of my blood had worshipped God for centuries. Their world was only
that which could be reached on foot or on an animal cart. St. František
Seraf was the true home for their souls, the center of their lives.

Within the past hour, in the small rectory down the hill from the
church, I had opened the leather-bound registry book to 1884. I traced
my finger over the name in the middle of the page of baptisms. Anna
Szalansky. The penmanship was elegant and flawless. The spelling was an
insult. It was a mandate of the Hungarians—their current overlords—that
the Slovak name of Salansky be "Magyarized." Or else it would not be
listed at all. My people were nonpeople, dispensable, faceless agrarian
serfs bound to the land owned by the royalty who lived in Spiš castle,
high on a real mountain. When my grandmother, teenaged and already
married, left Kolinovce before the turn of the twentieth century, it was a
village of fifty-nine homes, population 360. It is not much bigger today.

Grandmother Salansky lived with us, draped in a veil of bitter silence,
for all the years I was on Forest Avenue. She was born and married here
in Kolinovce, the records showed, but she never spoke of her village—then
again, I never asked. I was so obsessed with being American, I would have
gladly sided with the Magyars as they cleansed history, tradition, and language from these whom they deemed inferior. I too had run from my heritage, and, with a name like Wilkes, I never had to explain anything about
my lineage. Vlk was the name with which my father's people left Slovakia;
it became Vilk in the hands of an impatient immigration official at Ellis
Island. As my father was first a coal miner near Wilkes-Barre, Pennsylvania,
the name was transmuted once more. I was ashamed of my father, the coal
miner turned carpenter; my mother, the cleaning lady; each with their
sixth-grade educations. I was here in Kolinovce not only to better understand where I had come from but for Tracy to view up close at least the
shadows of the demons and angels that alternately inhabited me. But also
so that my teenage sons would drink in at least this part of their background, otherwise blended as they are of Irish, Scottish, and Russian
blood, with Jewish heritage. Fully one half of who they are is Slovak and
Catholic. One day, perhaps, they will remember this church, the narrow
street that runs through Kolinovce, the house the villagers said was my
family's, the wattle fences, the dusky outlines of the pine forests that circle
the village, the majestic Tatra range in the distance, the smell of onions
and cabbage, links of *hurka* hanging in the smokehouse.

I sat alone in a pew in the church of St. František Seraf. I looked to my
right and left. Here the Psalms were chanted for generations by men who

would have had my blue eyes; a head shaped like my mine, flat in the back; sandy hair eventually turning gray, but a full head of it to their dying day. Here women would have whispered the rosary through mouths toothless before they reached thirty, their rough hands smoothing the beads to a glistening brilliance. Svaty Boh, Svaty Boh, they would call to Holy God, help me, help me. How many prayers did these walls know?

My mind floated back to my first church, St. Benedict's in Cleveland, and I could smell once again the pungent odor of my father's chewing tobacco—probably stowed away in the corner of his mouth, even during Mass, for he rarely felt worthy to receive Holy Communion—and the smell of sawdust that seemed to invade even his Sunday clothes. It must have been in his pores. The smell of bleach on my mother's clothes, perfectly ironed, shapeless dresses, the fabric shiny with age.

Then I was back in Kolinovce, my heartbeat pulsing in my neck, in the veins at the top of my feet, in my temples. More members of my family sat here, prayed here, wept here than any place on earth that I will ever know of. These walls knew the happiness of a healthy baby, the agony of illness, bumper crops celebrated and failed crops bemoaned. Voices raised in pain, voices raised in celebration. Rote prayers in unison; silent, spontaneous cries to heaven that no one but God could hear.

This was their Father's house where they could come aside from life to be strengthened by one another's presence, the epicenter of a village's life, a spiritual organ through which everything flowed. No one was a stranger here; there were seldom visitors. The women's sturdy, thick-heeled shoes, the men's rough boots—and now some children's sneakers—that stepped across the threshold of that narrow door made a sound familiar to God. He was here, and his people knew that as firmly as they knew anything in their lives.

Vatican II had come and gone, and yes, the "Church" had changed. The Mass in the newly built church down on the main road was conducted in Slovak, not Latin; the priest faced his people, not the altar; but something beyond liturgical choreography and scripting was firmly rooted here. I had stood in St. Peter's Square in Rome—and I would stand there again, awed by Catholicism's magnificence, grandeur, and power—but it was here that I would truly feel Catholicism's true timelessness. Nothing at all had changed. God had not changed. The God whom my ancestors prayed to was no different from the God ready to hear my prayer that day. The Catholic Church I was born into, the Catholic Church I loved and railed against, embraced and rejected, was, after all, a piece of seamless cloth. So many weavers of the woof, but the warp stretched back beyond sight and ahead to where no one could see. A ragtag group of illiterate Palestinian fishermen, fired by a vision of a God among them, was now over a billion strong. From the dusty streets of the Middle East, that faith found its way here through SS. Cyril and Methodius, who had brought the message to my Slovak people.

I rose from my pew and knelt before the altar. I wanted to offer my small voice to all the voices of my family and my people. To the God to whom both they and I belonged. To the Christ who brought us together, at his altar, across the ages. I looked down at my hands clasped in readiness. I opened them to see my palms. They were so embarrassingly smooth and tender, not a good Slovak's hands at all. In recent days, they had not lifted more than an overstated adverb, done no more to harvest what I would eat than run a credit card through the reader at the Harris-Teeter supermarket at Independence Mall. These were not the hands of the men—or the women—of my blood who had prayed here. My eyes rested on the small, ashen marble tabernacle set inconspicuously within the back wall.

I would like to say that I thought great thoughts and crafted soaring words to offer in that stilled church. Actually, it was a simple enough prayer, little different from what I might say kneeling beside my bed any night.

> Dear God,
> Help me to be a good father and husband.
> Let the work of my hands be of good quality, honorable work.
> In whatever ways that are presented, let me make this world
> a better place.
> Let me not be tempted by easy answers.
> Keep my vices at bay.
> Control my arrogance, my impatience, my temper, my pride,
> my envy.
> Let me hear your voice.
> Help me meet the needs of my family. Let me help others with what-
> ever their needs might be.

As I rose to leave, I wondered: What were the prayers of my people in this church down through the centuries? Most likely, not that different from my own. My ancestors might have pleaded for help dealing with a demanding overlord instead of an unappeasable editor, a failed crop not a rejected article, but a sick child was a sick child, a marriage a marriage, temptation, temptation. Widening the scope, had the prayers of the people of Kolinovce done more for the Church and the world than

Merton's at Gethsemane, the people at Presentation in New Jersey, my own? Were the prayers intoned beneath Bernini's canopy on the high altar of St. Peter's in Rome and those of a peasant priest uttered here in Kolinovce of different valence? Of course, such a question is foolish. But when one measures—if this is possible to do—who is closest to God's heart, the answer becomes clearer. He always heard best those voices the world heard least.

I walked out into the overcast day, down the pathway leading to the main street where a small crowd had gathered. The crunching sound of my shoes on these ancient stones intoned a strangely beautiful melody, echoing far into a past of which I knew so little.

OO

"Americanov! Americanov!"

Any American visiting this out-of-the-way village in the east of Slovakia, Spiš region, in the district of Spišská Nova Ves, was immediately considered a bit of a celebrity, but our visit was even more of an event. My friend, Ladislav Lajciak, a dissident whom I met years before and who could now safely live in Slovakia after the 1987 collapse of the Soviet Union, had brought us here. I could hear him telling the villagers in whispered, almost reverential tones, that I was a *novinar,* a journalist, and a "VIP." I had already given a talk to an overflow audience of seminarians at Spišske Podhradi and at Matica Slovenská—the nation's cultural research center and national library. A reception had been held in my honor, complete with laudatory speeches; shots of *borovicka,* a breathtaking juniper-berry brandy; and a marvelous musician playing Slovak folk songs on the *fujara,* a six-foot-long shepherd's flute. Native sons, even a minor writer like me, were celebrated.

As we walked through Kolinovce and had our pictures taken, it didn't escape me that had it not been for my grandmother and grandfather's cadging enough money by selling a cow, plow, or some precious heirlooms—or maybe everything—and first buying train tickets to Hamburg, then steamer tickets to New York, and passing the health test at Ellis Island, I could be one of the smiling, toothless men standing next to me in the pictures. Women younger than Tracy looked decades older. One of them, in her babushka and characteristic black skirt—suspended by layers of stiff crinoline—could be my wife. The children of the village were not that different from mine: the global economy had outfitted them in team shirts, sneakers, and logo-emblazoned backpacks.

The afternoon Mass was held in a modern, well-lit church in the center of the village. The walls were a brilliant white, the statuary in keeping with Vatican II, with weeping Madonnas and saints' eyes fixed longingly on heaven replaced by plaster and wood images with confident eyes fixed directly on us, the congregants, as if to say, "You know the story; get on with it then." I was touched when, at the dedication, the Mass was offered for the "Vilk-es family."

The Vilk-es family. My mother and father did not openly seem too interested in their heritage, and I wonder what they would have thought of my coming back to Kolinovce. When Paul and Margaret Wilkes moved to Cleveland, they were members of a predominantly immigrant Slovak parish. They spoke in Slovak only when they needed to, so the children would not understand. This much they knew because of their own parents, but they seemed not to look back on what was always called the Old Country, focusing instead on the New World.

They did not have a rich history to pass on to us. Slovakia—or what they knew of Slovakia—had been a subservient pawn, trampled by the Ottoman Turks, ruled by the Hapsburgs, ethnically cleansed by the Magyars, dominated by the Czechs in the early part of the twentieth century, a sad war bride and puppet state of the Nazis under the firebrand priest, Jozef Tiso, during World War II, before falling under Soviet domination. But after all, what did they know of that history? Little, I think. There was something in the nature of Slovak people, a keep-your-head-down mentality that factored into their makeup. But there was another side to my people, something I needed to come to Kolinovce to witness. It radiated in the faces of the people who surrounded the Vilk-es family outside the church that afternoon. It was not the same glow as the one I first saw in the people at Presentation. That was a new, fresh wine, like fine, young Beaujolais. This was an excellent local vintage that had been drunk for centuries, mellower, fuller bodied, tried, tested, barrel after barrel, year after year.

∞

Nostalgia descends unannounced like a spell, attacks like a virulent virus that has sensed an opportunity, then stalks the weakest of the body's defenses, the mind. In those days, in the late 1990s, I found myself riddled with melancholy, longing for a simpler life, a simpler approach to God. My writing life was going well enough, my boys were wrestling with their testosterone and behaving alternately like fine young men and horrible beasts. Tracy had just begun DREAMS of Wilmington, an arts and character development center to work with disadvantaged inner-city kids. Years before, I had had a splendid midlife crisis, so it wasn't that. I wasn't dying, at least not immediately. I somehow thought that as I rounded the clubhouse turn and headed for the finish line, things would begin fall into place, this life of mine would make sense. God would, if not show his face, at least let me see the back of his head every so often.

I had this recurring vision of a stack of old IBM computer data cards. Those were from the pre-microchip days when, run through a sorting machine, their punched holes would compile data into neat categories. I was ready to call up such categories as Vocation, Spirituality, Catholicism, Integrity, Son, Father, Husband to see what my life amounted to. But no, try as I might, all I got was the same old jumbled mess, no clear answers. Nostalgia relentlessly stalked me, unimpeded by any antidote I could take.

What eluded me in the graveyard on the hillside behind the church in Kolinovce, where in vain I had searched the nameplates on rusted iron markers for members of my family, seemed to follow me to a grassy knoll at Calvary Cemetery in Cleveland. There I was looking for two small, smooth faces of granite I had visited so many times before. I brushed back overgrown grass and removed small branches when I thought I was in the right place. But the landmarks had changed, or at least were unfamiliar. Had I not been here for so long? Finally, there they were.

The tiny pine sapling that I first stood beside as a college freshman now reached overhead, gently shading the spot, its roots lovingly embracing the two caskets in lots 1737-1 and 1737-2. Side by side just inches apart, there lay my mother and father. Perhaps, I imagined, those roots even brought them closer together, year by year. I blew off withered grass clippings from the granite faces and, with the only tool available, my bare hands, removed the grass that crept over these, the simplest of gravestones. This was section 90 of the cemetery, where all stones had to be below ground level, to make mowing and maintenance easier. Yes, that would be typical of both of them. Don't waste money. Don't inconvenience anyone. Don't worry if a little ryegrass blocks the world's view of you.

My mother had left this life when I was about Noah's age. Like him, I was a rebel, my mouth two beats ahead of my brain. Nothing moved fast enough for me. I wanted so much more than what Forest Avenue offered. My father saw me go through college and graduate school, and the yellowed stack of magazines at the breakfast nook table indicated at least some degree of—if not quite pride—at least acknowledgment of what I did. He never could understand how I made a living, without having a boss or a company paycheck, but he was a working-class existentialist. If it some-how added up and a man paid his bills, what more was there to say?

What would they make of me now, brushing off their graves, my boys looking on, my half-Jewish, Protestant-born second wife, with eyes closed, saying a prayer for them? They would have loved the boys, vital and alert, and my Tracy they would have adored. Her straightforward-ness and lack of guile would have endeared her to them. Honesty counted. It would not have mattered the least bit that I appeared in the *New Yorker,* that my face was on the *Today Show* or CNN, that I was listed in *Who's Who in America,* that I could blithely walk into the offices of the *New York Times,* that I knew Kurt Vonnegut or Andy Warhol. "Butch," as they always called me, "Butch, are you doing okay?" they might ask, "okay" having nothing to do with how many bedrooms there were in my house or what year and make of car I was driving, the years of education I received, or the tax bracket I was in. They would never ask something as perfervid as "Did you make the world a better place?" No, that "okay" was a far deeper, all-inclusive litmus test. What kind of per-son are you? Do you keep your word? Do you not take more than your portion? Do you ever get "fancy," thinking you're more than you actu-ally are? Do you put in an honest day's work?

Tracy, Noah, and Daniel had wandered off now, and I was alone with my mother and my father, closer in a sense than I had ever been when they were alive. Because it was only now that I was beginning to under-stand them.

They might have used the word "okay," but they held themselves to a much higher standard. There was a kind of native excellence about them, a sacramental way of living that infused everything they did.

Like that day I was helping my father put in some flooring on a Satur-day job he'd picked up. It was blistering hot, he probably hadn't charged enough, and I was having trouble with a piece of molding beneath a radi-ator, bashing my knuckles and scarring the wood as I tried to nail it in. I pounded away, bending nails, splintering wood, but finally there it was, in place. My father stood back, saying nothing.

"Nobody'll ever see it," I said in my defense.

"*You'll* always see it, Butch," he said quietly.

Is this not how conscience is formed?

And my mother, who would hang out the wash for three adults and seven children on the lines in the backyard as if she were Monet at Giverny, carefully apportioning form and color and depth. First the whites, then in ascending pastels, followed by the darks. Each piece tautly stretched. Underwear would be discreetly hidden on the inner lines. There was no need for anyone to pierce our privacy by viewing these intimate articles of clothing.

Is this not about dignity, integrity, modesty?

And the tiny cores of toilet paper with but a few sheets left, the slivers of hand soap she brought back from her work as a cleaning lady for the Chadwick's in Shaker Heights.

Was this not sacred stewardship of the highest order?

My father was a model instructor, with his acts of kindness for which he wanted no thanks. He would teach me a generosity of spirit. Then my mother, who passed the serving plate to us even when she had not eaten enough—or even eaten at all—without a thought for herself. She would teach me that sacrifice for something worthwhile was no sacrifice at all and that with determination and faith, there was no night so dark that the dawn would not break. Their lessons were spliced into my DNA, there, indelibly stamped, even as I fought against them as a young boy and lived so profanely as an adult.

In the music world, the highest praise for a band or performer who gives the show everything is that "they left it all on the stage." So it was with Paul and Margaret Wilkes. They held back nothing. Each board my father cut, each sink my mother cleaned was done with dedication, attention, excellence. And it was this Petri dish of their virtues in which my tiny mustard seed of a Christian life—my Catholic expression of that Christian life—could flourish. Why had I not seen this before, seen it when I could have thanked them for the example they set? But they, like Father Greer, would have brushed off such gushy talk. There was nothing public about them. They sought neither praise nor recognition. As for their religious expression, it was never spoken, only lived. There were none of the "Praise the Lord" or "Jesus led me" prefixes to anything they uttered. I never remember the word "Catholic" being mentioned in my house. The word "God" was used sparingly, if at all, or with a ". . . dammit, son of a bitch!" tacked on when my father had reached the end of his patience.

∞

Our little family fell into a silent group as we trudged back up the Calvary Cemetery hill to our car. We drove across East 116th Street toward the old neighborhood. Like teeth that had gone rotten in a once healthy mouth, abandoned houses, houses with doors coming off the hinges, houses shedding paint revealed themselves as we turned onto Forest Avenue. The area was all black now, and 11412 Forest was still owned by the family my father had sold it to just days before he died. "He raised a family right here," said the current owner, a large black woman rocking back and forth on the uneven boards of the front porch, "and he said we should go ahead and do the same and raise ours. He was a *good* man."

We continued down Forest to what used to be East Boulevard, now renamed Martin Luther King, Jr. Drive. The soaring temple of St. Benedict's had changed hands. It was now grandly called Cathedral Church of God in Christ, with Bishop F. E. Perry Jr. its reigning prelate and pastor. Would Father Leo roll over, and over again, in his grave? My house, my church have gone on to other lives. They are no longer mine. Only the memories.

But those two souls, noted on unremarkable tombstones at Calvary Cemetery, they are not gone. They are not just memories. They, who achieved the exquisite balance between having their hands in God's own, meanwhile walking so justly, so softly, yet so solidly on this earth, they are so alive. I can turn to them and finally, after all the years, thank them for excellent lives that left it all here, on the stage. They gave me something beyond morality and religion. They gave me a way of walking in the world. And, the greatest gift, they gave me their faith, a faith they never once spoke about. They knew something so deep and so sure, something that my Ivy League schooling, my reporter's skills, my rubbing elbows with New York intelligentsia could never have taught me. It was freely given to me, because they could do it no other way. There could be no bargaining, no strings attached, no quid pro quo, because what they imparted was so ingrained in them that they could no more not pass it on than stop breathing. For their faith was like breath, natural, regular, and unconscious.

30

WORTHY OR NOT

"ARE YOU A PRIEST?"

I wheeled around to face a woman in a smartly fitted black smock. Her makeup was perfectly applied, from dark mascara in descending shades of azure eye shadow, rendered with pointillist artistry, to lipstick glistening to the outlines of her full lips. There I was at the Lancôme counter at Belk's, Wilmington's upscale department store, searching for the perfect perfume for Tracy, my hands bristling with tiny slivers of paper, each bearing its distinctive scent. And there she was, a visitor from the neighboring Chanel counter, as the distinctive logo on her smock noted. She looked at me intently through those well-etched eyes, awaiting my answer.

"N-no, I'm not a priest," I stammered.

"I remember you . . . ," she began hesitantly, as if this might not be the right place or time. She was not about to turn back now.

I held my breath; was my past life about to come back to haunt me? A priest? I once was an accomplished imposter, passing myself off as many different people; was this one of them? "When you came into my baby's room," she continued, "the helicopter was already on the pad ready to take him up to Duke Medical Center. He was sick, so sick. We thought he was going to die. I don't know your name, but I'll never forget that moment. You touched him so tenderly and blessed his tiny forehead with the sign of the cross. You gave me Holy Communion, and you said the most beautiful prayer I've ever heard. You said God would be on that helicopter with my son. And then they whisked us out of there. I don't know if that's all you said, but you brought a sense of calm in what must not have taken more than a couple seconds. I felt a sense of peace come over me. I did feel God was with us, and I knew," and here she hesitated, collecting herself, "I just *knew* from that moment on that he was going to be all right. He's now a rambunctious six-year-old, and I just want to say," her clouded eyes broke into a mother's proud grin, "thank you."

∞

One of the truly dramatic changes in modern Catholic life was set in motion with the repetition, four times, of the simple words "active participation." They appeared in the first document to come forth from the Second Vatican Council, *Sacrosanctum Concilium,* the Constitution on the Sacred Liturgy, officially promulgated by Pope Paul VI, in December 1963. "The people of God," who were members of the "priesthood of all believers," were no longer to be a passive audience at the Mass, but partners in raising up to God in song, word, and action. The days of a priest intoning Latin words, with his back oblivi- ously to the silent faithful, were soon to be over. The document desig- nated "Special ministers . . . constituted in order that they may give communion to themselves and to the faithful." This "special minister" was to be "A suitable person . . . chosen in this order of preference: sub deacons, clerics in minor orders, those who have received tonsure, men religious, women religious, male catechists (unless, in the prudent judgment of the pastor, a male catechist is preferable to a woman reli- gious), laymen, laywomen." With this three-page, quaintly chauvinistic document, a dam burst. Lay people, properly termed "extraordinary ministers of the Eucharist" (the priest was the "ordinary" minister), would now be allowed to distribute Holy Communion at Mass and to home- and hospital-bound sick. And, some thirty-five years later, *Sacrosanctum Concilium* would dramatically affect my life.

∞

One Sunday morning in the weekly bulletin at St. Mary, our Wilmington parish, the call went out for extraordinary ministers, and I assumed when I offered my name that, if accepted, I would be assigned to one of the local nursing homes. Instead, there was an opening for a person to visit New Hanover Regional Medical Center, our largest hospital, each Thurs- day morning. Not knowing exactly what that entailed, I agreed, and was schooled in the ritual of distributing the Eucharist by an unsmiling woman from the diocese, with all the compassion and pastoral skills of a Marine drill sergeant, who talked about the Eucharist as if it were fission- able material, which, if mishandled, would signal the utter and immediate destruction of the Catholic Church.

"Always ask if they are in the state of grace. Ascertain if they are in a proper marriage. At a minimum, be sure they have done their Easter duty. Under no circumstances . . ." She didn't so much frighten as exhaust me with her many admonitions. I would have to see for myself what being an extraordinary minister was all about.

Over the many Thursdays that followed, I gave Holy Communion to some four thousand people. I was honored to touch the face of the living and the newly dead. I was welcomed and was occasionally angrily told to leave. I stood with a spouse whose loved one had just received a terminal diagnosis. I was in the room when all tests came back negative. Tubes and pills and liquids brought sustenance and medications into these four thousand bodies, but I was there to tend to another, unseen, part of them that no medical chart followed. Each Thursday morning offered me a time to be humbled and dazzled by the deep faith of these men and women. Each Thursday morning offered the opportunity to reflect on the meaning of the mystery of Jesus Christ embodied in these tiny ovals of unleavened bread I offered. Through these patients I came to a clearer understanding of my own life, my Church, and my God.

∞

At the front desk of New Hanover Regional Medical Center, I exchange greetings with Buddy and Anne, who answer phones and direct visitors and new patients. There are usually fifteen to twenty Catholic patients to see. From the first day of my visits, I have kept cryptic notes about the patients, so that I might better remember them on later visits. What follows is taken from various visits, but let us call it a richly representative Thursday, for each Thursday presented its own unique chapter in the book of lives.

My first stop is the small chapel on the first floor. I approach the simple altar beneath a pane of backlit stained glass ubiquitous enough to offend none and embrace all. The Bible is open to Psalm 103, one of my favorites.

> Bless the LORD, O my soul,
> And all that is within me, bless His holy name.
> Bless the LORD, O my soul,
> And forget none of His benefits;
> Who pardons all your iniquities,
> Who heals all your diseases;
> Who redeems your life from the pit

Who crowns you with loving-kindness and compassion;
Who satisfies your years with good things,
So that your youth is renewed like the eagle.

Yes, the eagle. I bow my head and ask that I would be a worthy bearer of the gift borne in the tender talons of that mighty eagle.

In room 940 is Edna, a black woman in her fifties, who when I introduce myself ("Good morning; Paul Wilkes from St. Mary with Holy Communion for you") immediately apologizes that she's been away from the Church, but assures me she is coming back. It is a frequent first volley: guilt finely honed by my Church. I look into her bright eyes and say, "Well, I wouldn't worry too much about that right now, Edna; the Church has come to you. We deliver!" She smiles.

I come closer to her bed. Is this eight o'clock in the morning in room 940, or is it the vineyard at day's end? And didn't the vineyard owner see that the desires of those who hadn't had the opportunity to put in a full day's work are really no different from those who had worked all day long? Each needed to be fed, each acknowledged as having done their best, having given their time, with whatever abilities they had. Was Edna any more or less worthy than the woman I would see on the fifth floor who attends Mass each morning or the man in intensive care who—God forbid—married a Presbyterian?

The popular "What Would Jesus Do?" litmus test—both a subterfuge for appalling abuse and grounds for grace-filled acts—might seem a bit facile a way to guide my actions. But, quite honestly, it seems to make more pastoral sense than the third degree recommended by my exacting Eucharistic instructor. Well, what *would* Jesus do? I am not Jesus, so I can't know for sure. And I am not a priest, so I cannot hear her confession, which she might normally do before receiving communion. But does not a simple act of contrition rising up from this hospital bed from a woman in an advanced stage of respiratory failure and pneumonia not reach the ear of God?

"Edna, before we approach the altar together, so that you might receive this precious gift, let's lay down the burden of our sins," I say. We begin the Act of Contrition together: "Oh, my God I am heartily sorry for having offended thee . . ."

My prayer complete, I look down at Edna. I hold the host in the still air before her. The only sound is the muffled gurgling of the machine valiantly trying to cleanse her compromised lungs. "This is the Lamb of God who takes away the sins of the world. Happy are those who are called to this, his eternal banquet. O, Lord I am not worthy to receive you, but only say the word and I shall be healed." I add, "And you *are* healed, Edna. Your sins are behind you now. Even before you thought about whatever it was you did or didn't do that you felt was sinful, God forgave you. You are as pure and clean and sinless as you were the day you were born, and Christ awaits you with open arms." Edna takes the host. Her simple act of exhaling, audibly, is like a song wafted heavenward, a release of her worries and pain. The next inhalation will be purely divine.

What gives me the authority to offer the Eucharist without prior questioning, to speak like this to her? I wonder about that sometimes myself, but when I look into the eyes of someone like Edna—or Frank or Althea or Samuel or Blake or Miriam—I find myself carried along on the wings of something. Is this the Holy Spirit? I really don't know exactly what it is. But I am there in person; Christ is there, invisible. Although he is the one we turn to, I am the only physical presence, the only sound available. I must—I want to—as much as I can, bring the forgiveness of God I have felt in my own life. I want to impart something of the love that sends shivers down my arms. I want those I visit to experience the presence that is so palpable each time I open the pyx. I want them to know the abiding trust that washes over me in my lowest moments that somehow, someway, everything will be all right. He is with us; we are not alone.

In room 745 is Jewel, who cannot receive communion, as she is having tests later in the day. With a straight face to her husband of forty-seven years I offer, "Never a harsh word in all those years, right?" He rolls his eyes. "Just like my marriage," I add. I pray with them that the tests reveal exactly what Jewel needs and that healing will begin so she can go home soon. I touch the host to her forehead and pray that she receive Christ in her heart, and then give the host to her husband. "You are unified in marriage, and this morning you are once again unified in Christ," I pray.

I encountered this situation many times, where a loved one or family member was in the room, but the patient could not receive communion. Early in my Thursdays as a Eucharistic minister, I would simply pray with them, asking for healing and faith, but I always left the room feeling hollow. I searched for a way to make that moment more holy, more precious, more intimate, and one morning I found myself touching the host to a forehead and then giving it to a spouse. I don't know what the rubrics of the Church say about such a ritual, but it was the best I could do—physically, actually—to touch them with as much of the presence of God as was at my disposal.

As I enter a room, I never know whether it will be a crucifixion or the last hour of painless stay, whether the person's beliefs and makeup are standing her in good stead or failing her, whether he is close to

Catholicism or had long ago set it aside. Some are annoyed by my presence, but very few. Even those who prefer not to receive the Eucharist will most often accept a prayer, which I offer with as much specificity as I can, and quickly, so as not to overstay my welcome.

I have found that it is not the degree of pain, the seriousness of their disease or illness, the level of their religious practice, or even the imminence of death that separates those who seem somehow at peace and those who are not. All are afraid. Every one of us is terrified just being in a hospital bed. Early on, I would have said that it is faith that draws the line. But now I think it is something else.

It is anger, its presence or absence.

Anger that life was not fair to them, that people were not fair with them, that God seemed to look away just when they needed him the most. If they are not burdened by some variation of simmering resentment and they come to the conclusion that the germ, bad gene, virus, the cells multiplying too quickly or those too depleted to regenerate—even the shoe they tripped over that landed them here—were more sheer happenstance than evidence of divine wrath, then they seem to do better.

Such is not the case for Anna, in room 540. There is a rosary on Anna's bedside table, a book of spiritual reading on her lap, a crucifix wedged behind the bulletin board on the wall. But I find all these are of little avail, because there is so much anger in Anna's soul. I had seen her many times before that day, in fact almost from the first diagnosis of ovarian cancer. She was in and out of the hospital over a twelve-month period. An attractive, self-assured woman in her midfifties, she had lost her long, luxuriant auburn hair and regrown the stubble of a more curly variety. Her looks changed as she became more gaunt, but I had seen other cancer patients go through those horrible days and they seemed to soften, not harden, as the aberrant cells mutated and mutated again.

Usually, as a fatal disease dully marches on to its inevitable end, people release themselves from the unfairness of it all. Not Anna. Her husband had left her many years before, but the wound was still fresh. Her children didn't come to visit—or at least not often enough for her. Her jobs—to my mind, substantial—had never fulfilled her. "I have my faith," she says, clutching the rosary so tightly that her knuckles were white. "Thank God I have my faith."

Hers is not a faith that I can easily understand. Hers is a brittle pact with a hateful God who never allows anything to happen the way we might want and always frustrates us whenever we have even the least chance of being happy on earth. It is a faith that grasps at an unreachable God in heaven, a God who will not deign to walk with us on earth and share our burdens. A God who believes we must suffer in a vale of tears so that we might better appreciate the paradise that awaits us. It is a faith that offers obeisance to an unappeasable God of exactitude, the eye of the needle being so narrow that rich or poor, we'd best navigate so, so carefully and only then have the slightest chance of reaching him.

Anna recites again the familiar litany of grievances as I stand there, pyx in hand. I listen. I retrieve a host. She stops and stares at me. "Lord, you are present in the room with us today," I begin, and go on to pray that this would be a good and restful day for Anna and that she would sense Christ's presence as she takes the host, that she would feel him permeating her body with his holiness and that she would know that he stands by the bed all day long. At any time, all she needs do is reach out her own hand. His is already there. I place the host on her tongue and stand back, my head bowed, for a few moments.

"Anna, he's with you now," I say softly. "If there is anything at all, you can let him carry it. He loves you. He wants your happiness; he wants you to know that you can rest in him and there is nothing to fear."

"I'm not afraid of anything," she says defiantly. "But they should only know what they're doing to me, what they have done to me, what they . . ."

I stand at the door and wave back to her. She pulls the sheet up closer and begins the rosary.

In room 213, all I can do is cry.

For there is not-so-young Elisabeth with a baby boy nestled at her breast. To see the love in that woman's eyes, that sleeping child with unblemished skin and soul—I can't restrain myself. I touch his smooth cheek, play with his tiny toes, and finally bless the child's forehead with the sign of the cross. He stirs, as if he already feels God's presence. I begin my prayer. "Dear God, here we have this beautiful baby—a sign of your love, this mother's love, a father's love. Be with him to guide him so that he grows into a compassionate, kind, yet strong boy and young man. That he will always hear your voice even when the noises of the world tend to drown out everything. That he will be an obedient son, yet a man of his own mind. Bless him and this good woman Elisabeth, we pray in your strong name, Jesus. Amen."

I look at Elisabeth. "In this tiny piece of bread, Elisabeth, is the God of ages. Here. Right here in this room on the first day of your son's life. He comes to give you the strength to be the mother you know you can be. He'll be with you in those late nights when you don't think you have another ounce of energy. He'll never leave your side." I begin the Eucharistic prayer: "This is the lamb who takes away the sins of the world. Happy are those—"

"But, but I haven't been to church in so long, really since college," she says.

"And?"

"I'm Catholic, and I will have my son baptized, but my husband isn't much of a churchgoer. I don't know how God looks on all this. It's so confusing . . ."

I look down at her, the early morning sun turning the host almost translucent. "This is food for your journey of life, Elisabeth. It isn't a reward for good behavior. What kind of God do you think he is, to offer this beautiful food on this incredible morning and then say, 'No, Elisabeth, sorry—you don't qualify. I've checked your bar code and you're not in the system.' That's not the God that I know." After her Act of Contrition, Elisabeth receives, her tears mingling with the host, a tear, then another gently falling onto the cheek of her precious son.

Ten years ago, New Hanover Regional Medical Center built a hospice unit. Around a courtyard of semitropical plants and two reflecting ponds are twelve spacious rooms, each with a patio opening onto a beautifully landscaped terrace. The sign on room 6 says to see the nurse before entering, and I know what this usually means. I check with the nurse and then slowly open the door. The light from the reading lamp bathes Michael in a saffron-colored, ethereal glow. He is still, a not unfamiliar pose for the terminally ill. There is color in his face; his eyes are closed. He appears to be sleeping. I look for the telltale sign. The pressed sheet over what the cancer has left of his once broad chest (the pictures on the dresser show a robust Army corporal during World War II, in what appears to be a French village) is still.

There are so many moments of grace in the small ministry I perform, but this is a truly magnificent one. When death seems to have happened. I say it that way because death is not marked by the absence of a pulse or by a straight line on an electrocardiogram. Death happens over stages, and the dying are with us in the world one minute and in communion with God the next. Back and forth they travel. I have seen this over and over again. The face of someone who is seemingly comatose bears a beatific look that assures you that the person is already visiting the other side.

I feel honored to be with the earthly shell as the soul is finally released to go home. What is my prayer? First of all, I know I am praying to the newest saint in heaven. Now that Michael sees the face of God—and understands *everything*—I pray that he will intercede and pray for me, still thrashing through my days. I don't pray that he or I will get to heaven. That is a given. Could God deny anyone a return home? I pray that whatever this day will bring, I will do the next right thing. That I will be not so much husband as companion to Tracy, not so much father but honest friend to my sons, now in college, wisely helping them with midcourse corrections of praise and admonition. That I will not be, quite frankly, the jackass I have the propensity to be. The arrogant, the stubborn, the glib, the one for whom the garments of compromise too easily slip on and off. That I will walk the streets of Wilmington with the eyes of Christ, that Wilmington will be my Jerusalem or Galilee or Capernaum. That I will live as Christ lived, yet never uttering a word that that is my sole and simple objective.

Of course, that is a lot to ask of Michael, but I hope—no, I am sure—he understands my needs.

I walk out to my car, my rounds completed. I have just visited with a representative cross section of Catholic America. I have given the host to those considered "good" Catholics, marginal Catholics, and Catholics who would be considered outside the Church. It made little difference what their level of observance or supposed worthiness might be. The God of the ages, the Christ who promised his friends that he would not leave them alone, had once again fulfilled his promise. He had come to them, and whether they labored in the vineyard all day or for just a fleeting moment, they received the greatest gift my Church can offer them.

Once again, I had been given the privilege to see the scriptures come alive. I had felt the power of the presence of God.

31

RETURN TO ST. PETER'S

Even the ride from the airport lets you know you are in a place like no other.

There, off to the left, the Roman Forum, the Baths of Caracalla, the Circus Maximus. Beyond, the looming aqueduct—huge portions still intact—an engineering marvel that brought water to the seat of the greatest empire the world had ever known. This is Rome, so aptly called the Eternal City, now saying goodbye to a man who was here for but a sliver of its long life, but who so dominated this city's imagination that some wonder what it will be without his towering presence.

As I write this first blog as Beliefnet's Special Correspondent in Rome, the pope's body lies within the Vatican's Clementine hall, where his closest friends, staff, cardinals, Curia officials, and dignitaries are paying their respects. Two Swiss guards flank him left and right. His staff, with that now so famous crucifix, lies at his side. What is even more astounding is that even in death, he is still a media phenomenon. Live pictures have been broadcast of his still form, not only a precedent-shattering event, but an eerily real-time account of this, his final pilgrimage.

O

THUS BEGAN MY COVERAGE OF POPE JOHN PAUL II'S FUNERAL and the ensuing conclave that would elect Benedict XVI in April 2004.

I stood, a tiny figure lost in the long afternoon shadows of Bernini's sweeping colonnade, gazing out over the crowd overflowing the great expanse of St. Peter's Square. Two thick arteries of mourners moved slowly and silently toward the great basilica between parallel metal barriers that bisected the yawning expanse. These three hundred thousand in the square were but the vanguard of the hundreds upon hundreds of thousands more standing in lines that led out Via Conciliazione, splitting off to the north to snake through the streets of the bustling Borgo, and to the south to surge across the languorous Tiber.

Here I was, plastic press cards from CNN, NBC, and the Vatican press office dangling from my neck, a cell phone bringing urgent messages to come to television remote locations overlooking the Vatican, that I might offer my insights on the passing of one pope, the advent of another. Not to overstate my role—I was but a very minor player during a major event. I had covered a war or two, traveled to many places for stories; it did not escape me that this could be my last hurrah as a foreign correspondent. After all, I was now well into the autumn of my years.

Early the next morning, I entered the grand basilica of St. Peter's, a church on a scale as no other, almost six acres of open space, populated with some of the world's finest religious art. I approached the bier of John Paul II, whisked ahead of those who must wait—some of them twenty-four hours—by virtue of those little plastic cards. I looked upon the face of a world and spiritual leader, so commanding a figure that five kings, four queens, and seventy presidents and prime ministers would come to honor him. The funeral of Pope John Paul II saw the single largest gathering of heads of state in history. The privileged were here, but so were the poor. Some two million people would come to Rome to pay their respects in person, while hundreds of millions would watch the events on television.

I knew John Paul II's greatness and reach, but as I stood there, I felt embarrassingly devoid of emotion. I couldn't cry, as others did around me. There was a simple reason: I did not love the man. John Paul II was not what was best about the Catholic Church—at least in this Catholic's mind. Even as he traveled the world to adoring crowds, his papacy was cruel to many within his own house. He suppressed dissent as ruthlessly as the Communists had done in his native Poland. He promoted those most loyal to his views, those who passed his litmus test, not those who might be most pastoral to his people. He told those living outside the guidelines he drew and staunchly maintained that although they were still loved by God, they were not welcome at the table of his Eucharist.

As mourners passed by the bier and disappeared into the vaulted darkness of the side aisles of this cavernous basilica, continuing toward the great doors at the entrance, I broke off and turned sharply in the opposite direction. From a distance, the lights below the altar dedicated to St. Jerome are dimly olive-hued, as if merely another example of world-class bas relief sculpting awaits. But as you come closer, the light becomes purer, whiter, stronger, beckoning you to draw near. Only then do you see the body beneath the altar. There is a glass-faced sarcophagus, and within, the earthly remains of my beloved pope, John XXIII.

His face is waxen, unrecognizable really; only the great nose assures the pilgrim that this indeed is the right place. I joined a handful of others in the few rows of kneelers set before the altar. I bowed my head and folded my hands. Here I could express my love for a dead pope. And cry I did, huge, happy tears, not for this inert shape before me, but for the vision of the Catholic Church that he had implanted in my heart and the hearts of so many Catholics. I cried for a memory, like the wash of emotion on discovering a faded picture in an album while rummaging through the attic, a picture of life that was at once simple, straightforward, and charged with possibility. I spent a long, sweet time there, in silence, in reverie.

OO

I was not immune to the magnificence and sweep of history unfolding during those weeks in Rome. John Paul II's funeral was the largest Christian gathering, ever. And for those gathered and those watching on television, no religious body offers liturgical theatre with the power and beauty of the Vatican. To see the precise and resplendent rituals of waking and burying a pope, then selecting the next, is to stand in awe at the timelessness of my Church. When kids with tattoos on their necks stand next to Mother Teresa's Sisters of Charity who stand next to Polish miners in plumed hats next to Japanese businessmen who, in turn, offer their water bottle to the Australian backpackers, the word "universal" is enfleshed with new meaning.

But, as the days wore on and the pomp and ceremony continued, I found myself feeling more and more distant, more and more the outsider. Something was not quite right. To see Boston's Cardinal Bernard Law officiating at one of the nine commemorative High Masses, televised around the world, was more than I could take. The man whom I had written about in a recent New Yorker piece, who had arrogantly shielded and cavalierly moved priests known to be sexual predators, and who only resigned when fifty-eight of his priests pleaded to Rome to remove him, was even more powerful in exile. As archpriest of one of Rome's four major basilicas, St. Mary Major, Law was afforded a luxurious apartment, salary, and staff. As a member of eight papal congregations and councils, he wielded tremendous influence over everything from the appointment of American bishops to wording in the liturgy.

And to see cardinals and bishops floating through St. Peter's square in their medieval garb, bedecked in enough filigreed lace to please Marie Antoinette—the same cardinals so outspoken about homosexuals aspiring to the priesthood—began to sicken me. Greeting each other with the appellation "Your eminence," they seemed like children wearing some out-of-date tasseled curtains, playing a game of King and Queen. There was a Felliniesque quality about it all. I tried—as the Notre Dame sisters had taught me—to "avert my eyes" when confronted with a temptation (in this case, the sin of disdain or, more likely, rash judgment), but I was an utter failure. I sinned again and again.

And the self-importance of the American seminarians, who stood alongside me as we watched the funeral mass from a promontory on the Gianiculum Hill overlooking St. Peter's Square, was eventually more than this somewhat battered Catholic could take. Below us, the scene of a simple cypress casket surrounded by clerics in blazing red vestments was breathtaking. We chatted about things Catholic as the ceremony wore on, but the seminarians quickly assumed the role of teachers to a dull student. In their finely tailored soutanes, fingering their rosaries, they scolded me that my views were painfully wrong. Only those espousing the "fullness of faith" were worthy to be called Catholic. In other words, unless one assented to every edict from Rome, every word in the Catechism, and the pronouncements of one's bishop, and accepted that the Church spoke authoritatively as the very voice of Christ, then, inevitably, one was not sufficient. The rosaries twirled through their clean young hands. I said less and less and let them teach on.

On the afternoon of April 19, I was sitting in the CNN control center, rented years before for an ungodly amount and set within a huge hall in one of the seminaries on the Gianiculum. During the third conclave meeting of the elector-cardinals, the monitor trained on the Sistine Chapel chimney belched a schizophrenic mixture of smoke—white (a pope is elected) before turning to gray (bad pyrotechnical skills at the stove in which the ballots were burned), not quite black to show an inconclusive vote, and back to a murky white. All eyes focused on another monitor, showing the huge bell atop St. Peter's. As if rudely awoken from centuries of disuse, it began a slow, silent arch. By the time the first gong had sounded, I was racing toward the piazza. All of us in the control room knew, because of the quickness of the election, who the next pope would be. Within the hour, the 265th successor of St. Peter stood in the balcony above the great doors of the basilica. My cell phone was ringing. I was wanted as a guest on the Larry King show. It would be broadcast live, at

3 AM Rome time. It was now 6 PM. I needed some sleep, but before I got a few restless hours, I filed my report, which included my first impressions:

> The mood of the crowd in St. Peter's was in keeping with the man chosen to be pope—happy the election was over, but restrained. The man who is now Pope Benedict XVI extended his arms to the crowd, clasped his hands together in a victory grasp, but seemed almost to force a smile from time to time. Those who have seen him outside of his official capacities say he is a good dinner companion, extremely intelligent, but a man careful with his words and emotions. Chants of "Papa, Papa" rose up from the crowd, but died down after no more than a minute or so.

OO

It was windy and bitterly cold for a Rome spring—especially so in the dead of night—and once my hands were warm, I took off my leather gloves and handed them to the priest next to me in the frigid, three-sided CNN tent as we awaited the beginning of *Larry King Live*. This was the network's highest-rated show, and my priest friend, a member of the Legionnaires of Christ, an arch-conservative order that brooked no dissent from any Church teaching, eagerly told of his absolute bliss at the election of Cardinal Ratzinger. Once the show began, other interviewees chimed in, extolling the virtues of John Paul II, assured that his legacy would live on in Benedict XVI. When it came my turn, Larry King tossed me a canned question about Ratzinger's early involvement in the Nazi youth, a supposedly provocative inquiry that really had no intelligent response and a path I wasn't going down. And besides, all my pent-up emotions were about to be unleashed. After all, it was only a windy rooftop in Rome; the fact that millions of people were watching didn't occur to me.

"I've been doing a dangerous thing, Larry," I said after I had deflected his question with something about "youth."

"Paul, what's that," he said with at least feigned interest, leaning into the camera, his suspenders straining at the shoulders of his outlandishly striped shirt. I replied, "I've been reading the New Testament, Larry. And what I read in there and what I see going on down there," I turned toward St. Peter's Square, the magnificently illuminated backdrop, "well, sometimes they don't match up."

It was a crotchety, ill-tempered, and wrongheaded thing to say, in addition to being pompous and self-important. What was happening "down there" was an honest expression of the faith of over a billion people.

It was the orderly transition of governance, steeped in two thousand years of church history. Why had I been so flip, so dismissive? On the one hand, I loved the Catholic Church, loved that we had a definable structure—thanks to the model of imperial Rome—loved that there was a place to which we could point and where we could visit as a spiritual home. On the other hand, I hated the high-priest trappings as much as—at least from my reading of that New Testament I so defiantly thrust upon my host—Christ did, the phylacteries he railed against replaced in this era by the towering miters and yards of lace I had so unkindly noted. But why inflict such a low blow while posturing that I was taking a higher road?

My comment to Larry King was a crude attempt to say that I felt Catholicism was more about following the life of Christ than following the wiles of the "eminences." It was not God's hand that pointed to Ratzinger, as some other guests alluded. And that if Jesus had shown up in St. Peter's Square, preaching the gospel and condemning the high-priestedness of the Church, the *carboneri* would have arrested him in a heartbeat. My voice was largely drowned out over the hourlong show. I'm sure I seemed like a very ungrateful guest on this supposedly happy occasion.

The lights went down, and the guests dispersed. I pulled my trench coat tighter around me and walked over to the darkened edge of the roof. There I was alone with my thoughts, the great basilica before me. The statues of the saints astride the balustrade, which seem life-size from ground level but are actually over twenty feet high, ringed the colonnade, these magnificent, looming witnesses, most of whom I knew by name and vita. St. Cecilia, patron saint of music; St. Ignatius, the soldier turned founder of the Jesuits; St. John the Evangelist; St. Agnes; St. Frances of Rome; forty in all. Catholicism's Hall of Fame. And to the right were the darkened papal chambers, as yet unoccupied. Benedict poetically and humbly chose to spend his first night as pope in the simple quarters that he had occupied during the conclave. St. Peter's was bathed in a light I have never seen anywhere else in the world, an ethereal hue at once yellow and lime and gray; all of these and none of these, a color all its own.

What was it about me? Why was I so at war with this Church of mine? Why didn't I either accept its titles and lace and seeming indifference to the pain of so many people or simply send myself down some other path to God?

In a stiff blast of wind, it struck me. This was not "the Church."

How had I allowed myself to think that these sixteenth-century buildings—breathtakingly beautiful as they were—were anything more than so much stone and mortar? How had I imprisoned the Son of God within these cold walls and dressed him in such frivolous finery? How foolish of me. No, the Church was a billowing desert tent, once so tiny it held but a single man, wearing the simple clothing of the people of his time. It was now a vast tent, cobbled onto, ripped asunder, patched so many times in so many places, its poles bending in the wind, yet not breaking. A tent sweeping wider and wider so that no one would be denied shelter under its tattered roof. A tent not of man's work or devices but of God's.

In one corner of the tent, I could hear a feverish African drum Mass, in another, a Mass in Latin for those who would have it no other way. There, a great pipe organ; beyond, guitars and marimbas. In jungles and high-rise office buildings, this was a Church presided over and attended by saints and scoundrels. All under this vast tent. Theologians debating the fine points of the Incarnation; a peasant in a field of maize, kneeling at the sound of the Angeles bell. And those men in lace, Curia officials, going about their work. The saints, the molesters. This all-too-human Church, gathered under the great tent of God's love.

And there, over there was Father Greer. He was telling a young couple not to forget to invite Jesus as they planned their wedding. Next to him was Jacques Travers, touching Donald so tenderly on the check to calm him. Could it be? There was Thomas Merton recalling his profound experience of God at the Buddhist shrine of Polonnaruwa in Sri Lanka. There my own father, sharing a sandwich; my mother carefully patching the knees of someone's corduroys. Dorothy Day stirring a soup pot with one hand and holding a book by Dostoyevsky in the other. All of them, all here, all together.

Still more of the cloud of witnesses were here, earthbound yet heavenly. The Trappist monks high in the mountains of Kerala in Southern India, alternating the words of the Bagavad Gita and the New Testament. The Jesuits in El Salvador, forgiving those who killed their brothers. The flighty priest in Mostar, blessing a Muslim child before the One God of us all. Timothy Radcliffe, the wise Dominican superior general, advising that we must never let the Church get in the way of our relationship with God. The scriptures say it so well:

> Behold, the virgin shall be with child
> and bear a son, and they shall name him Emmanuel,
> which means "God is with us."

God *is* with us. And under this wide tent, he speaks with each of us, all wayfarers, pope to pauper, true believer with the fullness of faith to those—like myself—with but a fragmented portion. During this time in Rome, I had thought too much about "the Church," as if it were these dead, fixed buildings I was now looking at and not a living being, animated by a living God—the Christ—moving throughout the tent, consoling, prodding, whispering, listening, crying at our pain, laughing at the sheer humanity of us all.

Catholicism took in such an unruly, imperfect family. If you wanted to be part of it, you had to weather the crazy uncles and awful cousins because the whole was certainly greater than the sum of its parts. You had to weather your own storms and upheavals. You had to risk condemnation for what was in your heart.

The wind rose up again, coming from the southeast, from the Mediterranean, warmer now, as the dead of night had passed and morning was only a few hours away. I gazed down at St. Peter's Square for a last time.

Were Ratzinger's fine theological distinctions or Law's perceived arrogance all that there was to these men? Was that prissy Legionnaire of Christ any less worthy in the eyes of God than the gritty Jesuits who lived and died with the Salvadoran campesinos? Why ask such questions and, still worse, try to answer them? We were all Catholics, all hoping that we were somehow pleasing to God, that our lives meant something. Praying through the fog of our careful rationalizations, narrow-mindedness, and psychological short-circuits that somehow we were on, if not the right path, at least some path to him. But always with the quiet but blessed assurance that God's care for us would always prevail. For this is the mystery of the Mystical Body of Christ, each of us linked, unknowingly but surely contributing to the whole.

This is the mystery of Everyman and Everywoman. Each of us ordinary, yet placed in the extraordinary circumstances of our lives. And have I not been each of them? The people at Presentation parish, in Kolinovce, in the hospital beds at New Hanover Regional Medical Center? Here in Rome? Would my vaunted three-piece, custom-made Italian suit not match their phylacteries and miters and lace for ostentation? Sins against my body and the bodies of others? My lies and duplicities? Abuse of power? Squandering of gifts? I have lived each of their darkest lives and sinned their sins.

Yet there I was, still under the tent, and here I would stay, together with the assembled and sometimes fractious tribes and families. But I held the hope that at the end of the day, as usually happens at every huge gathering, I would get some choice of where to sit and with whom to talk. So I will wend my way to that corner of the wide tent of Catholicism where those of my spiritual tribe like Merton and Dorothy Day and Karl Rahner and Father Greer and Jacques Travers and John XXIII have found each other. Others may want to push us out, noisy, ungovernable bunch that we are. But, in reality, we have no place that we would rather be.

32

A LIGHT IN THE WINDOW

NO ONE WAS YET AWAKE IN THE HOUSE at 30 Inningwood Road. It was just after five o'clock. I crept down the creaky stairs and out the front door. It was fall in Ossining, a suburb of New York City, drenched with the early morning dew. The familiar scent of dead leaves on trees and ground is primeval and preconscious, I think, to a person who has spent most of his life in the North. I inhaled deeply.

Tracy and I were visiting her uncle, Rolf Kip, who had recently lost his wife, Barbara. Rolf and Barbara were sometimes more parents to Tracy than her own, divorced as they were soon after she was born.

The full moon cast a shimmering ribbon before me as I turned left at the fork and trudged up the incline on Ryder Road. At the rise of the road, about a half-mile further, the home of the Maryknoll order came into view. It was always an incongruous sight—even more so in the pale light—to see eight red-lacquered columns jutting out of a stout granite fieldstone tower to support a distinctively pagoda-style roof. Its green tiles, gently uplifted at the corners, bespoke a temple design so marvelously Buddhist. And yet it was a thoroughly Catholic building. Founded by Father Thomas F. Price, a priest born in my new hometown of Wilmington, North Carolina, Maryknoll represented American Catholicism's burning desire to bring the faith to the farthest corners of the globe. Built here on a knoll—thus the name—the order had triumphantly constructed a huge complex at a time when the Catholic Church attracted so many men and women to religious life that it could barely find room for them all. The main building was now but a relic, its once bustling seminary closed, many of its rooms and offices put to other uses or simply vacant. On the approach to the main building stands a poor relative, a squat, three-story red brick building, St. Teresa's. And there, on that fall morning, on the third floor, a single light shone. This was the residence for retired Maryknoll priests.

Had I followed the example of that sad-eyed Maryknoll missionary who stirred my fourteen-year-old soul in my freshman year at Cathedral Latin High, it could have been me in that room, reading the morning Office. Over fifty years ago, I had been so sure that this was my calling, my vocation. I would be, if God allowed, a Maryknoll priest, my passions subsumed into that bottomless pool of love that was Christ. Yet when the gypsy girl pressed her thighs against mine that night at CYO canteen, I found I had no control of my passions whatsoever. They were not to be subsumed by divine love after all. What an abject failure I soon proved myself to be. I was embarrassingly human, an ordinary man.

I stood in the shaded darkness of a huge oak tree and peered at that solitary light. I had once grandly dreamed of nothing less than "saving the world." I had yearned to take on the mantle of Christ, emboldened by his spirit to make his way known. But, as it came to be, I didn't take on that mantle. I didn't save the world. What kind of life had it been? On this moonlit autumn morning, it was the due season for an examination of conscience.

As for hearing a call, I had heard so many. I answered and pursued each with such intensity, only to find that the more effort I expended, the more elusive the call became. Early in life, I was so typically a Catholic of my time, one who believed that in the mind of God there was a very specific plan for me. I had only to decode his exacting prescription. Of course, never being a person who understood nuance or countenanced subtlety—consigning such traits to mere weaknesses—it necessarily was a plan writ large. Not that I would be famous or well known; no, not in that way. But that God's plan would ask everything of me. Every thing. Heroic. That always translated into a religious vocation; after all, why would a person who claimed to want to be close to God accept anything less than full-time service to him?

For more than half my life, I was firmly convinced that a vocation would call me to be something I was not. For what I was, was a talkative, nosey, overstated, shortcut-seeking, impulsive, insecure, often callow fellow. Yes, I sought God in prayer and tried to live with a moral code, but those were givens—I *had* those traits already. I had to work on what I did not have. I was convinced that that would take not only supreme acts of will but also an entire recasting of my very flawed nature. Where I was impatient, I had to learn to be patient; where impulsive, thoughtful. Where voluble, silent. Where inquisitive, so filled with faith that I would reach a point where I wouldn't need to ask a single question. The answers would be forthcoming only when God saw that I needed them.

Even when I married the first time, I had the gnawing feeling that I was doing something not so much wrong as entirely too easy. Leaving the Catholic Church was really the smaller part of my unease. I was giving into passion and loneliness. Where was the sacrifice here? The heroism? When that marriage was dying, I looked forward to the sacrificial make-over that would transform me into the saint I secretly wanted to be. I was happy to purge myself of the pretensions and possessions of middle-class life, wiping the slate clean for the hand of God to write upon. Then why did I weep into that wretched sofa on my first night of freedom? I should have known then.

With grim determination, I kept grasping just beyond my reach for that something that would make me different, better. I was trying to prove this to myself in the tragicomedic operetta that was my life, while God watched—bemusedly, I'll bet—from the wings. Why had it taken me so many years to discover that he was trying to work with what I was, not with what I was not? That my idea of holiness was not his. As Thomas Merton wrote in *New Seeds of Contemplation,* "Every one of us is shadowed by an illusory person: a false self. This is the man I want myself to be but who cannot exist, because God does not know anything about him." Indeed, God knew nothing of St. Paul of Forest Avenue, nothing at all.

Such a crooked path I traveled, through Hamptons parties and Oakham hermitage, taking my lead from Moondog Allen Freed and Trappist Thomas Merton. Talking to Kurt Vonnegut and Jacques Travers. Observing Andy Warhol and Father Joseph Greer. Sleeping on silk sheets and that wretched sofa.

Frederick Buechner's oft-quoted definition of vocation as "The place where your deep gladness and the world's deep hunger meet" puts it in Olympian terms, but Buechner's words happen to be right. I eventually came to know that happiness was, after all, a sign that I was coming closer to my calling. I realized that the past twenty-some years of my life were certainly the happiest. God took no pleasure in my desperate pursuits to be pleasing to him. My marriage to Tracy, the birth of Noah and Daniel, proved to be my postulancy and novitiate in the religious order I was called to join and, within this small community, to work out my salvation. Marriage, children— this was my consecrated religious life, brooking no escape whatsoever, but complete immersion into the deepest of mysteries. I had run from commitment, masking my altruism so well that I couldn't break through my own disguise. Finally, Tracy came into my life, a woman who, as the popular song says, "gave without taking," stripping away my pretenses and challenging me to lower my line of sight to the present, the ordinary.

For here was, if not a saintly or heroic life, a real life.

I was the father of children I really hadn't wanted, married to a woman who had no reason to say yes that day in New York. My life didn't add up; it was certainly not the sum of its parts. Founding CHIPS, writing some books, speaking about things Catholic. Living alone. Afraid to be alone. Average student. A good enough husband and father. My obituary will be a modest one: "Paul Wilkes, a writer and speaker on Catholic belief and practice, who won a few minor awards, died today at the age of _____." Something like that.

Every so often, when I get that faraway look in my eye, Tracy will ask, "Sure you still don't want to be a monk or go back to CHIPS?" No, I answer. But yes. I am a monk when I spend a few days alongside the lazy Cooper River at Mepkin Abbey with the Trappists there. I am ordained to take the Eucharist each Thursday morning. I've started a small foundation to help Home of Hope, a poor orphanage in India, which I now visit twice each year. I have Tracy and our sons. I have so much, more than I ever could have imagined, because I don't have any one thing.

I know my life isn't yet over and could in fact go on for a few more decades, but on the knoll dedicated to Mary, looking up at that window, I realized that it has been a life that grew deeper and better in spite of me. God was good enough to give me life itself. Christ kept his promise and stayed with me. The wind of the Holy Spirit ruffled my conscience and cooled my brow, filled my sails, sent me in directions I didn't seek and at other times calmed the seas just when I was about to drown.

I don't know if I pleased God, but as Merton's prayer assures us, the desire to please God pleases him. Through it all, I did have that desire. I do still have that desire. That much I know.

I looked up to the moon, brilliant in a cloudless, dark sky. The dew—so many droplets of grace—fell from the oak's bare branches onto my upturned face. I walked back down the hill and into what was left of my life.

ACKNOWLEDGMENTS

Thanks, and thanks again to John Thornton, my agent, for believing in this book and me.

To Sheryl Fullerton, my editor at Jossey-Bass, who carefully winnowed chaff from wheat.

To Michele Jones, a copyeditor every writer should be lucky enough to work with.

To Alison Knowles and Joanne Clapp Fullagar at Jossey-Bass, who deftly put all the pieces together.

THE AUTHOR

Paul Wilkes is one of America's most respected writers and speakers on religious belief and personal spirituality. Paul lectures across the country about the role of religious belief in individual lives as well the place and impact of religion in public life. As a commentator on religious issues, he has appeared on all major television networks and cable outlets.

His book *In Mysterious Ways: The Death and Life of a Parish Priest* won a Christopher Award. In addition to *Merton,* his PBS documentary, Paul was host and writer of the acclaimed television series *Six American Families,* which won a duPont-Columbia Award for documentary excellence.

He is the author of some twenty books and has written for the *New Yorker,* the *Atlantic,* and the *New York Times Magazine.* He has been a visiting writer and guest lecturer at many colleges and universities, including Columbia, Notre Dame, and the University of North Carolina at Wilmington.

Paul has been honored for his body of work with a Distinguished Alumnus Award from the Columbia University Graduate School of Journalism, where he received his advanced degree, and with a By-Line Award from Marquette University, where he graduated.

Paul lives in Wilmington, North Carolina, with his wife, Tracy, who founded an arts program for at-risk children. The Wilkeses have two sons, Noah and Daniel.

Paul founded Home of Hope India-US to assist the Home of Hope orphanage for girls in Kochi, India. He is a cofounder of CHIPS (Christian Help in Park Slope), a Brooklyn center that has served homeless young mothers and children and the poor for over thirty-five years.

Join Paul Wilkes in Helping
Orphan Girls of India

Prathyasha Bhavan
HOME OF HOPE

In early 2006, while on vacation, Paul Wilkes and his wife, Tracy, happened to visit Home of Hope, a poor orphanage for girls in Kochi, India. The seventy girls at Home of Hope – aged from five to twenty years old – had been abandoned or severely neglected. Too many of them had been physically and sexually abused. A good number of the girls had spent their entire lives on the street, begging. These were the poorest of the poor, now at least in a safe haven under the care of the Salesian Sisters of Don Bosco.

But the orphanage needed everything, barely having enough to feed the girls.

Looking into the innocent, upturned faces of these girls, whose lives had seen so much privation, something happened, something that Paul and Tracy still cannot explain to this day. They felt an overwhelming calling to help this poor orphanage in any way that they could.

In essence, they "adopted" the orphanage on the spot.

Since that day, Paul and Tracy have raised funds to help build a new dormitory (the girls had formerly slept on a concrete floor), sent girls on to college, provided clean water, better food, a playground, Jeep, computers, and many things the orphanage was unable to afford.

But so much more is needed. The work has just begun. Can you help?

You can find out more about Home of Hope at www.homeofhopeindia.org, or by contacting Paul at paulwilkes@ec.rr.com. You can help in many ways – through your financial support, through directing needed resources you may have available, or by employing your own skills when you visit and stay at Home of Hope, while assisting in its programs.

Paul Wilkes serves as the Executive Director of Home of Hope India – U.S., a 501(c)(3) tax-exempt charity, which has an eighteen-member board of directors. All donations to Home of Hope are fully tax-deductible and 100 percent goes to fund Home of Hope projects.